MAMA DADA

Studies in Modern Drama

Kimball King, *Series Editor*

Mama Dada

Gertrude Stein's Avant-Garde Theater

Sarah Bay-Cheng

Routledge

New York and London

Published in 2004 by
Routledge
29 West 35th Street
New York, NY 10001

Published in Great Britain by
Routledge
11 New Fetter Lane
London EC4P 4EE

Permission to quote from the following is gratefully acknowledged: "Plays" and "Portraits and Repetition" from *Lectures in America* by Gertrude Stein, copyright 1935 and renewed 1963 by Alice B. Toklas. Used by permission of Random House, Inc. From *Wars I Have Seen* by Gertrude Stein, copyright 1945 by Random House, Inc. Used by permission of Random House, Inc. *Four Saints in Three Acts, They Must. Be Wedded. To Their Wife., A Movie, Film. Deux Soeurs Qui Ne Sont Pas* from *Operas and Plays* by Gertrude Stein. Used by permission of Station Hill Press, Inc. "A Portrait of Constance Fletcher" and "The Psychology of Nations" from *Geography and Plays* by Gertrude Stein. Used by permission of the University of Wisconsin Press. "Composition as Explanation" and "What Are Master-pieces and why are there so few of them," by Gertrude Stein. Used by permission of Peter Owen Ltd., London. *Doctor Faustus Lights the Lights, Listen to Me, The Mother of Us All,* "A Photograph," and *Yes Is for a Very Young Man* from *Last Operas and Plays* by Gertrude Stein, ed. by Carl Van Vechten. Used by permission of the Estate of Gertrude Stein. Previously unpublished notes by Gertrude Stein on *Doctor Faustus Lights the Lights* and *Yes Is for a Very Young Man, Wars I Have Seen* are used by permission of the Estate of Gertrude Stein. *How Writing is Written* and "Reflection on the Atomic Bomb" by Gertrude Stein are used by permission of the Estate of Gertrude Stein. Robert Wilson's program notes for Gertrude Stein's *Four Saints in Three Acts* are used by permission of the Byrd Hoffman Water Mill Foundation.

Studies in Modern Drama, Volume 20

Library of Congress Cataloging-in-Publication Data

Bay-Cheng, Sarah.
    Mama Dada : Gertrude Stein's avant-garde theater / by Sarah Bay-Cheng.
      p. cm.—(Studies in modern drama)
    Includes bibliographical references (p.) and index.
    ISBN 0-415-96893-3 (acid-free paper)
    1. Stein, Gertrude, 1874–1946—Dramatic works. 2. Experimental drama, American—History and criticism. 3. Avant-garde (Aesthetics)—United States–History—20th century. I. Title. II. Series.
    PS3537. T323Z548   2003
    812′. 52—dc21

For Bert Cardullo

Contents

General Editor's Note

Routledge is delighted to publish *Mama Dada,* the first book to examine Gertrude Stein's drama within the history of the theatrical and cinematic avant-gardes. This book addresses the growing interest in Stein's theater by offering the first detailed analyses of her major plays, and by considering them within a larger history of avant-garde performance. Unique to this study is a three-part model of avant-garde drama, which argues that a significant and heretofore unrecognized relationship exists among the histories of avant-garde drama, cinema, and homosexuality. Using the posited connection among the avant-garde, cinema, and queerness as the foundation for this study, *Mama Dada* examines in detail Stein's major plays, distinguishing for the first time between her major and minor dramatic works. Finally, it considers the impact of Stein as a major influence on the American avant-garde, in particular her influence on The Living Theater, Richard Foreman, and Robert Wilson. Thus it is a fitting addition to Routledge's STUDIES IN MODERN DRAMA series.

Sarah Bay-Cheng received her B.A. from Wellesley College and Ph.D. in theater from the University of Michigan, Ann Arbor. She currently teaches in English and theater at Colgate University, and her co-edited anthology, *The False and Fallen Staff: A Collection of Falstaff Plays from Four Centuries* is forthcoming from the University of Delaware Press. This current volume, at last, credits Stein with the recognition her theater work deserves.

Kimball King

Acknowledgments

I wish to thank the following institutions for their generous support of this project: the Institute for Research on Women and Gender at the University of Michigan, which provided research support when this project was in its infancy; the Rackham School of Graduate Studies at the University of Michigan for their support of my early research; and the Colgate University Research Council for their generous support of research in the final stages of preparation. Thanks also to the staff at the Beinecke Library of Rare Books and Manuscripts at Yale University for access to Gertrude Stein's notebooks and papers, and for answers to numerous questions; Aaron Beebe, archivist for Byrd Hoffman Water Mill Foundation; and Clay Hapaz, archivist for the Wooster Group. I am further indebted to Anne Bogart, Mary Gearhart, and Paula Court for generously sharing their time and work with me. Thanks to the staff at Routledge who have done so much, and especially to Kimball King for his support, advice, and general enthusiasm for this project.

My special thanks to Bert Cardullo for his passion and guidance through the years; it is to him that this book is dedicated. I would also like to thank Anne Herrmann, Johannes von Moltke, and Leigh Woods for their comments on early drafts of this manuscript, and Amy Feinstein for helping me battle through the end of it. For their inspiration, I would also like to thank Larry Rosenwald, who profoundly shaped my studies in theater and the avant-garde, Robert Knopf, who first encouraged me to consider Stein, and Ellen Gainor, who was always willing to talk. Finally, my sincerest thanks to my parents, Mary Robinson and Richard Bay, who taught me to love theater, and especially to my partner, Laina Bay-Cheng, who took so much time and energy from her own work to help with this project.

Portions of Chapter 1 previously appeared as "An Illogical Stab of Doubt: Avant-Garde Drama, Cinema, and Queerness" in *Studies in the Humanities*

28.1–2 (June–December 2001): 82–93. An early version of Chapter 4 appeared as "Atom and Eve: A Consideration of Gertrude Stein's *Doctor Faustus Lights the Lights*" in *Journal of American Drama and Theatre* 12.2 (spring 2000): 1–24. I am grateful for permission to reprint these sections.

Chapter 1
Introduction

"Supposing no one asked a question. What would be the answer."
GERTRUDE STEIN, "NEAR EAST OR CHICAGO"

"I am violently devoted to the new."
GERTRUDE STEIN, *EVERYBODY'S*
AUTOBIOGRAPHY

Although Picasso's earlier painting *Portrait of Gertrude Stein* (1906) is better known, his later *Homage à Gertrude Stein* (1909) is the more prophetic of the two. The painting features several winged female figures bearing a still-life bowl of fruit and a trumpet. Picasso's honoring of Stein includes both the staples of figurative art, the fruit bowl and the female nude, and the classical image of the biblical herald—a winged figure with a trumpet. Picasso paints his version of Stein with visual references to painting's long history of biblical subjects (a style popular until the emergence of the Impressionists in the mid-nineteenth century). And yet, despite the references to classical figurative painting, the work is recognizable as an avant-garde painting. The bodies are disproportionate and abstracted; the color palette is muted and blurred with no discernible light source; and the relationship between the figures ambiguous. It is with this tension between the historical and the innovative, the figurative and the abstract, the classical and the modern, that Picasso honors Gertrude Stein. That he should also include a herald seems entirely appropriate, for while Stein embraced the past, she continually sought "the new." In her appreciation of art (as, arguably, the first great collector of modern painting with her brother Leo) and in her own artistic efforts, Stein foreshadowed much of the artistic progression of the twentieth century, though she would live to see less than half of it.

Figure 1   Gertrude Stein, 1934. Photograph by Rayhee Jackson. Used by permission of the
Estate of Gertrude Stein.

In Stein's writing in general and in her drama in particular, the dominant
artistic and cultural trends of the twentieth century emerge. Though she is
perhaps the least well known of America's twentieth-century playwrights, she
is the first genuine avant-garde dramatist of her country. As such, the history of
experimental theater and drama in America is virtually inconceivable without
her influence. One of America's earliest avant-garde theater groups, the Living
Theater, began production in 1951 with Stein's "Ladies Voices" (1916). Robert

Wilson produced her play *Doctor Faustus Lights the Lights* (1938) in 1993 and, in 1998, the Wooster Group performed its adaptation of Stein's *Doctor Faustus Lights the Lights,* titled *House/Lights.* Richard Foreman has credited Stein as the most significant influence on his work and has referred to her as "the major literary figure of the twentieth century" (Bernstein 108). Anne Bogart's theater and Stan Brakhage's films have built their respective aesthetics upon Stein's principles, and parallels can be made between Stein and such contemporary experimental dramatists as Suzan-Lori Parks and Maria Irene Fornes.

Yet despite her dramatic influence, Stein's plays are rarely studied, even among Stein scholars. Similarly, the field of theater studies to date has largely ignored her dramatic output, just as the field of cinema studies has ignored her two screenplays. This is not to say that there is no criticism of Stein's drama at all. Marc Robinson devotes a chapter to Stein in his book *The Other American Drama,* and Stephen Watson's *Prepare for Saints: Gertrude Stein, Virgil Thomson, and the Mainstreaming of American Modernism* offers a thorough consideration of Stein's only theatrical success during her lifetime, *Four Saints in Three Acts* (written 1927, produced 1934). Recently, Arnold Aronson in his *American Avant-Garde Theater: A History* cites Stein as one of three major influences on American avant-garde theater. Most studies, however, treat Stein as a literary anomaly, critiquing her plays as if they were mistitled poetry or abstract prose. Of the few books that consider her plays at all, even fewer examine these works as scripts intended for performance.

Of the two books devoted exclusively to Stein's drama, only one—Betsy Alayne Ryan's *Gertrude Stein's Theater of the Absolute* (1984)—treats these plays as if they were written for performance. Unfortunately, however, Ryan attempts to cover all seventy-seven of Stein's plays with little separating of one play from another critically, and fails to connect Stein to the larger history of drama. Conversely, the other of these two books—Jane Palatini Bowers's *"They Watch Me as They Watch This": Gertrude Stein's Metadrama* (1991)— claims that Stein's plays are primarily "literary" writings. Bowers contends that Stein's use of the label "play" is more a function of her attitude toward language—her *jouissance,* as Bowers calls it—than an indication of Stein's serious desire to write for the stage. For Bowers, these plays are *about* theater, not *for* the theater. Of the two, Bowers's analysis of Stein has had a more lasting critical impact. Martin Puchner's *Stage Fright: Modernism, Anti-Theatricality, and Drama,* for example, takes up Bowers's reading of Stein in his analysis of *Four Saints in Three Acts.* In accordance with Bowers, Puchner argues that Stein's dramatic literature is best understood as closet drama, in part because of what he identifies as her "suspicion of the theater" (103). However, he also acknowledges that *Four Saints* is not written exclusively for the reader, but occupies a third category: "closet drama that is to be performed" (111).

It is my contention, however, that Gertrude Stein's drama deserves consideration on its own terms, as drama and as theater. These plays have an interior logic as well as a dramatic progression in which Stein continually works out her vision of modernity and modernism, culminating in her greatest dramatic work, *Doctor Faustus Lights the Lights*. The development of her dramatic vision can only be fully understood, moreover, in relation to three dominant cultural and artistic trends of the twentieth century: the development of the avant-garde, the evolution of cinema, and the emergence of homosexuality as an identity. At the intersection of these artistic and cultural movements, Stein's theater is both a precursor of American experimental performance and a landmark in American dramatic history.

Avant-garde drama, cinema, and queerness all begin around 1895. Within one year, Alfred Jarry wrote and later performed probably the first avant-garde play, *Ubu Roi* (1896); the Lumière brothers produced their first—and *the* first—film, *Workers Leaving the Lumière Factory* (1895); and Oscar Wilde's highly publicized trials of 1895 brought into public consciousness the concept of homosexuality as an identity. These three events resulted from a burgeoning modernity that directly contradicted the late nineteenth-century belief in rationalism and science, often exhibited dramatically in the form of the well-made play. If late nineteenth-century realism and naturalism emerged as a dramatic response to such scientific "certainties" as Auguste Comte's positivism, Karl Marx's theory of capitalistic exploitation, Sigmund Freud's psychoanalysis, and Charles Darwin's theory of evolution, then early twentieth-century avant-garde drama and film was founded on such theories of unpredictability and chaos as Werner Heisenberg's uncertainty principle, Albert Einstein's relativity, and Georg Simmel's fragmentation of perception in the urban environment.

One of the earliest examples of such drama is *Ubu Roi* (1896), in which Jarry adapts the story of Shakespeare's *Macbeth* as a grotesque comedy. In this landmark play, Jarry's two protagonists, Père and Mere Ubu, attempt to usurp King Wenceslas, ruler of an imaginary Poland. Père Ubu, one of the more notorious figures in avant-garde drama, was based on an earlier parody of Jarry's high school physics teacher, Professor Hébert. *Ubu Roi* opens with Père Ubu's famous line, "Merdre" ("Shit"), and includes Père Ubu's poisoning of dinner guests with excrement flung from a toilet brush, flushing nobles down an enormous toilet, and emerging quite unscathed from the whole ordeal after having been driven from Poland. As an avant-garde pioneer, Jarry attacked institutions of government, killing kings, deposing nobles, and flushing military leaders; he offended his middle-class audience with vulgar language and humor that combined the sexual with the scatological; and, most disturbingly for the time, Jarry omitted any explanation or moral condemnation for Ubu's behavior. Whereas other late nineteenth-century drama attempted to account for human behavior through either psychological or sociological explanations, Jarry made no excuses for his characters and their behavior. In fact, Jarry's earlier play, *César-Antéchrist* (1895), clearly marks the emergence of Père Ubu as a new godless incarnation of humanity. As Roger Shattuck writes of Ubu in *The Banquet Years,* "He is what he is because God has existed and has died ritually and actually, because Antichrist has had his reign on earth, and because the powers of true deity will triumph" (226). It is this view of humanity in relation to its God and its own psychology that would distinguish avant-garde drama from all previous forms of drama.

In addition to eliminating God and predictable human psychology from his drama, Jarry further intended that the brutal vision of humanity personified in Ubu should reflect the theater audience. He writes in his essay "Questions of the Theater" that he "intended that when the curtain went up the scene should confront the public like the exaggerating mirror in the stories of Madame Leprince de Beaumont, in which the depraved saw themselves with dragons' bodies, or bull's horns, or whatever corresponded to their particular vice" (174). Jarry recognized that realism and naturalism similarly attempted to reflect their audiences, but noted that "Ibsen's attack on [the audience] went almost unnoticed" (175). Jarry's attack, however, would not only be noticed by his audience, but would also change the path of modern drama.

On December 11, 1896, the first production of *Ubu Roi* opened at Le Théâtre de l'Oeuvre in Paris. According to most accounts, the first word of the play incited a riot in which the audience eventually separated into two camps: enthusiasts and critics. In a stunning reversal for which the avant-garde would become renowned, the house lights were turned on in the middle of the outburst, allowing the performers on stage to watch the fighting below them. From the chaos of this one play, in both its writing and performance, the theatrical avant-garde was born. Bearing all the markers for the avant-garde to follow—nihilism, attacks on God and king, aggressive assaults on the audience, and the absence of moralizing and psychological explanations— *Ubu Roi* would inspire a generation of artists to follow. Most importantly, the play did what Jarry believed it could: it mirrored society and fundamentally altered that society's perception of itself.

Though not nearly as violent as the first production of *Ubu Roi,* the public presentation of the Lumière brothers' films were no less influential in the evolution of modern culture. Like Jarry's *Ubu Roi,* the Lumière brothers' films would fundamentally change the way people viewed the world. One of the most often told anecdotes of early cinema describes the first showing of the Lumière film *Arrival of the Train at the Station* (1895). Apparently, the image of the train rushing toward the camera startled early audiences, sending them shrieking back from the screen. As Gerald Mast coyly states in his *A Short History of the Movies,* "Audiences would have to learn how to watch movies" (19). The accuracy of the story has been questioned as in David A. Cook's *A History of Narrative Film,* in which he writes, "It is difficult to imagine that the Lumières' educated, bourgeois audiences seriously expected a train to emerge from the screen and then run them down" (11). However, as Dai Vaughan suggests, "the particular combination of visual signals present in that film had had no previous existence *other* than as a real train pulling into a real station" (emphasis in original, 126), allowing for the possibility of just such a response.

While there are no such stories to accompany the Lumières' slightly earlier film, *Workers Leaving the Lumière Factory,* audiences were no less enchanted. The film gave audiences a previously unseen view of the world—themselves in motion. Arthur Knight describes the effect most exuberantly in *The Liveliest Art* when he calls the Lumières' motion-picture camera "the machine for seeing better" (14). He writes that, "to the public, [films] were a revelation. It was not merely the fact that movement and the shadow of the real world were captured by these machines—that had been done before—but now everything could be seen as large as life and, curiously, even more real" (14). The Lumières' film itself is uneventful. A static camera films groups of people leaving a factory. To a modern viewer accustomed to film and television, the movement is repetitive and, as the faces are mostly obscured in shadow, there is little to attract the eye other than the movement of the figures. Nevertheless, the film is a vital document of modernism and is intimately related to the theatrical avant-garde. The film achieves what few avant-garde performances would accomplish, despite repeated attempts. *Workers Leaving the Lumière Factory* transforms people, particularly the crowd, into objects. On film, especially in the work of the Lumières, people are repetitions of each other and their movement creates the unified flow of a mass, obscuring individuality.

Two important ideas are introduced through the Lumières' representation of their workers. First, the Lumières capture humanity in what Siegfried Kracauer would later call "the mass ornament." In his 1927 essay of the same name, Karacauer first coined this term in his critique of the Tiller Girls, an all-female precision dance team from the 1920s and 1930s. He writes, "These [performers] are no longer individual girls, but indissoluble girl clusters whose movements are demonstrations of mathematics" (76). Although the workers leaving the factory are much looser in their organization than the precision-trained Tiller Girls, the workers also become human "clusters" rather than individuals. The image is one of mass—a group that becomes an aesthetic object. Secondly, the people represented in the film become mechanical and the group movement parallels the movement of a machine because of its uniformity. To quote again from Kracauer's "The Mass Ornament":

> Although the masses give rise to the ornament, they are not involved in thinking it through. As linear as it may be, there is no line that extends from the small sections of the mass to the entire figure. The ornament resembles *aerial photographs* of landscapes and cities in that it does not emerge out of the interior of the given conditions, but rather appears above them. (emphasis in original, 77)

As with Père Ubu in *Ubu Roi,* film of mass spectacle eliminates individual psychology. In the films Kracauer identifies, humanity is presented as less grotesque than Ubu, but the filmic representation lacks the individualism to be found in realistic and naturalistic characterization. Furthermore, the film presents a mechanized way of viewing humanity. Because individuals are so similar in the Lumières' film, they begin to appear as copies of each other, as a few people duplicated or repeated. No matter how real the image seemed, the representation was unlike any that audiences had previously seen—full of people, yet devoid of individual personalities, and seemingly real, yet two-dimensional and mechanized—thus altering modern society's perception of itself. As awareness of this altered perception increased, film would eventually merge with the avant-garde, creating self-reflexive works that specifically addressed the role of vision and modes of seeing throughout the twentieth century.

This change in modern perception was simultaneously echoed in the trials of Oscar Wilde for "gross indecency." Ironically, Wilde initiated the very proceedings that would eventually send him to jail by filing a libel suit against the father of his lover, Lord Alfred Douglas. In a letter, the Marquess of Queensberry referred to Wilde as a "Somdomite" [*sic*], prompting Wilde's suit. The trial eventually turned on Wilde, however, and Queensberry was found to be justified in his derogatory reference to Wilde a sodomite. Shortly after losing the lawsuit, Wilde was arrested for "indecent acts" in April 1895. His trials were marked by public attention from the beginning. Newspapers from all over the world covered the scandal, including the *New York Times.* Before the first trial, a sale of photographs of Wilde caused such a riot that the police were called and the sale had to be stopped. English newspapers in particular relished the event, in one case calling Wilde the "High Priest of the Decadents."

It was during his first trial, which began on April 26, 1895, that Wilde first admitted to the "Love that dare not speak its name." In this now famous speech, Wilde defended this love as "the noblest form of affection" and "intellectual," equating such relationships with those described in Plato's philosophy and the sonnets of Michaelangelo and Shakespeare. His reply, however, was taken as an admission of indecency. Although his first trial failed to end with a unanimous verdict, his admission would eventually be his downfall. His second trial resulted in his conviction and he was subsequently sentenced to two years at hard labor. But more significant than the actual event of Wilde's trial was the effect of his conviction on the public. The emergence of a homosexual identity fundamentally changed society's perception of sexuality and its relation to being. As a recognizable homosexual, Wilde fundamentally destabilized assumptions not only about "normal" sexuality, but also about normal society. Similar to the effects caused by avant-garde drama and cinema, the emergence of the visible homosexual caused a fundamental shift in cultural perception. Moreover, this shift in perception was not simply the result of the assimilation of new information, as had occurred in the intellectual revolution created by such figures as Freud, Darwin, and Marx; rather, this new shift was the realization of an invisible, threatening, and essentially random universe.

It was these events of 1895–1896 in avant-garde drama, cinema, and homosexuality that, at least in part, set the course for culture in the twentieth century. Coupled with the emergence of mechanized warfare in World War I, early twentieth-century drama reflected the increasing tensions and uncertainty of a conflicted and ambivalent modern world. As a result of these cultural developments, the histories of the theatrical avant-garde, cinema, and queerness share more than just a mutual point of origin. These three echo the unpredictability and instability of the early twentieth century in several shared formal devices: repetition, fragmentation, nonlinearity, and, perhaps surprisingly for film, the nonreproduction of reality.

Avant-Garde Drama, Cinema, and Queerness

Attempting to categorize or classify the theatrical avant-garde of the early twentieth century is, consequently, problematic at best. As J.H. Matthews points out in his *Theater in Dada and Surrealism,* "No guaranteed criterion exists that, cutting across misleading chronological boundaries, would permit us to classify this play of unquestionable Dada inspiration and that play of a purely surrealist derivation" (4). Considering that most avant-garde movements, both in drama and the plastic arts, sought to explode conventional ideas, labels, and categories of genre and form, it seems rather unfair to impose rigid limits on the artistic products of such movements. Furthermore, the very instability of the form itself has accounted for a variety of contradictory definitions over time. However, despite the radical differences among various plays of the period, there are two specific elements that provide a basis for evaluating works as products of the historical avant-garde and as examples of an avant-garde theatrical style.

The first element present in nearly all products of the avant-garde is its negation of organized religion and belief in God. As Jacques Derrida writes in his analysis of Artaud's Theater of Cruelty, a key reference point for much of the avant-garde theater:

> The theater of cruelty expulses God from the stage. It does not put a new atheist discourse on stage, or give atheism a platform, or give over theatrical space to a philosophizing logic that would once more, to our great lassitude, proclaim the death of God. The theatrical piece of cruelty, in its action and structure, inhabits or rather *produces* a nontheological space. (emphasis in original, 235)

Similarly, in the introduction to his *Theater of the Avant-Garde: 1890–1950,* Bert Cardullo argues that avant-garde drama can be identified, in part, by its elimination of faith in the providential designs of an omnipotent, omniscient, and omnipresent God or a divine monarch. He further extends this argument to account for the many deviations from conventional drama in the theater of the avant-garde. So vital is the anti-theism of the avant-garde that this negation of God triggers a further breakdown of logic or rationality in drama, "Modernist or avant-garde drama, however, took modern drama a step further by demonstrating that a play's movement could be governed by something completely outside the triad that links motive to act, act to logical sequence of events, and logical outcome to divine or regal judgment" (5). According to Cardullo, the elimination of God ultimately creates, in addition to a non-theistic space as argued by Derrida, a space in which all previous rules have been abolished, including those that govern both human psychology and behavior and the rationality or causality humans would impose on any sequence of events. Consequently, the avant-garde not only eliminates God, but it also directly refutes the logocentric scientific certainty that underlay both naturalism and realism in the late nineteenth century. As John Weightman notes in his *Concept of the Avant-Garde,* "the term *avant-garde* is not simply a military metaphor . . . it is basically connected with science, and with what is sometimes called the scientific revolution, the replacement of the medieval belief in a finished universe by the modern scientific view of a universe evolving in time" (20).

The second unifying element of avant-garde drama is its nonrepresentational use of language. As Christopher Innes notes in his essay "Text/Pre-Text/Pretext: The Language of Avant-Garde Experiment," "The search for a new form of theater language can be seen as one of the defining elements of the theatrical avant-garde as a whole" (58). In his overview of some of the major performances of the American avant-garde in the 1960s, Innes argues that such performances demonstrate the limits of a purely physical theater precisely through their reliance on scripts and the centrality of text. Erika Fischer-Lichte further defines this "new form of theater language" in her "The Avant-Garde and the Semiotics of the Antitextual Gesture." She lists the criteria of avant-garde language as follows:

1. It lacks a stable repertoire of signs.
2. The combination of elements used as signs results from rhythmic principles.
3. The elements that are used as theatrical signs lack an independent semantic dimension, that is, they bring no previously established meaning into production. They are in a sense floating signifiers, to which signifieds can be attributed to—internal and external—contextualization. (93)

Although such definitions have been used to label the avant-garde as anti-textual, it is important to note that avant-garde drama is not against all forms of text; rather, it opposes the logical progression of plot that characterized representational drama. Just as the avant-garde worked against the idea of a God-created and ordered universe, so too did avant-garde language resist the rules of grammar and syntax on stage.

Because of these two major elements—the elimination of God and the elimination of words as representational signifiers—the avant-garde as a concept can be considered, among other things, nonreproductive. By dismissing belief in a divine creator, avant-garde drama ruptures the fundamental relationship between humanity and a Judeo-Christian God—that is, the idea that man is made in God's image. Consequently, humanity is no longer the offspring of a benevolent patriarchal figure, obedient to His will. Instead, humankind is robbed both of its lofty origins and its destiny of redemption or damnation. It is this loss, epitomized most famously by Friedrich Nietzsche's "God is dead," that the theories of Marx, Freud, and Darwin attempt to make up for with their entirely causal explanations of the world's and humankind's secular origin, development, and destiny. Although the existence of God had been disavowed, it was believed that sociopolitical conditions, the subconscious, and evolution could account for human existence and behavior in the absence of God. But, as previously noted, faith in such scientific explanation was similarly discounted by the avant-garde theater. According to it, the chaos of the world could not be rationalized or resolved by an understanding of socioeconomic conditions, psychology, or biology. Human psychology and behavior cannot be fully comprehended because the human mind does not always produce predictable emotional responses and behaviors, but instead, at times, human beings appear to act and react without reason. With cause and effect, reason, and scientific understanding thus challenged, the avant-garde theater was faced with representing a chaotic and incomprehensible universe in which humanity could find no direction. Language itself could no longer adequately represent the world of objective reality, nor, as a communication device, could it enable human beings to transcend their own existential isolation. Not only had humanity lost faith in its divine origins and secular reasoning, but it had also lost faith in its linguistic ability to describe those twin losses.

Given this perspective, realistic representation was considered abhorrent to the artists of the avant-garde, resulting in the flagrant violation of basic principles of conventional drama and speech and the appearance of anti-textualism. In response to the radical changes in perception at the end of the nineteenth century, artists of the avant-garde, most especially the Dadaists, proclaimed themselves "anti-art"[1] and embraced ideals of destruction and negation as the principles of their movement. It is precisely the rejection of God, king, and soul that Dada's founding father, Tristan Tzara, advocated for the group. In his "Dada Manifesto" (1918), Tzara specifically called for the negation of the traditional family, the future, memory, authority, and sexual mores, among others. Considering Dada's attack on such social institutions as marriage and family, it is not difficult to draw a parallel between the aesthetic principles of the avant-garde and queerness, despite the overwhelming heterosexuality and misogyny within Dada itself. In fact, despite Dada's (and later Surrealism's) almost exclusively masculine culture, gender transgressions preoccupied many in the avant-garde. For example, Marcel Duchamp was fond of cross-dressing as his feminine alter ego Rrose Sélavy, and Man Ray frequently experimented with gender ambiguity in photography, beginning with portraits of Gertrude Stein and later creating a series of male portraits concluding with the cross-dressing dancer, Barbette. With their vehement attacks on institutions of sexuality, avant-garde movements such as Dada and Surrealism are fundamentally related to queerness in their mutual attack on bourgeois sexual and social conventions.

As early as Carl Westphal's 1870 essay, "Contrary Sexual Sensations," homosexuality was emerging as an identity as opposed to merely an act. As Michel Foucault writes in *The History of Homosexuality,* "Homosexuality appeared as one of the forms of sexuality when it was transposed from the practice of sodomy onto a kind of hermaphrodism of the soul. The sodomite had been a temporary aberration; the homosexual was now a species" (42). Although this notion—that an origin of modern homosexuality can be identified—has been widely critiqued in queer studies, it is possible to point to an historical moment at which public discourse widely recognized the homosexual as an identifiable body.

A defining moment almost certainly seems to be the public trials of Oscar Wilde in 1895. These trials mark a profound shift in the concept of homosexuality. Although Foucault cites the origin of the homosexual as an identity with Westphal's essay, the spectacle of Wilde's three trials introduced this concept of sexual identity to a much broader public. As previously mentioned, it was Wilde himself who struck the first legal blow. By filing suit against the man who called him a sodomite, Wilde was not denying a particular behavior, but rather rejecting the identity cast upon him. Importantly, it was for this identity that he would ultimately be convicted, more so than for any individual act. As has been frequently noted, the authorities at Wilde's trial were hardly ignorant of homosexuality. Adolescent same-sex relationships were relatively common in the English public schools, which most of the legal persons present had attended. However, it was not for Wilde's participation in an act that he was convicted—an act in which many in the court may have engaged—but for his corrupting presence as a homosexual person, independent of any particular sexual involvement.[2] The presiding judge of Wilde's third and final trial, Mr. Justice Wills, stated that Wilde was "the center of a circle of extensive corruption of the most hideous kind among young men" (Ellmann 477). Wilde as a homosexual was threatening precisely because his homosexuality was not merely a sexual act, but rather an attack on social norms and a *visible* model for others to follow. As Jonathan Dollimore notes, "Wilde's transgressive aesthetic simultaneously confirmed and exploited [the] inextricable connection between the sexual and the (apparently) non-sexual, between sexual perversion and social subversion . . ." (223).

It should come as no surprise, then, that the social upheaval created by Wilde's trials in London and the riots at Jarry's *Ubu Roi* at the Théâtre de l'Oeuvre should occur within a year and a half of each other. Laurence Senelick, in fact, cites *Ubu Roi* as perhaps "the first 'queer' play" because "Whatever Jarry's own sexuality . . . the whole ethos for the Ubu cycle is 'queer' in its refusal to play by the rules of the universe" (24). If the avant-garde drama is against the institutions of family, marriage, nobility, and the church, so too is homosexuality. As Harold Beaver writes in his essay "Homosexual Signs (In Memory of Roland Barthes)":

> The primal injunction was formulated long ago by none other than God: "Be fruitful and multiply." Homosexuality defies that injunction; it transgresses against breeding. With cannibalism and incest, it appears the very incarnation of social distraction, seeking whom it may devour. Like cannibalism, it threatens to turn abundance to sterility. Like incest, it irrevocably defiles genital desire. But homosexuality alone achieves the dual distinction (and penalty) of simultaneously contravening both "nature" and "culture," fertility and the law. It transgresses not merely against breeding but against the institution of marriage and of the family. (99)

Queerness fulfills a function similar to that of the avant-garde in its rejection of social convention and a divine order. Neither reproduces reality—the avant-garde in its rejection of realism and naturalism, queerness in its refusal (or inability) to bear offspring—and each consequently violates the biblical edicts of God. Both homosexuality and avant-garde drama, like that of Jarry, implicitly reject the belief that God created man in His own image and united Adam and Eve as the first family.

In addition to these similarities, queerness and the avant-garde theater share certain formal techniques. Many of the plays of the avant-garde are notable for their repetition of sounds and language and for their simultaneous action. With its same (homo)sexuality, queerness creates a kind of sexual repetition, breaking down the binary logic of sexual intercourse. Furthermore, the queer body can be seen as simultaneously being two sexes. In his eighteenth-century novel *Memoirs of a Woman of Pleasure* (1750), John Cleland writes of his protagonist, Fanny, looking through a peephole in the wall of her hotel. Through the hole, she observes the sodomy of the two men next door. She reports that "His red-topt ivory toy, that stood perfectly stiff shewed, that if he was like his mother behind, he was like his father afore" (158). In his

Homographesis, Lee Edelman interprets this sentence as recognition of the fundamental illogic of queer sex:

> [T]he sentence...seems to signify...that the man who from the front, is like his father from the front, is also from the back, like his mother *from the front.* The sodomite, therefore, like the moebius loop, represents and enacts a troubling resistance to the binary logic of before and behind, constituting himself as a single-sided surface whose front and back are never completely distinguishable as such. (emphasis in original, 184)

Importantly, Edelman identifies the gender-blended body as the product of homosexual intercourse, and it is this conflation of gender-confusion and sex that may best be understood as queer. The queer body, then, is simultaneously mother and father, masculine and feminine, in direct contradiction to the "natural" binary order of two distinct or opposite sexes, coupling but never completely integrated. This queer relationship of gender to sex is fundamental both to Stein and the theatrical avant-garde. And this queer deviation from the binary is a breakdown of logic that even the overwhelmingly heterosexual Dadaists surely would have appreciated.

In a final point of comparison, one may consult the origins of the word "queer." According to the *Oxford English Dictionary* (OED), the first use of the word "queer" as an adjective comes in 1508, when it means "very inferior." In 1740, the word was used as a synonym for "counterfeit" and "odd." In 1922, according to the *Oxford Dictionary of Slang,* queer was first used to designate a male homosexual. Most interesting, however, is the evolution of queer as a verb. First used as such in 1790 (OED), the word meant "to quiz or ridicule, to puzzle, to impose or swindle or cheat"; and in 1812, queer meant "to spoil, put out of order." In their loosest usage, these definitions for queer have all at one time or another been attributed to the products of the avant-garde: very inferior, counterfeit, odd, ridiculous, puzzling, spoiled, out of order. But considering what the theater of the avant-garde was attempting, it can justifiably be said that the avant-gardists "queered" the drama. In relation to the well-made play, performances and texts of the avant-garde wanted to "spoil" realistic drama and put it out of order. For example, Georg Büchner's drafts of *Woyzeck* (1836)—perhaps the major precursor of the avant-garde—successively move further away from a linear plot line, putting the titular protagonist's story more and more "out of order." Thus, it may be argued, queerness is avant-garde, just as the avant-garde is queer.

Nonreproductivity, nonlinearity, and fragmentation are not limited to the avant-garde and queerness, but are shared by a third major trend of modernity—cinema. Of the three, cinema is the least likely to be considered nonreproductive. On the contrary, cinema (like its forerunner, photography) was originally heralded as the epitome of realistic representation. So exact were the reproductions of cinema and photography, that artists such as Laszlo Maholy-Nagy believed that cinema would liberate all other arts from attempting to replicate reality. In his 1925 essay *Painting, Photography, and Film,* Maholy-Nagy wrote, "In the exact mechanical procedures of photography and the film we possess an expressional [*sic*] means of representation which works incomparably better than did the manual procedures of the representational painting we have known hitherto. From now on painting can concern itself with pure color composition" (9). However, even the most realistic film is not an entirely accurate reproduction of reality. In early cinema, the black-and-white, nonverbal (though not silent, as these early films included musical accompaniment) image was hardly a mirror image of the "real." Even the advent of sound and color could not eradicate the two most abstract qualities of the cinematic image: its limit to two dimensions and its framing. These two nonrealistic characteristics are present in every film (except perhaps the occasional 3–D film). Though individual films attempt to diminish the viewer's awareness of the constructed nature of their reality, the masking and the flatness of the image are never totally obscured.

Additionally, cinema shares several characteristics with the theatrical avant-garde. First of all, both are fundamentally visual arts. This is not to discount the aural presence in film and avant-garde performance; it is only to say that visual communication was always the primary mode of communication in both forms. Film, because of its early technical limitations, and the avant-garde because of its disdain for literary or bourgeois drama, used visual codes, cues, and designs to affect their audiences. Even in Dada play scripts, which place a great deal of emphasis on sound, careful attention is paid to the arrangement of the words on the page and to the overall visual effect. Since many of the earliest avant-garde performers were also visual artists, their costumes, sets, and physical stunts often overshadowed the texts they were enacting. Their performances developed coterminously with film, and their live stage acts were often based on or related to American silent films widely available in the Paris of the 1920s, as well as on the increasing number of avant-garde films being produced in Paris at the time.

Perhaps the most famous (or infamous) Dada performances, *Relâche* ([1924] literally, "relax" or "no performance") and *Soirée di coeur à barbe* (Evening of the Bearded Heart, 1925), included the films *Entr'acte* (1924) by Francis Picabia and René Clair and *La Retour de Raison* ([1923] *Return to Reason*) by Man Ray. Man Ray's film consisted of moving "rayographs," created without a camera by covering unexposed film with objects—salt, nails, etc.—then exposing the film to light and developing it. *Return to Reason* is an entirely silent film, containing only abstract moving images (the shadow of the objects in negative) and devoid of theme, character, dialogue, or plot. Although it is not quite as abstract as *Return to Reason, Entr'acte* is little more than a series of visual puns and gags embellished by trick photography.

Buildings and rooftops are shot at impossible angles, columns and streets are superimposed over and intercut with images of a ballerina, an ostrich egg, and Marchel Duchamp and Man Ray playing chess. The second half of the film is devoted entirely to a runaway coffin, vigorously chased by its fretful pallbearers. According to Clair, the film "respects nothing except the desire to burst out laughing" (Kuenzli 5).

Film privileged visual elements over others, not only because of its early limitations in terms of sound, but also because of its history in optical devices. Cinema's origins in series photography and devices like the zoetrope illustrate the prominence of the image over sound, text, and even narrative. As André Bazin writes in his "The Evolution of the Language of Cinema," "If the art of cinema consists in everything that plastics and montage can add to a given reality, the silent film was an art on its own. Sound could only play at best a subordinate and supplementary role: a counterpoint to the visual image" (26). In fact, although Bazin is best known as an emphatic proponent of realism in film—the long take, deep focus, and a static camera—even he sees a connection between cinema as a visual art and the work of the avant-garde. In his "The Ontology of the Photographic Image," Bazin writes:

> Wherefore, photography actually contributes something to the order of natural creation instead of providing a substitute for it. The surrealists had an inkling of this when they looked to the photographic plate to provide them with their monstrosities and for this reason: the surrealist does not consider his aesthetic purpose and the mechanical effect of the image on our imaginations as things apart . . . Every image is to be seen as an object and every object as an image. Hence photography ranks high in the order of surrealist creativity because it produces an image that is a reality of nature, namely, an hallucination that is also a fact. (16)

Thus, it is cinema's emphasis on the visual that connects it to the aesthetic principles of the avant-garde, even though film appears to exactly record reality.

Most importantly, both the theatrical avant-garde and cinema construct their visual landscapes according to the same aesthetic of collage. Expressed in films such as Dziga Vertov's *Man with a Movie Camera* (1929), and in the visual creations of Dada artists Raoul Hausmann and Hannah Höch, the technique of collage—and its cinematic twin, montage—dominated the avant-garde in visual art and cinema, and eventually emerged on stage. Specifically, both cinema and the avant-garde (especially avant-garde cinema) create works out of fragments. The principles of editing in film are no different from the principles of collage in art. Both involve the layering of visual fragments in relation to one another to create a cohesive whole. Höch aligns a photograph of a baby's head on top of an advertisement's picture of a doll's body and a single figure is created. Similarly, D.W. Griffith's parallel editing aligns two simultaneous events into a single narrative moment that articulates the complete event in time, even though it is occurring in two distinct places. The very essence of film is its assembly of fragmented images (each individual film frame) run together quickly before the human eye so as to create the optical illusion of movement. This is true of all film, whether avant-garde or narrative. The most linear Hollywood film uses shot-reverse-shot techniques that fundamentally fracture the otherwise straightforward progression of the narrative. The theatrical avant-garde similarly constructs its early performances in fragments: spontaneous, dynamic spurts of activity that are layered upon one another until the wholeness of the image is formed.

Even the advocates of cinematic realism recognized the fundamental fractured essence of film. As the title of his *Theory of Film: The Redemption of Physical Reality* suggests, Siegfried Kracauer argued that the essential purpose of film was the straightforward recording and revealing of the visible world. According to him, cinema, as the derivative of photography, favors unstaged reality, random events, and a "tendency toward the unorganized and diffuse which marks [it] as [a] record" (20). His language alone here bears a strong resemblance to avant-garde performance with its emphasis on randomness and chaos. However, Kracauer also argued that in order to reinforce its role as objective observer of this unstaged reality, cinema must necessarily allude to world outside its frame, a quality he referred to as "endlessness." But what is most intriguing about Kracauer's argument is that despite his insistence that film is fundamentally the representation of physical reality, he describes film as a fragment of that reality. He writes:

> [P]hotography tends to suggest endlessness. This follows from its emphasis on fortuitous complexes which represent *fragments* rather than wholes. A photograph, whether portrait or action picture, is in character only if it precludes the notion of completeness. Its frame marks a provisional limit; its content refers to other contents outside that frame; and its structure denotes something that cannot be encompassed—physical existence. (my emphasis, 19–20)

In other words, for film to present reality, it must simultaneously draw attention to its own lack of reality. Kracauer is not dissimilar to Bazin when he notes that film is not "real," but rather points to a physical reality that it cannot fully embody because of its limited frame and two dimensions.

Kracauer, quite rightly to my mind, thus establishes film as a fundamentally fragmented art form. As has previously been discussed, film is certainly fragmented in terms of its individual frames and its incorporation of editing techniques, such as montage, parallel editing, and the shot-reverse-shot format. However, Kracauer's language here suggests that even in its most static, linear, and realistic form, film is still fragmented because it is a fragment of the real, which constitutes a whole outside the borders of the film frame. It is only logical then that the avant-gardists should have admired the dynamic and fragmented quality of film enough to incorporate its principles into their texts and performances. So much are cinema and the avant-garde related, that what is presently considered culturally mainstream—rapid-cut music videos, the tangential dynamism of the Internet, and contemporary films such as *The Matrix* (1999), or *Waking Life* (2001)—has far more formal similarities with the early avant-garde than with realist drama, which by comparison seems unnaturally static.

But if the cinema and the avant-garde relate primarily through their manipulations of the visual and their conventions of editing, then queerness completes the triangle as the human embodiment of the visual collage by combining both masculine and feminine, male and female, into one body. Queerness, like cinema and the avant-garde, is primarily visual. All three can be seen as codes that must be cracked in order to understand the text/image/body. To return to Edelman, "homosexuals have been seen as producing—and, by some medical 'experts,' as being produced by—bodies that have a distinct, and therefore legible, anatomical code . . . [Homosexuals] are subjected to a cultural imperative that viewed them as inherently textual . . ."(5–6). The queer identity is seen as one of inherent multiplicity. Homosexuality in the last century (and still today) has been feared both because of its excess of signification and lack of overt signifiers. On the one hand, queerness is seen as the "flaunting" of sexuality itself, as something inherently lewd and perverse. (Note, for example, the resistance on the part of many parents to informing their children about the existence of homosexuality.) On the other hand, homosexuality can also be seen as a threat precisely because it can exist without the observer's being aware of it. Unlike the more recognizable ethnic or racial minority, the homosexual is doubly to be feared because he "looks just like us!" Not only do homosexuals look like "us," they can covertly look *at* us. The power inherent in a sexual majority can be threatened both by the overt mocking of prescribed sexual and gender roles (drag queens and kings, public kiss-ins, etc.) and by the potential infiltration of straight culture by the homosexual, where the heterosexual can be made into an unwitting (and unwilling) sexual object.[3] Under this threat of becoming a sexual object, the queer body (like the avant-garde) can be seen as inherently duplicitous and threatening unless the "signs" of queerness appear overtly *on the body*. But the assumption of most early twentieth-century commentary is that these signs are not overt and therefore must be read and interpreted to discover the "truth" underneath. Like avant-garde drama, and perhaps even more so avant-garde film, queerness presents an ambiguous set of signifiers and codes to be deciphered by the viewer. All three present seemingly confusing visual images that nevertheless demand to be interpreted.

The avant-garde, cinema, and queerness thus evolve and function in continuous relation to one another. Though important concepts in their own right, each has a fundamental connection to the other two, and as such cannot be completely appreciated without first understanding this tripartite relationship. In the drama of Gertrude Stein these three concepts come together powerfully, and although her writing has been studied in terms of its modernism and her lesbian identity, it has rarely been compared to cinema or the avant-garde and never discussed in relation to cinema, queerness, and the avant-garde as interrelated phenomena. As I intend to demonstrate, Stein's drama is more than just a series of sexual euphemisms; it is in fact a profound body of work and it further represents a significant contribution to the aesthetics of the avant-garde and cinema. As demonstrated by the fundamental similarities among these three cultural phenomena, no study of one is complete without at least a consideration of the other two.

Gertrude Stein: A Cinematic, Avant-Garde Queer

The influence on Stein of avant-garde plays and performances, film, and her own queer identity can explain many of the most puzzling aspects of her drama: namely, her use of the nonlinear plot, repetition, the fragmentation or complete elimination of character, simultaneity, and her own unique, "continuous present." Though often treated as literary (rarely dramatic) anomalies, these techniques are no different from the wordplay, indeterminate meaning, and disorienting imagery of avant-garde theater and film. Like the avant-garde theater and cinema of the early twentieth century, Stein's plays are filled with ambiguous images, fractured and multiplicative characters, and words collaged or edited in nonlinear progression or, more often, stagnation.

Although Stein is nearly always regarded as a prominent literary figure, she was fascinated by the visual and by ways of seeing. How else does one explain her early (and unprecedented) fascination with modern art and with Cubism in particular, which specifically addressed different and simultaneous perspectives of reality? Dramatically, one need only read the opening stage directions from *Doctor Faustus Lights the Lights* to find evidence of Stein's visual imagination: "Faust standing at the door of his room, with his arms up at the door lintel looking out, behind him a blaze of electric light" (89). The image of Faustus brilliantly silhouetted in a doorway is undoubtedly a visual opening that can only be fully realized in performance. As exemplified by her fascination with modern art, Stein believed that the modes of seeing were changing. The multiple, simultaneous perspectives of Cubism; the repetition of frames and the inherently fragmented editing in film; and the fractured identities of queerness all surface in her dramatic writings. As she herself states in the opening to her first screenplay, *A Movie* (1920), "Eyes are a surprise."

Though Stein's plays have frequently been called "nonsense" and "anti-art," they are not dissimilar to other drama of the period. Like Stein's plays, Guillaume Apollinaire's *Breasts of Tiresias* (1917), Tristan Tzara's *Gas Heart* (1920), and Roger Vitrac's *Mysteries of Love* (1924), all flagrantly violate the construction of the well-made play. Indeed, Tzara, as the founder of Dada, specifically attempted to make "anti-art" theater. As I will show in detail in Chapter 3, Stein's dramatic form deviates from the norm in precisely the same way as the drama of these other playwrights and, as such supports her role as "the mama of dada."[4]

In 1895, Gustav Freytag documented linear structure or form in his *Technique of the Drama: An Exposition of Dramatic Composition and Art*. Freytag conceives of the drama as a pyramidal structure with five points:

> [The plot] rises from the *introduction* [a] with the entrance of the exciting forces to the *climax* [c], and falls from here to the *catastrophe* [e]. Between these three parts lie (the parts of) the *rise* [b] and the *fall* [d]. (emphasis in original, 114–115)

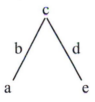

The symmetry of Freytag's illustration echoes the predictability of the well-made play structure. In their deviation from causal connection, Stein's plays work against this structure, extending suspense without benefit of climax or eliminating suspense altogether. She nearly always deprives the reader or viewer of the final resolution, or what Freytag terms the "catastrophe." Stein's drama not only exhibits both the deviations common to other avant-garde drama, but also clearly incorporates the formal techniques of cinema and a queer sensibility, particularly in terms of gender, into her work.

The purpose of my study is systematically to examine Stein's major plays—those works with the greatest thematic scope and best artistic execution—within what I am identifying as three dominant cultural movements of the twentieth century: the avant-garde, cinema, and queerness. My primary criteria for selecting these plays from her rather large body of drama are relatively simple: to what extent does the play address the major social, philosophical, and ethical questions of its time; to what extent is the dramatic form of the play aesthetically innovative; and to what extent is the play thematically innovative in comparison with other drama of its time. Of secondary importance is the "stageability" of the play; in other words, does Stein seem to indicate an understanding of theatrical staging in her plays and an intention to have her work staged.

The intersection of the avant-garde, cinema, and sexuality provides a useful foundation for exploring Stein's drama as avant-garde theater. Take, for example, a short passage from Stein's play *They Must. Be Wedded. To Their Wife.* (1931):

Josephine

      and

Ernest   It is mine. When. Is it. Mine.

      and

Guy.

Josephine

      and

Julia

      and   When is. It mine.

Ernest

      and

Guy.

Josephine

      and

Julia

      and   When is it. Mine.

Ernest

      and

Guy.

Josephine

      and

Julia

      and

Ernest	When is it mine.
and	
John	
and	
Guy.	
Josephine	
and	
Ernest	When is it mine.
and	
John.	
Josephine.	Or which. Is mine.
Josephine.	Is it mine.
Josephine	
and	They may be. Thought. As well.
John.	
Josephine.	Naturally. (174–175)

If one initially ignores the series of names on the left, the text of the scene (labeled "Scene II," though it is neither the second scene of the play, nor the only scene labeled as such) reads as a seemingly arbitrary dividing of words into two sentences. Stein begins the series with a clear statement followed by a halting questioning of that statement: "It is mine. When. Is it. Mine." This question (though lacking a question mark) is repeated in three slightly different forms: "When is. It mine./When is it. Mine./When is it mine." This last sentence is repeated once more before Stein changes the nature of the question to: "Or *which*. Is mine" (my emphasis), followed by the simplest construction of the central question, "Is it mine." Thus, Stein frames the text of this scene between the statement, "It is mine," and the question, "Is it mine."

What "it" is, Stein never reveals. Earlier in the scene she refers to a wheelbarrow, "a pleasure," a wall, action, a noise, interference, and willows. But there is no clear antecedent for "it." So, having no clear subject with which to discuss her sequence of questions, this short scene becomes about the act of questioning, rather than actively seeking an answer. Like a child sounding out words and phrases, Stein laboriously puts the elements of the question together, slowly building to a unified question. Ultimately, the question cannot be answered. Rather, the very nature of what needs to be asked changes. The questioner stops pursuing a unified "it," and instead deliberates between two or more "its"—"Which. Is mine." Here, the questioner appears temporarily to have lost ground in the struggle to produce the appropriate question.

It is this use of language that best makes the argument for Stein as a dramatist—as opposed to an exclusively literary author—for such a progression of words is most effective when spoken. The rhythm of the language, its hesitations and stutters, best conveys the overall theme of the play: the external struggle between men and women in relationships and the individual's internal struggle to unify the male and female halves of the self. To illustrate the fundamental difficulty of human communication, Stein has characters repeat words or phrases when they speak. This technique of playwriting is not unlike Caryl Churchill's in her one-act play *Not Not Not Not Not Enough Oxygen* (1971), in which a lack of oxygen on the earth has made speaking in full sentences virtually impossible. Churchill uses the repetition of a single word to connect a character's struggle for air and speech with the emotional isolation of that character. Similarly, the halting quality of Stein's dramatic language, slowed to an excruciatingly slow pace by an abundance of periods, makes the act of questioning—and hence of genuine communication—a highly belabored process.

This technique of Stein's similarly echoes the progression of frames in a filmstrip. As Stein herself noted, each individual cinematic frame appears to be identical to the one immediately preceding and following it. And as I have previously stated, a film is nothing more than nearly identical fragments throughout, moved quickly in front of the eye to produce the illusion of both unity and movement. Watching a movie, one perceives neither the black separations between the frames, nor any hesitation in the movement of the actors and objects on screen. In Stein's essay "Portraits and Repetition" (1935), she states quite plainly the influence of cinema on her work: "I cannot repeat this too often anyone is of one's period and this our period was undoubtedly the period of cinema and series production. And each of us in our own way are bound to express what the world in which we are living is doing" (177). Thus, one can see a parallel between the progression of Stein's fragmented language and the filmstrip running slowly enough so that one may perceive its divisions, yet still behold the progression of images and the illusion of movement.

If the spoken text illustrates a frustrated search for understanding, Stein's names reflect a quest on her part to unite the fragments of identity into a cohesive self. Though initially confusing, Stein's use of character names follows a steady progression toward the questioner's cohesive identity. The initial tendency when reading Stein's drama (or any other play, for that matter) is to associate character names with the written text in the traditional horizontal alignment: character name on the left, followed by a colon, leading to the spoken text assigned to that particular character. But as is clearly evident in

Stein's dramatic work, the text rarely cooperates. In the passage from *They Must. Be Wedded. To Their Wife.*, for instance, one cannot assume that each name is a separate character. Stein connects the names with the conjunction "and" and ends each list of names with a period. Thus, the series of names does not reflect multiple characters, but a fractured identity—one person split into multiple names. Tellingly, each series is completed by a period and the spoken text associated with the names is always directly in the center of the group of names.

The purpose of the text makes much more sense if one accepts that there are not four individual people—Josephine and Julia and Ernest and Guy—but rather one person, fragmented, a single character called Josephine- and-Julia-and-Ernest-and-Guy. This character further splinters into Josephine-and-Julia-and-Ernest-and-John-and-Guy, then gets compressed into Josephine-and-Ernest-and-John, then Josephine-and-John, and finally simply Josephine, "Naturally." This technique is not uncommon in Stein's work. Her primary female character in *Doctor Faustus* is a single woman with four names and the conjunction "and"—"Marguerite Ida and Helena Anabel." In *They Must* it is the collection of names speaking, not one character among many. There is one character talking to herself. As the names culminate in "Josephine," one can assume that this is the core identity for the character, around which all the other character names revolve.

While this segment of the play is both avant-garde and cinematic because of its fragmentation, repetition, and the complicated character psychology, the key to understanding the meaning of the scene (and, as I will argue in Chapter 3, the meaning of the play) is primarily Stein's depiction of a queer identity. The character names represent the fragmented queer (perhaps her own) identity, specifically the masculine and the feminine, and attempt to reconcile the disparate parts of the self into a single identity. It is entirely possible that the searching question of the text, the elusive "it," is in fact that single identity. What is at first assumed to be owned, "It is mine," is lost in the confusion of multiple names, "When. Is it. Mine." The "it" that is Josephine's identity must ultimately be chosen from among many. Finally, however, Josephine learns that to believe the identity is hers is all that is necessary to own "it." "Is it mine. They may be. Thought. As well." The ending with only the single word, "Naturally," is ironic, for nothing in this short segment (or indeed the entire play) appears "natural." That Stein concludes in this way only further implies her own awareness of the *unnaturalness* of her endeavor—her belief that the search for a self-evident identity is itself "unnatural." In advance of contemporary feminism Stein experiments with identity as a social construction, not an innate or biological designation.

More important than the definitive "meaning" of the play, however, is the dramatic struggle that Stein portrays—a struggle that can only be fully understood if the words are spoken, not merely read. Through her depiction of a character attempting to find a unified identity, Stein, like so many avant-gardists, turns this very human struggle—to discover the self, to communicate, to find answers—into nearly total abstraction. Drawing on Freud's theory of the subconscious and the myth of the integrated personality, the concept of self in the avant-garde is viewed as fundamentally fragmented. For Dada, Surrealism, and Futurism, and later modern dramatists such as Luigi Pirandello, this fragmented self was the root of their art and their representation of humankind. For the Surrealists, articulating the dream state and the subconscious mind became a prominent dramatic exercise. The Futurists and Dada explored the mechanization of humanity in modern urban life by representing the individual in society as a fragmented and often technologically enhanced body as in the Weimar paintings of Otto Dix, photomontages by Dadaist John Heartfield, and plays like "Feet" by the Futurists. In the avant-garde, psychologically as well as physiologically, the idea of the complete person became an antiquated myth.

But for Stein the fragmentation of self was not just about fragmented psychology or mechanized humanity. In both Stein as an individual and her work as an artist the rupture of identity was split along gender lines. As I will show in my analysis of such works as *The Mother of Us All* (1945–46), and *Yes Is for a Very Young Man* (1944–45), Stein wrote from alternating male and female perspectives. Her own gender identity as expressed in much of her writings was remarkably fluid. She was in the habit of calling herself the "husband" to Alice B. Toklas's "wife," though the extent of their relationship was known only to their inner circle of friends. Both within and outside this circle, many took note of Stein's gender ambivalence. Virgil Thomson, for instance, referred to Stein as, "The *homme de letters, homme* not *femme*" (Sprigge 140). This gender ambiguity, particularly as it relates to individual identity, appears in nearly all of Stein's major drama and in many of her minor plays as well. For example, in her 1935 play, "Identity," Stein writes:

I am I yes sir I am I.

I am I yes madame am I I.

When I am I am I I. (593)

While one might read the above passage as talking to two different people, the repetition of the "I" forces the reader to simultaneously consider the gender (sir or madame or both) of the author. But the presence of queerness in Stein's work is evident not only in her personal gender-confusion: it is also evident through her representation of relationships among people, particularly between men and women. Her final play *The Mother of Us All* most directly attacks the institution of marriage, but Stein's earlier work similarly demonstrates a cynicism toward heterosexual relationships. Like the Dadaists, Stein presents a vision of humanity in which simple communication—connection, understanding—is difficult, if not impossible. Stein, who considered herself both masculine and feminine, cannot reconcile her belief in herself as an artistic genius (a domain she and her contemporaries saw as exclusively male) and her female identity. Indeed, it is possible that Stein's disdain of James Joyce and Ezra Pound had less to do with her distaste for their writing, than with her resentment of their ability to work outside mainstream literary conventions to great international acclaim, while her own writing was dismissed as ludicrous nonsense. It is also possible Stein believed that, had she been writing as a man, her work and her role as a "genius" would have been recognized much sooner.

That this recognition eluded her was an increasing frustration as her drama developed. In her opinion, cinema in the early twentieth century was changing the way people saw the world and how they would read books and see performance. Therefore, that few seemed able to appreciate her "cinematic" work was a continual puzzlement and frustration to Stein. Thus *They Must. Be Wedded. To Their Wife.* reflects not only the frustration of trying to reconcile the different aspects of one's personality, but also the crisis of being unable to communicate with the world at large. The multiple "they" wedded to the singular "wife" may be the masculine and the feminine halves of Stein attempting to connect romantically with a single other, but the halting nature of the writing of this play, especially when spoken aloud, implies the difficulty of articulating in words these disparate parts of the self. In terms of gender, of course, there is no word in English or French that fully explains Gertrude Stein's gender. Not a "he" exactly, but certainly not a "she" in the traditional sense, Stein falls somewhere between these linguistic absolutes. Mina Loy perhaps best expresses this limitation of language in a letter to Stein, when she eschews the customary "Miss" in favor of Stein's full name, claiming that the term "Miss" was too general. One might also agree that the traditional address was also too gendered for Stein.

Though Stein is often regarded as someone who loved language and played with it like a toy, her attitude toward language in her later plays evokes a communicative despair similar that of Samuel Beckett. Whereas Beckett's belief in the futility of language led to the progressive elimination of the spoken word from his plays, favoring increasingly longer silences and eventually totally silent works, Stein articulates the same belief through an *over*-abundance of language. In Stein's view the world was not becoming increasingly silent, but increasingly verbal, and this deafening roar of language inevitably obscured its meaning. As Stein writes in "Reflection on the Atomic Bomb," "People get information all day long. They listen so hard they lose their common sense" (179). Though moving in opposite directions, Stein and Beckett ultimately came to the same conclusion that language was no longer an effective means of communicating—that communication itself had become impossible.

Most of Stein's dramatic work subscribes to this pessimistic worldview. As I intend to show through a consideration of her dramatic works between

1920 and her death in 1946, her opinion of the world became increasingly dark, culminating in her final avant-garde work, the opera *The Mother of Us All,* at the end of which Susan B. Anthony contemplates the futility of her "long, long life." Ironically, however, Stein's penultimate play, *Yes Is for a Very Young Man* (written while she was slowly dying of cancer), is a relatively upbeat, realistic melodrama, the first and only example of this genre in Stein's body of work. While simultaneously writing the dour *Mother of Us All,* Stein manages to write a rather simple romance set against the backdrop of the French Resistance and liberation. Although not entirely uplifting, *Yes* projects a hope for the future through its optimistic young men.

At its core, Stein's drama is prophetic, an artistic herald for the latter half of the twentieth century. Through her use of nonlinear language, fragmented characters, and nonnarrative "plot," Stein seemingly predicts the rise of nonlinear communication (as found on the Internet) even as her art itself was influenced by the horror of weapons of mass destruction and the increasingly technological landscape of the "developed" West. That she has never completely disappeared from our collective theatrical and cultural imagination is only one testament to her enduring influence and artistic significance. The other is her work itself, which continues to excite the imagination, challenge the conventions of language as well as thought, and reflect the state of humanity more than half a century later.

Chapter 2

"Eyes Are a Surprise": The Origins of Gertrude Stein's Drama In Cinema

"I understood the qualities of Dailiness in [Stein's] first works and her final writings, the playfulness of her dramas and rhetoric . . . She inspired much daily filmmaking of mine, a whole oeuvre of autobiographical cinematography in non-repetitive variations. But I then was, as was she, infected with Drama as an assumption; and assumptions always pre-suppose *some* sense of repetition."

STAN BRAKHAGE, "GERTRUDE STEIN: MEDITATIVE LITERATURE AND FILM"

Among Gertrude Stein's major writings, two texts are written explicitly for film: *A Movie* (1920) and *Film. Deux Soeurs Qui Ne Sont Pas Soeurs (Two Sisters Who Are Not Sisters* [1929]*)*. Often considered among Stein's plays, these two scripts are notably different from her other dramatic work. Less convoluted in plot, noticeably lacking in dialogue, and more explicitly visual, these texts provide the most tangible link between Stein's dramatic work and the cinema. Despite Stein's assertion in her lecture "Plays" (1934) that she never went to the cinema, the screenplays demonstrate not only Stein's awareness of and interest in cinema, but also her knowledge of different film forms, specifically silent film comedy and the avant-garde cinema of Paris. Whereas her first film script, *A Movie,* imitates the slapstick technique and gag structure of silent film comedy, her second script, *Film. Deux Soeurs Qui Ne Sont Pas Soeurs,* like many of the Parisian avant-garde films of the 1920s, questions the relationship between reality and cinematographic representation.

Although Stein's embrace of avant-garde principles is evident throughout her dramatic writing, it is only after her cinematic experiments in 1920 and 1929, respectively, that Stein's drama shows evidence of her mature style. It is my contention that this development in her writing was a direct result of her exposure to and experiments in cinema. Her avant-garde drama is thus

Figure 2 *Identity.* Created by Donald Vestal. Detroit Institute of Arts, 1936. Used by permission of the Estate of Gertrude Stein.

inseparable from the evolution of both the theatrical *and* the cinematic avant-garde in Europe of the 1920s. As previously noted in Chapter 1, there is a fundamental connection between Stein's dramatic writing and that of her avant-garde contemporaries, especially the Dadaists and Surrealists. This connection can further be expanded to include her dramatic relationship to cinema as well. Although Stein's dramas, especially her later, more mature works, deviate from the conventions of traditional drama—such as the elimination of God in her *Doctor Faustus Lights the Lights* (1938), or her use of repetition and nonlinear speech patterns in *They Must. Be Wedded. To Their Wife.* (1931)—Stein's plays are equally recognizable by their resemblance to avant-garde cinema. Her verbal collages, multiple names for characters, disembodied voices, puns, and non sequiturs follow the technical innovations of the avant-gardes both in cinema and theatrical performance. In addition to appropriating techniques of the cinematic avant-garde in her creative writings, Stein articulates in her theoretical essays many of the cultural issues at stake for avant-garde film artists: namely, the possibility of reproducing reality, the effect of mechanical reproduction on human perception, and the representation of an increasingly mechanized society. For Stein, as for avant-garde artists throughout Europe, this shared ambivalence about modernity and anxiety about the future of a technological humanity is expressed largely through film. It is the centrality of cinema to Stein's theatrical expression of modernity that in part establishes her as a major writer of one of the most significant theatrical and cultural movements of the early twentieth century.

Even before writing her film scripts, Stein had already begun experimenting with cinematic elements in other forms of writing. Her first references to the film form appear in relation to her early textual portraits, short prose poems written about her friends. Stein claimed that she called these short essays "portraits" because of her attempt to capture the essence of a person in language, rather than oils and pigment. It is also likely that at this time, surrounded as she was by painters and having painters as the subjects for these early writings, she wanted to create something akin to the work that filled both her house and her social life. In her portraits Stein sought to represent her own act of verbally recording a person, even as she revealed the person in question. For example, in "Portraits and Repetition," she explains the origin of her use of repetition as her attempt to record the written image of a person, to make visible both the existence of that person and, simultaneously, its representation. Significantly, to achieve this, Stein imitated cinema. In cinema, she found the solution to this question of how to portray both the individual subject and the artistic representation of that subject. Stein writes:

> Funnily enough the cinema has offered a solution of this thing. By a continuously moving picture of any one there is no memory of any other thing and there is that thing existing, it is in a way if you like one portrait of anything not a number of them. (176)

It is Stein's act of linguistically recording a person that bears a close comparison to cinema. In these portraits she wanted to represent the subject both as an individual and as the product of artistic creation. For Stein these two distinct qualities were temporal. The individual as a person exists in time, as does the creation of their representation, whether visual or textual. Much in the same way that Cubism introduced temporality to the two-dimensional canvas through its multiple, simultaneous perspectives, Stein worked very carefully to include a similar sense of time in her writing. But whereas the canvas produces its multiple perspectives within spatial limits, Stein had no such constraint in her writing. To create a verbal analogue for spatial limitation or constriction, Stein employs her most characteristic technique, repetition.

Perhaps the clearest connection between Stein's unusual dramatic style and the cinema can be found not in her creative writing, but in a series of lectures delivered in the United States in 1934. This lecture series, published as *Lectures in America* in 1935, addresses many of the most perplexing aspects of her writing, including an entire lecture on her drama, titled "Plays." Three of the six lectures in this series make some reference to cinema. Written as elucidations of Stein's earlier work, these lectures provide a unique insight into Stein's own reasons and understanding of her work both as product and process. As noted in "Portraits and Repetition" it was in the cinema that Stein located her continuous present and, importantly, she did so *visually*. Whereas the written word can be reread and reconsidered, thus entrenching language in memory, on the screen the continuously moving image offers no memory of the image before. Because each film frame so closely resembles the one before and after it, one can see these frames as identical repetitions of each other. However, each one is, in fact, very subtly different. When these individual frames are moved quickly in front of the eye, the seams between them fade away and the image perceived is one of unity in perpetual motion. Stein recognized that in film the eye has no memory of the individual frame, seeing only the images run together in movement. Based on this effect of cinema, Stein concluded that there was, in fact, no such thing as true repetition:

> existing as a human being, that is being listening and hearing is never rep-
> etition. It is not repetition if it is that which you are actually doing because
> naturally each time the emphasis is different just as the cinema has each time
> a slightly different thing to make it all be moving. (179)

Stein repeats this connection between cinema and repetition a year later in her "How Writing is Written" (1935), in which she writes, "There is no such thing as repetition . . . The cinema goes on the same principle: each picture is just infinitesimally different from the one before" (153).

Stein's repeating of words and phrases creates two significant effects in her writing. First, by using repetition, Stein draws attention to a particular qual-ity of a person, while simultaneously diverting the reader from the meaning of the words. That is, Stein tries to eliminate the history of the words—previous usages or contexts—in order to to attach them exclusively to the person being examined. For example, in "A Portrait of Constance Fletcher" (1911), Stein creates a portrait of a woman looking back at her "family living." Constance, referred to almost exclusively as "she," is continuously posited in relation to this family living through a series of past progressive verbs. Over the course of the portrait, one loses concern for the definition of "family living" (a type of living or family members still alive?) and instead focuses on Constance Fletcher's act of remembering her life "when she was a young one." Con-stance is rendered in verb form: having, thinking, and feeling, among others. The repetition of these verbs records the individual in moving fragments, much like frames of film, thereby making the reader aware of Stein's presence as the creator of the piece and drawing attention to the words as fragments of Constance's identity, not merely bearers of meaning.

In the portrait Stein further writes:

> She was then feeling in being one loving, she was then thinking in being one loving. She was then living in being one loving. She could be then one being completely loving. She was filled then, completely filled then, she was then feeling in being loving, she was then thinking in being loving. She was completely filled then. She was feeling, she was thinking, she was feeling and thinking then in being one loving. (158)

Stein's repetition of the verbs draws attention to Constance Fletcher in a state of "being" that alternately includes thinking, living, loving, feeling, and being filled. Stein uses the past progressive tense to create a continuous present for Constance Fletcher, although the portrait itself is set in the past. Important too, are the interactions of the verbs with each other. Constance Fletcher is simultaneously feeling, being, loving, and thinking as well as thinking about feeling, feeling loving, loving living, and a living loving being. Thus, her emotions and states of being are simultaneously represented as a single moment (the immediate present) fractured into a variety of interdependent relationships among these different states of "being filled" with feeling. Stein's repetition of verbs represents a single moment, but not a static moment. Rather, she creates a dynamic moment shifting within static time, much like the cinema itself.

The second major effect of Stein's repetition is its impact on time. In the critical commentary on her writing, much has been made of what she called "the continuous present." This concept clearly develops out of her fascination with cinema, as the cinema, like Stein's ideal subject, can only be perceived in the present tense. Even flashbacks, which may be said to portray the past of the film narrative, are experienced only in the present tense. Thus, in addition to recording her act of representation, Stein slows time to the point where a reader or viewer perceives her subject as a collection of instants made visible. Stein's ideal reader is not interested in the past or future of the subject, but perceives it only in the continuous present, a present that is interminably stretched out over time. It is this process that creates a dramatic effect similar to the one created by montage in cinema. Just as Stein repeats words and phrases to create a single, dynamic moment on the page, cinema uses repeated and simultaneous images to create the same effect on screen. Thus, the accumulation of images creates the integrated work of art. The whole is created as the sum of its fragments.

This principle of fragmented unity and repetition is central to the avant-garde cinema. In Ferdinand Léger's seminal avant-garde film *Le Ballet Mécanique* (1924), a woman climbs stairs toward the camera. Léger replays this shot over and over, such that the woman repeatedly ascends the stairs but never reaches the top. Because an identical moment in time is repeated, the progression of time within the space of the film is stunted. The viewer of the film is locked within the woman's movement as an endlessly repeating present moment. Film's ability to record and interminably replay a single moment, as Léger does, is a visual analogue to what Stein called the "continuous [verbal] present." This technique also appears in Man Ray's film *L'Etoile de Mer* (literally, star of the sea, 1928). In this film he composes a shot that presents not only repeated action, as in *Le Ballet Mécanique,* but also displays images from different spaces in the single frame of a shot. In the shot, multiple images of starfish spinning in glass bottles are juxtaposed with spinning gears and a man repeatedly sheathing and unsheathing a sword. Man Ray thus repeats identical moments in time while violating the limits of space. This use of repetition both temporally and spatially would find its way into Stein's writing. In the wake of such cinematic experimentation, she attempted to create images in her writing that imitated these uniquely cinematic techniques, using many fractured moments and images to create a unified whole. As Stein writes, "I was making a continuous procession of the statement of what that person was until I had not many things but one thing" ("Portraits and Repetition," 176–177).

While cinema clearly influenced much of Stein's writing after 1910, including her poetry and short prose, the innovations of film most profoundly affected her drama. This influence suggests that Stein's interest in drama and theater was more than as written language, but that she also conceived her drama as visual works of art. Accordingly, her lecture "Plays" contains the most references to cinema of all her explanatory essays and lectures in the mid-1930s. Ironically, she repeatedly claims ignorance of film even as she asserts its importance in her work. These denials and double-talk no doubt account for the lack of critical attention Stein's interest in film has received to date.[1] For example, she claims in "Portraits and Repetition" that she "did not think of [drama] in terms of the cinema, in fact I doubt whether at that time I had ever seen a cinema," while also writing on the same page that "any one is of one's period and this our period was undoubtedly the period of the cinema and series production. And each of us in our own way are bound to express what the world in which we are living is doing" (177).

This perception places Stein squarely with her avant-garde contemporaries working in photography and film. Most avant-garde artists shared Stein's perception that cinema and series production dominated the cultural landscape of the early twentieth century and drew similar comparisons between such visual representations and repetitions. As Laszlo Maholy-Nagy writes in *Painting, Photography, Film* (1925), "Repetition as a space-time organizational motif . . . could be achieved only by means of the technical, industrialized system of reproduction characteristic of our time" (51). Like her avant-garde contemporaries, then, Gertrude Stein believed that the cinema—with its inherent repetition, continuous present, and reproductive ability—would transform not only the visual arts, but also writing and thinking and seeing.

Not surprisingly, Walter Benjamin's foundational essay "The Work of Art in the Age of Mechanical Reproduction," would appear less than a year after Stein's lectures in America echoing Stein's observations about film and repetition. According to Benjamin, the cultural significance of mechanical reproduction in photography and cinema is that "the technique of reproduction detaches the reproduced object from the domain of tradition. By making many reproductions it substitutes a plurality of copies for a unique existence" (221). These plurality of copies without a "unique existence" creates mass accessibility to multiple, identical art objects, and therefore destroys what he terms the authority or "aura" of the original object. Throughout the essay Benjamin articulates his ambivalence about the loss of an object's aura, considering both the benefits and the detriments of its loss of uniqueness. One of the detriments that Benjamin identifies concerns the film actor, who through the process of being filmed, becomes alienated from his own identity. By capturing an actor's performance the film creates a record of performance, which can be re-cut and reshaped according to the whims of an editor. Thus, the film actor watches himself acting, but is alienated from the performance through the mechanization of his body.[2] Significantly, Benjamin quotes an avant-garde playwright and theorist to bolster his argument for the alienation of the actor on film. In his essay, Benjamin cites Luigi Pirandello's novel *Si Gira* (*Shoot!* [1916]). Pirandello writes, "The film actor feels as if in exile—exiled not only from the stage but also from himself" (Benjamin 229). In film, particularly avant-garde film, the human body becomes an automated object, capable of infinite and exact repetition.

There is no evidence that Stein read, or even knew of Benjamin's essay, but its central argument is eerily similar to her dramatic work, particularly her recognition of the loss of "aura" in relation to individual identity. In much of her drama and cinematic writing in the 1920s and 1930s Stein renders her own version of mechanized humanity, fragmented, duplicated, and alienated from itself. For example, many of Stein's characters both in her film scripts and plays appear in multiple versions. Multiple characters bear the same name, thereby seemingly repeating each other and creating, at least as written, exact copies of one person, while single characters frequently have multiple names. Stein's frequent references to twins reflect a fascination with the biological repetition of identity and she often equates this biological repetition with the ability of photography and cinematography to mechanically duplicate people. Stein's writing implies that just as the visual work of art is no longer unique, human beings, too, are becoming merely replicas of one another. (This observation would also have a significant impact on her thinking about sexuality in film and drama.) Because of its combination of visual and aural elements presented by live bodies, theater became for Stein a kind of testing ground for her theories about cinema. Her plays vastly outnumber her screenplays, but the ideas she first explores in her writing for film would continually echo throughout her theatrical texts.

In her essay "Plays" Stein offers an explanation for the importance of cinematic repetition in drama. Significantly, her reasons are firmly based on theater as performance, rather than merely closet drama. Although Stein is almost always viewed as a literary writer, two aspects of live performance preoccupied her thinking about drama. First, it bothered her that the emotions of the audience were often asynchronous with the progression of a play. In the theater Stein claimed that the audience was "always behind and ahead of the scene at the theater but not with it" (103). And, secondly, she attributed this emotional syncopation, in part, to the competing roles of sight and sound in theater, and questioned the relationship among its various visual and aural elements. "Does the thing heard replace the thing seen does it help it or does it interfere with it. Does the thing seen replace the thing heard or does it help or does it interfere with it" (103).

Stein's considerations of drama go beyond simply the reading of a dramatic text. The hearing and seeing in theater is quite different than reading, but not unrelated. She acknowledges that "In connection with reading an exciting book the thing is again more complicated than just seeing, because of course in reading one sees but one also hears" (102), but she recognizes that this relationship is different in theater where reception occurs temporally and where action is closely akin to "real" events. Stein asks, "does as the scene on the theater proceeds does the hearing take the place of seeing as perhaps it does when something real is being most exciting" (103). For all of Stein's deviation from conventional theater practice, these questions remain central to the production of any play and its coordination of elements to convey meaning, emotion, or both. Stein further distinguishes between reading and seeing/hearing modes of perception. Reading a play—even with its elements of "seeing" and "hearing"—is quite different from seeing and hearing theater. It is clear from "Plays" that Stein's emphasis is on the latter. That she finds possible answers to these questions in the cinema further accentuates her emphasis on performance over reading as a representation of "anything real . . . happening" (103). Her consideration of perception and representation in the theater emerged out of the cinema, which she claimed had caused a new perception of sight, sound, and emotion in audiences. Stein's experiments in drama thus derive from her thinking about film:

> I may say that as a matter of fact the thing which has induced a person like me to constantly think about the theater from the standpoint of sight and sound and its relation to emotion and time, rather than in relation to story and action is the same as you may say general form of conception as the inevitable experiments made by the cinema although the method of doing so has naturally nothing to do with the other. (104)

Although Stein argues that the methods for creating sight, sound, and emotion in the cinema and the theatre "had nothing to do with each other," the cinema made a profound impression on her dramatic writing after 1929. The methods of making movies and staging plays are obviously different, but ironically it was the cinema that helped her to understand how to manipulate time and meaning on stage.

Her dramatic writings before 1920 are distinctive for their anti-theatricalism. They contain no list of dramatic characters, no discernible actions, and no plot. There is nothing, in fact, to indicate that these writings are plays other than that Stein says so in the titles. This is perhaps most true of her first play, *What Happened. A Play in Five Acts* (1913), in which, of course, nothing happens. Throughout the 1920s, however, this style of writing gradually disappears and by the end of the decade such texts virtually disappear from her oeuvre. It is surely no coincidence that her self-published *Geography and Plays* (1922) indiscriminately mixes Stein's poetry and portraits with these early plays. As many have argued previously, these early texts labeled "plays" are not terribly stage-worthy (though numerous productions have been attempted). Indeed, these early plays have much more in common with her other poetry and prose than with her later drama. After her experiments with film, however, her drama becomes much more sharply focused and much more theatrical. For the first time, Stein begins to "see" her plays, not merely read them.

Although she wrote several dramatic texts over the years between her two screenplays, most significantly *Four Saints in Three Acts* in 1927 (itself a kind of bridge between her earlier more poetic work, and later more developed drama), Stein's best dramatic writing emerges only after her second, more adventurous film experiment in 1929. Through her cinematic experiments, Stein explored the effect of series production and mechanical reproduction on character and dramatic structure. Indeed, while writing her first screenplay, Stein was also creating what she termed "series production" in her play *A Photograph* (1920). Written seven years before Siegfried Kracauer's essays "Photography" and "The Mass Ornament," and fifteen years before Benjamin's "The Work of Art in the Age of Mechanical Reproduction," *A Photograph* attempts to capture and explain the change mechanical reproduction had wrought on humanity. This short play follows the form of Stein's early dramatic experiments and, as such, contains few discernible characters or events. However, the play does represent an important transition between Stein's thinking about drama as language and theater as visual, mechanical representation. It is therefore useful to consider *A Photograph* as Stein's first mechanical, if not cinematic, experiment in drama.

A Photograph explores the relationship between mechanical duplication and human reproduction. Doubles crowd the text, as they do in her later *Film. Deux Soeurs Qui Ne Sont Pas Soeurs.* Multiple copies of photographs and people in the form of twins populate the drama. Stein makes little or no distinction between mechanical and human reproduction, and both challenge the uniqueness of creation, as evidenced by Stein's abundant references to twins.[3] Stein writes, "A photograph. A photograph of a number of people if each one of them is reproduced if two have a baby if both the babies are boys what is the name of the street" (346). This second sentence clearly implies a connection between photographic and human reproduction. However, Stein answers the question "what is the name of the street" with the apparent non sequitur "Madame" (perhaps also "Ma dame," or "my wife"). Through her use of this single word Stein genders the act of mechanical reproduction. "Madame" may also function as a means for Stein to insinuate herself into the process of reproduction as neither a photographer nor a mother, but as a kind of fusion of the two. For Stein, the words of the play are her offspring—both organic in speech and mechanical in typescript. Though seemingly repetitive, her language is utterly unique, much like her example of twins and the individual frames of film.

The influence of film on her dramatic writing is one that Stein shares with her avant-garde contemporaries. Even one of her harshest critics took note of Stein's writing and its similarity to cinema. In his critique of Stein, *Art by Subtraction: A Dissenting Opinion of Gertrude Stein,* B. L. Reid writes that, "This is not art; this is science. Miss Stein would turn the artist into a recording mechanism, a camera that somehow utters words rather than pictures" (168). Though reserved exclusively for Stein, Reid's criticism could easily be applied to many avant-gardists, particularly German Dadaists, like Grosz and Heartfield, Futurist playwrights, and members of the Bauhaus, like Walter Gropius and Oskar Schlemmer. Many in the theatrical avant-garde, be they Futurist, Dada, or Bauhaus embraced a machine aesthetic and wanted to replace the artist of old (in Dada's case through "anti-art") with a modern mechanized artist. Members of Dada in particular aspired to be like machines themselves—to utter words as if they were pictures. Dadaists such as Georg Grosz and Hannah Höch actually portrayed themselves and their Dada friends as machines. Several of Grosz's self-portraits depict him as a human/machine hybrid. His body is recognizably human, but often his head is replaced by various kinds of machines, with his mouth as the source of a tickertape of numbers. He is not an artist, but a machine. He does not produce "art," but a seemingly endless stream of digits.

Though an attempt to discount Stein artistically, Reid's assessment of her writing is entirely accurate. Many of Stein's plays do "utter words" much as a camera records pictures without necessarily telling a story. But her choices are neither arbitrary nor nonsensical, as Reid implies. Stein attempts to capture the essence of an event without telling the story behind it. Her dramatic writing is not unlike a group of photographs that presents the viewer with a series of related images, without the contextual details. In photography, avant-garde cinema, and the works of Gertrude Stein, it is the viewer or reader who must assemble the pieces of the story into a coherent whole. As Louis Aragon wrote in "On Décor," "Film extends the art of Picasso, Georges Braque, and Juan Gris in the use of 'scraps' of everyday material" (165). Stein herself admits in "Plays" that, "I concluded that anything that was not a story could be a play and I even made plays in letters and advertisements" (119). Just as Kurt Schwitters made his "merz" art out of letters, advertisements, and scraps of printed materials he found in trashcans, Stein also appropriated fragments of culture, gleaned from popular and personal sources and reworked in her screenplays and drama. As such, Stein's plays exemplify the cinematic form by mimicking its process of editing and montage, while at the same time they also employ the avant-garde technique of collage. The moving montage of film and the static collage of the visual arts meet in Stein's unique language, which echoes both the cinematic and painterly techniques of her contemporaries.

Like Stein's drama, Dada writing was visual and fragmented, using none of the literary techniques Reid values: metaphor, illustration, and analogy, to name only a few. Consider, for example, Tristan Tzara's famous publication "How to Make a Dada Poem." In Tzara's formula, one cuts up a newspaper story, word by word, places the words into a paper bag, shakes the bag, dumps the words out, and writes them down in the order in which they fall from the bag. For obvious reasons, then, both Stein and Dada were drawn to cinema. Even at its most representational, the film form was inherently nonlinear. Parallel editing, flashbacks, and fantasy sequences combined to make even narrative cinema more dynamic than the climactic structure of the well-made play. Mechanical and new, potentially subversive and modern, visually and literally fragmented, the cinema was attractive to the artists of the avant-garde, who began experimenting with the medium almost immediately.

While Stein's plays exhibit many of the formal devices of cinema—collage/montage, repetition, and nonlinear plotting—her two film scripts illustrate most completely Stein's knowledge of cinematic structure. Considering Stein's use of language in *A Movie* and *Film. Deux Soeurs Qui Ne Sont Pas Soeurs,* it is clear that she intended them primarily to be visual works of art. In contrast with her dramatic writing prior to 1920, these two scripts feature short, remarkably clear sentences. For example, Stein opens the script of *A Movie* with the following "establishing shot": "American painter painting in French country near railroad track. Mobilisation locomotive passes with notification for villages" (395). Unlike most of her other work, which creates complication and tension through the nonsequential nature of individual words, Stein's sentences in these two works are uncomplicated, though her images in *Film* are more complex and ambiguous than those in the surprisingly straightforward *Movie.*

At the time of Stein's first screenplay, the presence of American films in Paris was common, largely due to the increase in the number of what were known as cine-clubs. These clubs, and the international collection of films they imported to Paris, would have a profound effect upon the French avant-garde cinema, as Jacques Brunius (Luis Buñuel's collaborator on *L'Age d'Or* [1930]) details:

> Romantic and expressionistic German films (*Caligari, Nosferatu*) stimulated a research into composition; American so-called comics, that ought rather to be qualified as poetic or lyric (Mack Sennett, Charlie Chaplin, Hal Roach, Al St. John, Larry Semon, Buster Keaton, Harry Langdon) prompted a re-consideration of logic and reason; Swedish films (especially *La Charrette Fantôme*) released a wave of dreams and super-impositions; and later Soviet films (*Potemkin*) added fresh fuel to the preoccupation with cutting and editing. (Curtis 10)

Like much of the French avant-garde, Stein's first writing for film, *A Movie,* reflects the influence of American comic cinema. Action, visual humor, a car chase, a spy plot, a love story, and a last-minute-chase-and-capture scene are all included in Stein's short script. In Stein's simple action-adventure story, an American painter-cum-taxi driver-cum-spy races through the French countryside with his female servant, suffers a car crash, and recovers in time to capture two American crooks. Stein's writing style in the screenplay, quite different from her other writing of the period, is reminiscent of popular American films of the early 1900s, including the physical comedy in Max Lindner's *Troubles of a Grass Widower* (1908), the parallel editing of D.W. Griffith's *The Girl and Her Trust* (1912), and the action sequences of Henry "Pathé" Lehrman's *The Bangville Police* (1913). The rhythm of the writing is quick, even abrupt, and largely driven by action. Stein's sentences are short, remarkably clear, and, as previously noted, include a number of purely visual establishing shots. Rather than establish and maintain an evolving plot, the script is composed of a series of visual moments or exchanges: the painter trying to sell his artwork; teaching his servant to drive; evading the police; and visiting with American soldiers. These moments only loosely connect to form the basis of the simple plot. It is as if Stein is imitating the gag structure of American silent film comedy, initiated by early production houses such as Mack Sennett's Keystone Company (home of the Bangville Police series, also known as the Keystone Kops) and later popularized by such artists as Charlie Chaplin and Buster Keaton—but without the humor. She clearly eschews narrative, but her "gags" lack physical humor or wit. Like her "undramatic" drama, or her victimless murder mysteries, *A Movie* is a jokeless, humorless gag film.

Significantly, the very structure of Stein's script indicates an awareness of her cinematic sense. For example, paragraph breaks frequently occur on what would be major cuts in the film, including change of location or perspective, whereas minor cuts—different shots within a montage sequence—are contained within a single paragraph. Consider the following passage:

> American painter painting in French country near railroad track. Mobilisation locomotive passes with notification for villages.
>
> Where are American tourists to buy my pictures sacre nom d'un pipe says the american painter.
>
> American painter sits in café and contemplates empty pocket book as taxi cabs file through Paris carrying French soldiers to battle of the Marne. I guess I'll be a taxi driver here in gay paree say the american painter. (395)

In the above passage, three paragraphs correspond to three major edits: exterior shot of French countryside; shot of painter with intertitle text; painter in café watching taxis pass by, with intertitle. The images Stein conveys here move from a wide establishing shot to a closer, perhaps even a close-up, shot of the painter, to a new location in a café with each major cut accompanied by a paragraph break.

Stein's visual structure also indicates the use of a minor cut or montage sequence. Whereas a major cut indicates a new action, location, or idea, minor cuts separate distinct, but interrelated shots. The next example describes three different shots as part of a montage sequence detailing the painter's progress from landscape artist to taxi driver: "Painter sits in studio trying to learn names of streets with help of Bretonne peasant femme de ménage. He becomes taxi driver. Ordinary street scene in war time Paris" (395). Although the text (like the camera for which it substitutes) changes location and time, the brief sequence primarily depicts the visual progress of the painter. We "see" him study and become a taxi driver. The last sentence implies a larger scene containing numerous taxis, one of which (the shot implies) is driven by the painter.

This writing style heightens the presence of action within the screenplay. Whereas other Stein texts remain static, her *Movie* positively brims with activity, especially when the short screenplay reaches its rather dramatic climax. After the painter's servant, a woman referred to as "the Bretonne femme de menage peasant girl" (abbreviated by Stein as "Bretonne f. m."), receives telegrams and letters from family in Avignon, she and the painter decide to visit:

> Its snowing outside but no matter we will get there in the taxi. Take us two days and two nights you inside and me out. Hurry. They start, the funny little taxi goes over the mountains with and without assistance, all tired out he is inside, she driving when they turn down the hill into Avignon. Just then two Americans on motor cycles come on and Bretonne f. m. losing her

head grand smash. American painter wakes up burned, he sees the two and
says by God and makes believe he is dead. The two are very helpful. A team
comes along and takes american painter and all to hospital. Two Americans
ride off on motor cycles direction of Nimes and Pont du Gard. (396)

Contained within a single paragraph, or major cut, this series of actions
conveys a physical journey with (for Stein) an uncharacteristic economy of
language. The turning point in the script is the car crash, perhaps inten-
tional against the painter as spy. When he awakens in the hospital, the painter
valiantly leaves in search of the motorcyclists, who, after an "exciting duel,"
are discovered to have robbed the American military stationed in Paris. In an
ending worthy of Hollywood, the painter is rewarded for his efforts with the
special honor of driving his taxi at the end of the parade celebrating the Al-
lied victory. The final image of the screenplay describes the Bretonne woman
driving the taxi with the painter waving an American flag.

Following Stein's first attempt at cinematic writing in 1920, the cinematic landscape of Paris transformed radically. Whereas the 1910s witnessed
the emergence of screen melodrama in the work of D. W. Griffith and come-
dies like those of Max Lindner or the Keystone Kops, the 1920s saw the birth
of the avant-garde film. This new direction in cinema, based in part on the
dramatic and visual experiments of Dada and Surrealism, would remain a
major form of artistic production throughout the 1920s and no doubt had a
profound impact on Stein's writing, both cinematic and dramatic. If one compares the prevailing films available in Paris between 1920 and 1929 (including
the numerous films produced by Stein's friends and colleagues) to her own
cinematic writing, it is clear that the scope of influence on her writing extends
far beyond her collaborations with poets and composers, and must necessarily
include filmmakers and photographers as well.

Most notably, Stein maintained a friendship with one of the most prolific
cinematic and photographic artists of the 1920s, Man Ray. Though cordial,
their relationship was often one of mutual exploitation: Ray met many of his
portrait clients through Stein's salon, and she gained notoriety as the subject
of his photographs. Man Ray himself credited Stein as a major influence on
his work in photography and film, and at one point claimed to be her "official
photographer." In 1926, he wrote to inform Stein of his new work with cinema
(perhaps alluding to his forthcoming *Emak Bakia* [1926]), and in a letter from
July 1933, he described Stein as a crucial part of his artistic development.
Although there are varying accounts of the strength of their relationship (they
had a falling out over money in 1930), there is no doubt that they were in
frequent contact throughout the 1920s—during which time Ray produced his
major avant-garde films: *Return to Reason; Emak Bakia* (1926); *L'Etoile de
Mer* (1928); and *Les Mystères du Château de Dés* (1929).

But Man Ray was only one of a number of important artists to visit Stein during the 1920s. As avant-garde cinema reached its peak in Paris of the 1920s, so did Stein's literary and artistic salon. Filmmakers such as Buñuel, as well as visual artists such as Picasso and Cézanne, not to mention such cultural figures as Marcel Duchamp (who created the film *Anemic Cinema* [1925–26]), André Breton, Francis Picabia, and Tzara, were visitors to Stein's famous 27 Rue de Fleurus address. A few letters to Stein demonstrate that she and her circle discussed the latest filmic endeavors of the avant-garde. And although though there is no mention of Stein's attendance at the famous Dada performances, *Relâche* (literally, "relax" or "no performance") in 1924 and *Soirée di coeur à barbe* (Evening of the Bearded Heart) in 1925, it is likely that she at least knew about them since she knew nearly all the participants personally. "Relâche" and "Soirée," which featured the films *Entr'acte* and *Return to Reason,* as well as André Breton's violent outbursts, represented the height of Dada performance and cinema in Paris. Not only were these major films shown at the two performances, but at *Relâche* Tzara and others also performed their plays, including Tzara's *The Gas Heart* (1920).

Only a few years after these avant-garde films and performances first appeared in Paris, Stein was approached regarding her interest in the cinema. Kenneth Macpherson, editor of the newly formed cinema journal *Close-Up,* wrote on June 24, 1927, asking Stein to contribute a piece for publication in the journal. In his solicitation, Macpherson writes that "The most modern tendency seems so linked up in this [filmic] way and the kind of thing you write is so exactly the kind of thing that could be translated to the screen that anything you might send would be deeply appreciated" (14). In response, Stein sent two pieces, "Mrs. Emerson" and "Three Sitting Here," published in August and October 1927, respectively. Although her statement in "Plays" that "I myself never go to the cinema or hardly ever practically never and the cinema has never read my work or hardly ever" has been used as evidence of her cinematic ignorance, "Mrs. Emerson" seems to suggest that Stein had at least some familiarity with cinema houses. The poem begins: "I cannot see I cannot see I cannot see. I cannot see" (28) and refers to a house without windows, but filled with "kindly amazing lights," and exceptionally produced "cheerful shapes." These references have been read as oblique references to cinema and certainly given the context of "Mrs. Emerson" in the film journal opposite Man Ray's description of his *Emak Bakia,* the poem can be read as a description of film viewing, regardless of Stein's original intention in 1914. In this cinematic context, the repetition of "I cannot see" can be read as the experience one has sitting in the movie theater as the lights first go down before the film has begun. This darkness is then punctuated by the "kindly amazing lights," which may be a reference to film similar to Man Ray's description of photography and film as "painting with light," Laszlo Maholy-Nagy's film

Lichtspiele (1926), and perhaps even the French pioneers of cinema, Auguste and Louis Lumière.

But perhaps the most significant evidence of the avant-garde cinema's influence on Stein is her second and final attempt at writing for the screen. Only after perhaps the most important decade of major avant-garde filmmaking and her inclusion in *Close-Up* does Stein attempt her second screenplay, *Film. Deux Soeurs Qui Ne Sont Pas Soeurs,* in 1929. This second and final screenplay deviates radically from the gag structure of her first cinematic composition. This complex screenplay has much more in common with Stein's drama of the 1930s and 1940s than her earlier *Movie* and represents a dramatic shift in Stein's thinking about representation, language, and performance. Even the most cursory comparison of the two scripts demonstrates the impact of avant-garde cinema on Stein's writing. Whereas *A Movie* follows the plot structure of American comedy and is written in English, *Film* (French for "movie") abandons this cinematic structure in favor of a less linear, less representational series of images and is one of Stein's few publications in French. Although some credit Stein's collaboration with Virgil Thomson and the French poet Georges Hugnet as the reason for her shift in cinematic emphasis,[4] a more likely reason for the shift is Stein's increased exposure to avant-garde films of the 1920s (many of which were French) that transformed not only her screenplays, but also the remainder of her dramatic writing as well.

Film not only reflects Stein's interest in avant-garde film, but also marks Stein's thinking about gender and sexual identity. In *Film,* Stein returns to her original interest in photography and its duplication of reality. Rather than creating a single autonomous protagonist, Stein's *Film,* like her earlier play, *A Photograph,* concentrates on doubling and reproduction. The primary character—a protagonist only in the loosest sense—is a washerwoman "of a certain age," who will soon be joined by a younger washerwoman. The older washerwoman becomes entranced by a photograph of two white poodles. Suddenly, she is joined by two ladies, who see the photograph and are filled with admiration for the dogs. After a series of distractions, the washerwoman realizes that her photograph is gone. It will reappear finally as a live dog driving by with its new owners, the two ladies in an automobile. Within this simple story, Stein returns to her fascination with copies and doubles. Throughout the screenplay, there are two washerwomen, two women in the car, two poodles in the photograph, two appearances of the photograph, two appearances by a young woman and young man, two parcels (never opened), and one live dog, who himself is a duplicate of, (perhaps the product of?) the two dogs in the photograph.

It is this "Film," in particular, which takes up the division between cinema as realistic representation and as a "real" image itself. Maya Deren, who would later refer to this division in her essay "Cinematography: The Creative Use of Reality" (1960), writes that "if realism is the term for a graphic image which precisely simulates some real object, then a photograph must be differentiated from [a real object] as *a form of reality itself"* (emphasis in original, 64).[5] Unlike Stein's first screenplay, in which the world was self-evident, *Film* reflects her emphasis on the simultaneity of appearance and reality in the photographic and now cinematographic image. The title indicates immediately a discrepancy between what one perceives and what is true. As the story of *Film* is based on Stein's adoption of her and Toklas's first poodle, Basket, the title is often thought to refer to Stein and Toklas. Walking through the streets of Paris, they might appear to be sisters, when in fact they were lovers. It is here that Stein first begins to connect the potential multiplicities of meaning in cinema with the apparent duality of homosexuality. In both cinema and homosexuality, what first appears to be true may not in fact be "real." Further, homosexuality's sexual doubling echoes cinema's duplication of images. Just as cinema repeats nearly identical images in the individual frames of film, the partners of same-sex coupling are thought to repeat each other, much like the twins of *A Photograph.*

Not only Stein and Toklas ("two ladies"), but all of Stein's characters in *Film* are split between their perception and reality. Stein defines her characters by their appearance, but this is often misleading for readers or potential viewers. For example, while the older washerwoman and the two ladies from the automobile are gazing at the photograph, a young woman appears who "est coiffée comme si elle venait d'voir un prix dans un concours de beauté" (is made up as if she had just won a prize in a beauty contest, 399). While the viewer might expect such a striking figure to become prominent, she remains marginal in the narrative. The beauty queen gets into the empty automobile and, without reason or explanation, begins to weep. Strangely, no one responds. Eventually, the two ladies throw the young woman out, though their motives are similarly unclear. Stein is acutely aware of the expectations of the visual, and through *Film* she constantly works against the reader's or potential viewer's assumptions.

Stein's cinematic emphasis has clearly shifted (though she remains enamored of car chases, including one in *Film* as well) from the humor and excitement in a filmed visual spectacle to the inherent ambiguity or faultiness of film's representation of reality. Most striking in the film is the metamorphosis of the photograph of the two poodles into a single live dog, presumably Basket I.[6] But, as Stein realized, the live dog on film is barely different from the photograph of the dog on film. Both are photographic copies, despite the illusion of reality and movement created by the "live" dog. As Stein would later write in "Plays," "there is yet the trouble with the cinema that it is after all a photograph, and a photograph continues to be a photograph and yet can it become something else" (117). Thus, in a film there can be no real difference between the photograph of a dog on film and the image of the live dog on film. As Beth Hutchinson states in her assessment of the screenplays, "The transitory reality of the scene is long past; what the spectators of a film see is simply the procession of a series of photographs. That series of photographs has a minimal relation to 'reality,' despite appearances, just as a photograph of a dog has a tenuous relationship with the dog itself" (37). With camera tricks, super-imposition, slow motion, and repetitive editing, the cinema of the avant-garde also used the apparent reality of film as a means of questioning the concept of reality itself. Stein's manipulation of the doubles, and her photograph within a photograph, are no different from these other avant-garde cinematic pursuits, except that Stein has expanded her experiments to include identity and sexuality, two concepts often taken for granted by her male counterparts.

But perhaps Stein greatest affiliation with avant-garde film is her deliberate and repeated emphasis on looking. Her characters here are constantly engaged in the act of seeing. *Film* opens with the older washerwoman gazing "avec ardeur" at the photograph of the dogs. The characters all look at the beauty queen and she herself is defined by how she looks. The older washerwoman is so taken with the look of the beauty queen that she does not realize her photograph has been stolen. Whereas the plot of *A Movie* is driven by action—what characters do—the plot of *Film* is created by what characters see. It is as if, in her second screenplay, Stein fulfills the promise of her prelude to *A Movie,* "Eyes are a surprise." What characters see in *Film* often surprises them and is often incomprehensible both to the characters and to the audience. The last line of her script reads, "Les trois [older washerwoman, younger washerwoman, and young man] sur le trottoir le regarde [*sic*] passer et n'y comprennent rien." (The three on the sidewalk watch him [the dog] pass and they do not understand anything, 400). Thus, the characters, despite their progression throughout the film are left in the pessimistic state of seeing, but not understanding.

This screenplay recalls such self-reflexive images as the superimposed eyes in the camera lens of Man Ray's *Emak Bakia* and the reflection of Léger's camera in the swinging metallic ball in his *Le Ballet Mécanique,* and it prefigures such works as Samuel Beckett's *Film* (1968). Self-reflexivity, often visually represented through devices such as a mirror, appears in most of Stein's dramatic work after these early film scripts. Stein's questioning of reality and its representation deepens as her writing progresses and increasingly raises questions about identity and appearance, which are only briefly touched on in these early screenplays. For example, her later short play, "Three Sisters Who Are Not Sisters: A Melodrama"(1943), focuses almost exclusively on the relationship between the sisters and "two brothers who are brothers." In this odd murder mystery, the brothers and sisters play dead, pretend to kill one another, and dress up as various law enforcement officers trying to solve the crime. Just as *Film* contains a photograph within a photograph, Stein's other "Sisters" will enact a play within a play. In cinema, then, Stein finds an ideal form for representing the fragmentation, multiplicity, and simultaneity of modernity. If rapidly changing visual stimuli characterize modern urban experience, cinema seems uniquely able to capture the speedy, visual, and fractured quality of this life. With its inherent movement and multiple perspectives, cinema embodies these perspectives that, for Stein, are essential to life in the twentieth century.

It is therefore somewhat surprising that she did not pursue an interest in film beyond these two screenplays. Certainly in Stein's work there is a profound shift after this year. Compared with her screenplays and *Four Saints in Three Acts* (1927), her major dramatic work in the 1930s and 1940s is much more focused and more subtly executed. As her plays become more focused, they also become more theatrical. Most important, her increased subtlety of theme or idea articulates connections between gender and technology, names and identities, and rhythm and meaning. As one can see from a close study of her next major plays, *They Must. Be Wedded. To Their Wife.* (1931), and *Listen to Me* (1936), Stein's interest in human and gender identity, as well as the dramatic representation of character, becomes central to her work. Furthermore, her manipulation of dramatic form evolves from early exercises and experiments into an innovative and successful style, representing the human struggles of the modern world on stage. As opposed to screenplays that address gender identity but do not extend beyond the simple technique of repetition and doubling, Stein's later works establish her as a major American playwright by incorporating her early cinematic experiments into larger considerations of all humanity living in the shadow of technological "progress" and two world wars.

While it is possible only to speculate on Stein's real motivation, it seems likely that after her second film, Stein had taken her understanding of film to the limits of the form. As she would note in "Plays," the methods for cinema and the theater were radically different. In film, she would always be bound by the technology—the camera, the filmstrip, the projector. In theater, Stein found that she could abandon almost every convention—except, of course, her beloved words. For as visual as she believed the twentieth century to be, her real love was reserved for language. Most scholars who have examined Stein have articulated this same perception. But Stein would not neglect cinema and the visual in her later dramatic works. Rather, she would begin to treat her words as images and sounds themselves, as individual film frames. Stein did not continue in cinema because she had nothing more to say within what she perceived as its limitations. Instead, she would incorporate the lessons of cinema into her plays, creating works that not only transcended the limitations of both theater and film, but also transformed both media in ways that would resonate throughout the twentieth century.

Chapter 3
"Listen to Me": Stein and Avant-Garde Theater

"Every man must shout: there is great destructive, negative work to be done. To sweep, to clean. The cleanliness of the individual can appear only after we've gone through folly: the aggressive, complete folly of a world left in the hands of bandits who have demolished and destroyed the centuries."

TRISTAN TZARA, "DADA MANIFESTO" (1918)

"The twentieth century is a century which sees the earth as no one has ever seen it, the earth has a splendor that it has never had, and as everything destroys itself in the twentieth century and nothing continues, so then the twentieth century has a splendor which is its own."

GERTRUDE STEIN, *PICASSO* (1938)

After her experiments in film, Stein's plays incorporate not only elements of the cinematic, but also those of the theatrical avant-garde. Although she had been writing experimental drama since her first play, *What Happened* (1913), following the 1920s and major productions of the Dadaists, Surrealists, and Futurists, Stein's work became more recognizable both as performable drama and as a direct descendent of major avant-garde plays of this period. Her plays in the late 1920s and 1930s reflect an ever-increasing interest in the themes, techniques, and effects of the drama and theater of the early avant-gardists. As Stein's style progressed through *Four Saints in Three Acts* (1927), *They Must. Be Wedded. To Their Wife.* (1931), and *Listen to Me* (1936), her use of fragmentation, repetition, and negation increasingly resembled the deployment of these devices in avant-garde plays and productions during the interwar period. Although much has been written about Stein and the visual avant-garde—specifically Cubism—in such books as Michael Hoffman's *The Development of Abstractionism in the Writing of Gertrude Stein* (1965), Marianne DeKoven's *A Different Language: Gertrude Stein's Experimental*

Figure 3 *Wedding Bouquet.* Adapted from Gertrude Stein's *They Must. Be Wedded. To Their Wife.* Composed by Lord Gerald Berners. Sadler's Wells Ballet, 1937. Used by permission of the Estate of Gertrude Stein.

Writing (1983), and Randa Dubnick's *The Structure of Obscurity: Gertrude Stein, Language, and Cubism* (1984)—little to date has been written connecting Stein's drama to avant-garde performance and dramatic writing of the early twentieth century. As a literary figure, Stein has been classified as experimental, nonsensical, even "anti-art," but rarely has she been included in discussions of the theatrical avant-garde, despite sharing the ideas and methods of her more widely recognized contemporaries.

There are a variety of possible reasons for Stein's exclusion, not the least of which is her rather isolated position as a financially independent Jewish American lesbian among the financially struggling European men who constituted the majority of avant-garde writers and artists. In fact, Stein is often recognized not for her own artistic work but for her influence on, or recognition of, other artists: direct in the case of avant-garde painters such as Picasso, Matisse, and Braque, and young American writers Ernest Hemingway, Sherwood Anderson, and F. Scott Fitzgerald; and from her lingering influence on nontraditional American theater figures and movements of the 1960s and 1970s, including the Living Theater, Richard Foreman, and Robert Wilson, among others. Additionally, Stein's plays are often considered more literary than dramatic. In one of the first examinations of Stein's dramatic works, for example, Donald Sutherland wrote that "Her operas do take music and staging well, but they are first of all *literary* works embodying the essential qualities of opera—lyrical dramas, if you will—as her plays are literary works embodying the essence of stage plays" (my emphasis, 107). Most recently, Martin Puchner has argued for Stein as a closet dramatist who follows not the principles of the "distracting and interruptive nature of theater as it was systematically celebrated by the avant-garde," but rather ascribes to the "high modernist values of engulfment and solitary reading" (103). However, such statements ignore the progression of Stein's drama over three decades and unnecessarily group nearly everything she called a "play" into one category. Stein's dramatic writing as a body of work is much more nuanced than such categorical claims suggest. Certainly Stein was a literary author who devoted much of her energy to the effect of language on the solitary reader. However, as her dramatic career progressed, her work becomes progressively more theatrical and she turns attention increasingly to the role of the audience in theater. Although *Four Saints in Three Acts* is far better known than the works that followed it, it is perhaps the last of her "early" experiments in drama and as such represents the end of one phase in her dramatic career and the beginning of her more explicitly theatrical writing.

The perception of Stein as an exclusively (or at least primarily) literary author further distances her work from that of the theatrical avant-garde. Specifically, definitions of the historical avant-garde are often founded on the belief that avant-garde theater is explicitly antitextual—something Stein's plays clearly are not. While Christopher Innes, for example, claims that the search "for a new form of theater language" (58) is a defining element of the avant-garde, he specifically identifies this "new language" as separate from and independent of any written text. Similarly, in his introduction to *Contours of the Theatrical Avant-Garde,* James M. Harding argues that the anti-textualism of the avant-garde is essential to its ideology: "As the object against which the avant-garde was able to define itself, that text-based theater served not only as a foil for the avant-garde's anti-textualism but more generally for its opposition to the institutions of bourgeois culture" (9). Despite her radical reformulations of language, Stein consistently remained devoted to written language and to the centrality of the text, even in her plays. Given this commitment, it is not difficult to see her as outside an explicitly anti-textual avant-garde.

Finally, Stein's work has not been considered avant-garde for another reason unrelated to her literariness. In addition to being too "literary," Stein's plays are often thought to lack the antagonism found in the plays of other avant-garde artists. David Graver, for instance, argues in his *Aesthetics of Disturbance* that avant-garde drama "cultivates an aesthetics of disturbance, lashing out at the world around it, altering the composition of its aesthetic material in unexpected, unorthodox ways" (41), and by this definition he excludes not only Stein from consideration, but also Apollinaire, Cocteau, Tzara, Marinetti, and Mayakovsky, among others. Graver describes Stein's plays as "more surprising than disturbing" (209). The combination of these objections—literacy and non-antagonistic—may be found in Jane Palatini Bowers' book-length study of Stein's drama, in which she argues that Stein's work is both too literary and not aggressive enough to be counted among the work of the theatrical avant-garde. Her argument sums up much of the criticism that has placed Stein outside the avant-garde and is therefore worth citing at length.

> While Stein's plays, like those of the antagonistic avant-garde, present us with an unfamiliar and potentially alienating theater experience, I would argue that they are not antagonistic or nihilistic. Whereas the Surrealists sought to terrorize, the Dadaists to offend, and the Futurists to shock the audience, Stein wished for a theater experience that would allow the audience to "rest untroubled" in the performance of the play . . . The second and more important difference between Stein and the antagonistic avant-garde playwrights resides in the texts themselves and in the importance accorded to the text by the playwright. For the antagonistic avant-garde, the text is of minimal importance. Instead, the visual, spatial, and dynamic elements of performance are valorized. In fact, these theater texts are almost always antiliterary (either implicitly or explicitly). (130–131)

This is not to suggest, however, that Stein is never considered in light of the historical avant-garde. However, when Stein's drama *is* linked to the avant-garde, she is most often compared to avant-garde painters rather than avant-garde dramatists. In his essay "Gertrude Stein und ihre Kritik der dramatischen Vernunft" ("Gertrude Stein and her Critique of Dramatic Reason"), for example, Andrej Wirth argues that the confusion an observer might feel upon viewing or reading a Stein play is "the same uncertainty [one feels] when facing a collage by Picasso, Braque, or Heartfield" (my translation, 66). He goes on to state that "the programmatic and frequently disruptive Stein text is not unlike the strategy of a collage, in which the symbolic decoding is left to the respective observer" (67). Even Marc Robinson, who otherwise links Stein to other American playwrights claims that in Stein's plays, "'Act' and 'scenes' function like frames around paintings directing and focusing our attention on discrete sections of the perceived world" (14). Of course, both Robinson and Wirth are correct—Stein does have much in common with the visual avant-garde, but what they ignore is that the use of collage and the structure of the frame are not limited to the visual arts. Not only did avant-garde filmmakers of the period use the juxtaposition of images as a major principle of their work, but so did avant-garde performers and dramatists such as Hugo Ball, André Breton, and Roger Vitrac. These dramatists drew heavily from the visual arts and early cinema, creating theatrical texts and performances that violate expectations of theatrical realism and experiment with language in ways that echo Stein's drama.

What all of the objections to Stein as both a theatrical and an avant-garde writer ignore are the strong formal and thematic similarities between Stein's drama and the theater of the avant-garde, aside from the relationship of her work to avant-garde painting and photomontage. Techniques such as fragmentation and the creation of multiple or conflicting meanings are found both in Stein's theater and in Dada and Surrealist performance. The simultaneity so integral to the Futurists' vision of performance dominates much of Stein's dramatic writing. Moreover, the disruption of audience expectations that Wirth finds in Stein's drama was an essential component of avant-garde theater beginning with Alfred Jarry's *Ubu Roi* (1896), and continuing through nearly all of the avant-garde's first hundred years. Although it has been suggested that Stein was purely a literary oddity and modern art collector, she frequently entertained some of the most notable avant-garde *theater* artists including Tzara, Breton, and Apollinaire. Significantly, it was only after a period of approximately ten years of major avant-garde performance and filmmaking in Paris that Stein began seriously to write for the theater. Before 1927 she wrote short experimental pieces and called them plays, but it was not until the late 1920s that Stein began to write stageable drama. While there is no direct evidence that Stein attended avant-garde performances or read such scripts, the fact that her drama changed so noticeably following major avant-garde productions in Paris would suggest that she was influenced by them—either by seeing these shows or hearing them discussed. Indeed, it is unrealistic to assume that modern performance or, say, the Futurist theory of Filippo Tommaso Marinetti was never debated in Stein's company.

In fact, there is implicit evidence to the contrary. As Annabelle Melzer documents in her book *Dada and Surrealist Performance,* Marinetti was well-known to the Parisian literary circles and would have been known to Stein. Two of his manifestoes were published in Paris in 1909 and 1912 and his play *Le Roi bombace* [*sic*] was produced at the Théâtre de l'Oeuvre, with accompanying scandal, in 1909. In fact, Stein herself acknowledges in *The Autobiography of Alice B. Toklas* (1933) that, "It was about this time [1910s] that the futurists, the italian [*sic*] futurists, had their big show in Paris and it made a great deal of noise" (117). So similar is Stein's drama to that of Futurism, that Hugo Ball's writings on Futurism and the era from which it emerged read much like a description of Gertrude Stein's plays. In 1915, Ball writes, "In an age like ours, when people are assaulted daily by the most monstrous things without being able to keep account of their impressions . . . all living art will be irrational, primitive and complex; it will speak a secret language and leave behind documents not of edification but of paradox" (Melzer 30). Stein echoes this sentiment when she writes in her "Reflection on the Atomic Bomb" that "Everybody gets so much information all day long that they lose their common sense" (179). Given the dissemination of Futurist philosophy in Paris, then, as well as the number of visitors to 27 Rue de Fleurus who had connections not only to the avant-garde in Paris, but also to experimental movements in Zurich, Italy, and Germany, it is impossible completely to discount the influence of the theatrical avant-garde on Stein's plays.

In addition to the historical prominence of the avant-garde in Stein's social life, analyses of her plays further reveal the influence of the avant-garde. Although Bowers claims, quite rightly, that Stein was focused on "the language and language-making activity of the poet," she was not interested in language merely for its own sake; rather, she used language as an avant-garde tool to dissect and critique issues of gender, technology, and war in the modern era. Stein attacked the rules of grammar and syntax as vehemently as the Dadaists attacked their audiences' moral sensibilities. Although Stein never overtly provoked her audience, she repeatedly unnerved its members by distorting sentence structure as well as defamiliarizing words and phrases. Given the repeated attacks on Stein both privately and in print, her approach seems to have worked. Thus Stein can be considered an antagonistic playwright in Graver's sense, if only because she so passionately deconstructed the simplest component of communication—conversational speech. In the wake of World War I, Stein's drama echoes precisely the breakdown of human communication and of the ability to comprehend an increasingly chaotic and disturbing world. As with nearly all her avant-garde contemporaries, Stein's dramatic techniques mirror the automatization, atomization, and anomie of a Europe devastated by the first mechanized war.

World War I, Science, and the Avant-Garde

Although Stein has been excluded from considerations of the avant-garde because of her perceived lack of aggression or antagonism toward her audience, she was fully aware of the relationship between art and war. In fact, in advance of such critics as Renato Poggioli and Peter Bürger, both of whom argue for a fundamental negativity in the avant-garde, Stein clearly recognized the destructiveness of World War I as a significant influence on modern art (or the "modern composition," as she called it) and its reception. She believed that the experience of World War I had created a way of seeing that not only artists, but also their audiences could appreciate and understand. In her 1926 essay "Composition as Explanation," Stein wrote that war had brought popular views of modern art, or as she called it "contemporary composition," in line with the works themselves. She argued that war accelerates the "natural" process of appreciating avant-garde artists. Whereas before the war, these artists had to forge new directions with little or no recognition until after their deaths, now war had compressed this process allowing audiences to see and understand the artists' vision without needing history to inform it.[1] War had, according to Stein, created an avant-garde audience. It is with this audience in mind that Stein began writing plays. Although she stated (many

years after these early plays) that she wanted her audience "to rest untroubled" in her drama, the works themselves do not reflect an untroubled world.
Rather, Stein attempts in these plays to convey the chaos and confusion of the
modern era, represented not through the orderly progression of a well-made
play, but through language as distorted and twisted as the terrain of war-torn
Europe.

Both Stein's drama and the theater of the avant-garde may be perceived
as antagonistic and nihilistic because both were influenced by the frightening
new technologies of war. It is nearly impossible to discuss the avant-garde
without simultaneously considering the tremendous effect on human perception caused by World War I. Aerial bombing, machine guns, nerve gas, hand
grenades, tanks, and trench warfare scarred the European psyche as much
as they did the European countryside. And Stein, like many artists living in
Europe during the "Great War," believed that it had irreparably changed human consciousness. If the postwar audience had finally caught up with the
modern artist, it was because the war awakened in both artist and audience
a similar sense of chaos, irrationality, and ambivalence or indecision. The
logic of realistic and naturalistic drama no longer reflected the daily reality
of European citizens, and the science that was thought to enlighten humanity
and improve civilization turned out to have horrifying technological consequences. As Hugo Ball glossed the scene in 1916:

> The image of the human form is gradually disappearing from the painting of
> these times and all objects appear only in fragments. This is one more proof
> of how ugly and worn the human countenance has become, and of how all
> the objects of our environment have become repulsive to us. (Melzer 31)

But not only were Stein and other avant-gardists writing drama influenced
by the most destructive war in history—"the war to end all wars"—they were
also writing in response to radical transformations in science. Although the
term "avant-garde" originated as a military term—and indeed retained its aggressive connotation throughout much of the early twentieth century—it also
began to reflect a deep connection with science. In the wake of theories like
Darwin's, it came to reflect a belief in an unstable and unfinished universe. As
much as the drama of the avant-garde was shaped by the events of World War
I, it was also influenced by such scientific developments as Einstein's theory
of relativity, Max Planck's quantum physics, Heisenberg's uncertainty principle, and Freud's theory of psychoanalysis and the subconscious. Each new
scientific theory introduced greater uncertainty to an already unstable model
of the universe. With each new discovery or theory, the concept of a knowable
world was further eroded. Just as war had uprooted faith in technology, so
did each scientific discovery further challenge the existence of absolute, fixed
knowledge.

It seems no coincidence, then, that many of the founding members of the avant-garde were doctors or had scientific training, as did Richard Huelsenbeck and André Breton. Stein herself trained as a medical doctor in psychology, studying under William James ("the father of American psychology") and Hugo Münsterberg at Harvard and completing all but her final year at Johns Hopkins University's medical school. Like Breton, Stein pursued her interest in psychology in the drama, in the form of "automatic writing." Stein's first published essay documented her early experiments designed to uncover the subconscious through such writing—the same style promoted by Breton some years later as a major tenet of Surrealism. In fact, Breton had remarkably similar experiences to Stein in his first attempts at automatic writing. After Breton worked with shell-shocked victims of World War I, he "concluded that the investigation of the unconscious should also remain open to poets who could use relational methods in pursuit of what he called the 'marvellous'" (Gale 218). As a result of their psychological experiments, both Stein and Breton explored the role of an unpredictable and often disturbing subconscious or unconscious mind in their plays. Although Stein herself claimed never to have engaged in the technique of automatic writing—most likely, to avoid claims that her work was not sophisticated—many of her characters speak as if directly from their own subconscious. These characters frequently repeat themselves, stutter, and launch into expositions of their own thoughts, which are frequently indecipherable both to other characters as well as the audience. Furthermore, Stein begins even in her earliest plays to break down unified characterizations by dividing one character into numerous names.

Strongly influenced by "progressive" scientific and technological developments, then, Stein's plays developed in ways very similar to those of her better-known avant-garde contemporaries, the Dadaists, Futurists, and Surrealists. Although avant-garde traces are evident in Stein's earliest dramas, she would best use these techniques—fragmentation, collage, and automatic speech—to create her first full-length—and first major—drama, *Four Saints in Three Acts.* This and Stein's subsequent plays of the late 1920s and 1930s clearly mark her not only as a remarkably dedicated member of the dramatic avant-garde, but also as a deeply profound one.

Four Saints in Three Acts (1927)

In January 1926, Virgil Thomson approached Gertrude Stein with the proposition that they should collaborate on an opera. Thomson had already set some of Stein's shorter pieces to music and he now wanted to create an original opera for which Stein would write the libretto. Stein agreed and the result was *Four Saints in Three Acts,* a work that has since become the signature work in Stein's dramatic oeuvre, despite its somewhat transitional position in her dramatic progression. One of only three works to be produced during her lifetime, and certainly the most significant given its run on Broadway, *Four Saints* is nevertheless a quite marginal play in Stein's collected work. In it she makes her first real foray into theater, but it is an uncertain entrée. Since the project was proposed by Virgil Thomson, a young and relatively unknown composer at the time, one suspects that Stein may have tested the commitment of the young man. Certainly, she presented Thomson with a seemingly unstagable text. As Martin Puchner notes, "The transformations that were necessary for staging *Four Saints* can serve as a measure for the distance Stein's text maintains from the theater" (111).

Given that *Four Saints* was written to be an opera and is explicitly subtitled "An Opera to Be Sung," it is perhaps questionable to consider the work purely as drama, independent of its music and production. However, my investigation into the play is less a consideration of the end product in performance, than an inquiry into the text as a stage in the evolution of Stein's dramatic writing.[2] First, although she may have desired, and possibly even counted on, the opera's eventual production, Stein was mostly absent from the creation of that production. Stein gave her libretto to Thomson, who wrote the music and later employed the painter Maurice Grosser to create a "scenario" for the piece. Grosser's scenario gave Stein's words a visual context or setting, which he admitted to creating with considerable liberty. As a result of this rather loose collaboration, most of the production choices were made without Stein's influence or comment. Thus, to consider Stein's text in the context of its eventual production, including music, setting, and story (none of which she created), is to read her words as part of a collaboration in which she had no direct participation. To examine the libretto strictly as drama, independent of its score or production, is to understand Stein's dramatic purpose before that purpose was shaped by Thomson and Grosser.

Furthermore, Stein's text for *Four Saints* has much more in common with her other drama of the time, namely *They Must. Be Wedded. To Their Wife.* and *Listen to Me,* than with her second and final opera, *The Mother of Us All* (1945–46). While writing *Mother,* Stein obviously had a much greater understanding of how her text might be interpreted and staged, having already seen Thomson's production of *Four Saints.* Conscious manipulation of the text for performance, including crucial silences in the last scene of *Mother,* are largely absent from *Four Saints.* On the page, *Four Saints,* with its lists of character names, abundant punctuation, and odd repetitions clearly prefigures her next two plays with little or no connection to her later opera. It may be that Stein titled *Four Saints* an opera ironically. The director, Robert Wilson, greatly influenced by Stein, called his *Einstein on the Beach* an opera, not because it was a literal opera, but because it did not fit any conventional genre. According to Wilson, it was not a narrative play, nor a musical, nor a painting; hence he titled it an opera after the word's etymological root, "opus" or work. Just as likely, of course, is the possibility that Stein titled *Four Saints* an opera because that is what Thomson said he wanted to compose. Given Stein's own limited involvement in creating the musical aspects of *Four Saints* and the similarities between her libretto and her nonmusical drama, it thus seems most useful to consider this work as a stage in her dramatic progression, independent of the music that was later added to it.

Despite its apparent unstagability, *Four Saints* differs significantly from Stein's early experimental "plays," and includes unprecedented stage directions (however obliquely written), characters, recognizable dialogue, and dramatic conventions of act and scene, although their use is distorted almost beyond recognition. One need only compare *Four Saints* to its thematic predecessors to see how far Stein has evolved in her sense of drama. *Lend a Hand or Four Religions* (1922), for example, demonstrates Stein's earliest thinking about the relationship between saints and performance. Although not identified as a play, *Lend a Hand* explicitly mentions actors and actresses and much of the text is presented as action. In a paragraph seemingly labeled (or attributed to) "Third religion" she writes, "On Thursday [Third's-day?] actors and actresses are arriving. As she counts ten are her lips moving or is it Thursday and are actors and actresses arriving" (171). The performance of the actors is directly parallel to the performance of prayer: "[she is] kneeling in a way in that way, in that way kneeling and being a chinese [*sic*] Christian meditatively" (171). Throughout this text, unnamed people (typically referred to as "he," "she," "they," and "I") constantly *do* things. The text is full of descriptive verbs none of which can be attributed to any recognizable characters. Importantly, *Four Saints* takes these verbs and begins to embody action, or more precisely inaction, in recognizable characters. Though largely descriptive, *Four Saints* represents a shift in Stein's thinking about theater from the abstraction of idea to the physical embodiment of performance. For instance, in her opening Stein writes, "Four benches used four benches used separately" (12).

In her attempt to create performance texts, Stein borrowed from the techniques of avant-garde theater and cinema. Perhaps the strongest evidence for this assertion is in the structure of the play itself. Often termed a "landscape play," *Four Saints* is a remarkably static text with little character or plot development. This static quality, together with Stein's own misleading analogy between her plays and landscapes, has often led critics to compare *Four Saints* with painting. Norman Weinstein writes in "Play as Landscape" that "Dramatic tension is created by the contrasts between different verbal masses ... Set in contrast with each other they create tensions analogous to the color of painted masses in Kandinsky or Pollock" (120). But this same dramatic tension is found in Futurist drama and Dada performance as well. In fact, several Futurist plays bear strong resemblance to Stein's. The Futurist Remo Chiti's play "Words," for example, uses discontinuous phrases to create its static drama. To cite only a few lines from the play:

> ... and why ARE THEY also a ...
>
> ... exactly! And in FIFTY YEARS not ...
>
> ... go there! THAT IS enough ...
>
> ... of him who WAITS something more ...
>
> ... that is SOMETHING that doesn't work ...
>
> ... he put it BY THE DOOR and he said ... (258)

This use of nonsequential dialogue to create a single, yet disjointed, moment is common throughout Stein's drama as well as that of other avant-garde writers. In fact, such verbal collisions probably have less in common with avant-garde painting than with the visual techniques of avant-garde cinema, which, as previously mentioned, sought to create a similar effect on the viewer through rapid montage. Both in Stein's plays and in avant-garde cinema and theater, the discontinuity of action and images, whether read, heard, or seen, creates a sense of confusion similar to what Georg Simmel described in "The Metropolis and Mental Life" as human experience in the modern city: "the rapid crowding of changing images, the sharp discontinuity in the grasp of a single glance, and the unexpectedness of onrushing impressions" (410). In *Four Saints,* Stein also creates a disorienting effect through her use of punctuation and repetition. In her longer passages, she frequently combines sentences without punctuation, forcing the reader or speaker to move through the language without cues indicating where to pause, breathe, or place emphasis. To quote from *Four Saints:*

> Settled passing this in having given in which is not two days when everything being ready it is no doubt not at all the following morning that it is very much later very much earlier with then to find it acceptable as about about which which as a river river helping it to be in doubt. (29)

Although the words and some phrases are familiar—"everything being ready it is no doubt"—this passage as a whole creates the impression of language in chaos. With careful reading, one can discern a vague meaning in Stein's text, but read only once or spoken aloud even at a slow pace, the passage seems to have been written in another language. Stein defamiliarizes even the most ordinary language, and this defamiliarization is integral to understanding her work.

Throughout *Four Saints,* Stein's language is never totally inaccessible—the words are easily recognizable and many of her sentences are short—but, the context is highly ambiguous, and the writing as a whole creates the impression of nonsense. In her manipulations of language, Stein experiments with ideas that derive not from logical progression, but from spontaneous thought or unpredictable act. It is less Stein's language that is broken and disjointed, then, than the mental as well as physical world her language represents. As did most avant-gardists, Stein uses the verbal fragment to represent her sense of a fractured reality. She also seems to be aware here, for the first time, of her effect on an audience. For example, her title claims that she offers four saints and three acts, whereas in fact there are many saints and a structure that makes keeping track of the number of acts virtually impossible. Stein begins her play with the misleading promise of a well-made, three-act play structure and then devilishly dismantles the audience's formal expectations throughout the drama. The only way to describe the play's structure, absent characteristics of both climactic and episodic form, is as a collection of fragments. Fragments of biography—from the lives of saints as well as from Stein's own life—of realist play structure, and of language combine to create the disorienting world of Stein's *Four Saints in Three Acts*.

This use of the fragment is common to many of her plays, but for the first time in *Four Saints* this fracturing of the world in general extends to her individual characters as well. Perhaps influenced by artists such as Kurt Schwitters and certainly by film, Stein represents characters as fractured and multiple identities, a concept that extended to the staging of *Four Saints* through Virgil Thomson's casting of two women to play Saint Therese. But one could conceivably cast dozens of women to play Saint Therese, as Stein suggests early in the play by drawing specific attention to potentially simultaneous versions of Saint Therese:

Saint Therese. Not this not in this not with this.
Saint Therese must be theirs first.
Saint Therese as a young girl being widowed.
Saint Therese. Can she sing.
Saint Therese. Leave later gaily the troubadour plays his guitar.
Saint Therese might it be Martha.
Saint Louise and Saint Celestine and Saint Louis Paul and Saints Settlement Fernande and Ignatius.
Saint Therese. Can women have wishes. (18)

Stein's seemingly inconsistent verb choices create the impression of several images occurring simultaneously. Saint Therese must belong to someone, is being widowed, leaves a troubadour, might be Martha, and also questions the audience with the poignant last line, "Can women have wishes." This decentering of Saint Therese is directly related to both technology and representation. Stein took her inspiration for this representation of Saint Therese from photography and its unique ability to stop time and render a sequential event in a single, isolated moment.

In *Four Saints,* Stein describes a photographic progression of Saint Therese from a "lady" to a nun: "Saint Therese could be photographed having been dressed like a lady and then they taking out her head changed it to a nun and a nun to a saint and a saint so" (17). In her essay "Plays," Stein describes a photography display in which a young girl is gradually transformed into a nun through a series of still photographs. It is within this photographic sequence that Stein locates the evolution of Saint Therese's identity from girl to nun (130). Thus, Stein transforms the icon of Saint Therese into a modernist construction—a picture in sequence, with each stage of the development from girl to nun simultaneously represented. For his adaptation of Stein's text to the stage, Virgil Thomson chose to have a single performer (alternating between the two women who simultaneously played St. Therese) say each of the lines attributed to Saint Therese on a particular page, regardless of how many times her name appeared on that page. But it is impossible to know if this was actually Stein's intention, particularly since Thomson communicated with Stein very little during the rehearsal process. It is highly possible that, for Stein, each repetition of Saint Therese's name represented an entirely new character (or at the very least a different aspect of the same character), coincidentally also named Saint Therese. By using repeated names in the text, Stein creates a fundamentally fractured world in which there is no real cohesion even at the most basic, individual level—in other words, an avant-garde image of history and humanity.

Finally, Stein's use of repetition distorts time in an experimental manner. She repeats not only phrases and names, but also entire acts, as in the stage direction, "Repeat First Act" (16). In addition to stage directions, Stein also repeats scene numbers, as in her series of Scene Fives (V):

Scene V

There are many saints.

Scene V

They can be left to many saints.

Scene V

Many Saints.

Scene V

Many many saints can be left to many many saints scene five left to many many saints.

Scene V

Scene five left to many saints.

Scene V

They are left to many saints and those saints these saints these saints. Saints four saints. They are left to many saints.

Scene V

Saint Therese does disgrace her by leaving it along and shone.
Saint Ignatius might be five.
When three were together one woman sitting and seeing one man lending
and choosing one young man saying and selling. This is just as if it was a tribe.

Scene V

Closely.

Scene V

Scene five Saint Therese had a father photographically. Not a sister.
Saint Therese had no mother and no other appointed to be left at hand. (25–26)

In a number of ways, this series of scenes illustrates the effect of
avant-garde principles on Stein's dramatic writing. By repeating Scene V,
Stein effectively stops time, and by repeating the "many saints," Stein strips
them of their uniqueness and what Walter Benjamin called "aura." Stein traps
her audience in a repetition of scenes akin to a broken record, though, as
she would later argue, the list of Scene Vs is not a true repetition. Although
in written form (and in Thomson's production) these scenes occur sequen-
tially, it is possible to imagine that all the Scene Vs occur simultaneously.
By thus constructing a "continuous present"—a scene that neither progresses
nor concludes, but rather continuously cycles—Stein creates her own kind
of simultaneity on stage. She employs this technique throughout her drama,
creating a body of work that plays endlessly with time as a fluid dramatic
element. Stein's use of repetition, simultaneity, overlapping images, nonlinear structure, overlapping speech, and non sequitur dialogue in *Four Saints*
indicates a new direction in her work and firmly places that work within the
scope of avant-garde drama. But for Stein, the techniques of the avant-garde
not only offered her a means to reflect the world around her; they also enabled
her to project her own inner turmoil and division.

They Must. Be Wedded. To Their Wife. (1931)

In the 1930s Stein's drama became less about the world around her and increasingly focused on her own psyche and fractured gender-identity. Just as Breton
submitted his dreams to meticulous examination and dramatic portrayal, Stein
began to dissect her own interiority, particularly in terms of gender. In *They
Must. Be Wedded. To Their Wife.* and many of her other dramatic writings
of the same period, this fracturing of identity is primarily articulated through
the manipulation of names. Throughout Stein's career, character names were
of constant interest to her. She often repeated names, borrowed names from
friends, and frequently used names that created puns. It is possible that what
may initially have attracted Stein to drama was the listing of character names

on the left margin of dramatic texts, before the dialogue; and the repetition of names, particularly in scenes with only two characters, must have intrigued her. Or perhaps what interested her was the fact that, in drama, the names stand in for the physical character, who is listed in detail at the beginning of the script but exists only as a name for the remainder of the text. Or perhaps, as Randa Dubnick argues in her *The Structure of Obscurity,* drama attracted Stein's attention because it followed the vertical format, or lists, that she had previously explored in poetry. Whatever the reason, Stein goes farther in her treatment of names than most avant-garde (or even non-avant-garde) dramatists, working systematically to separate the names from their automatic association with character. In her 1931 essay "Sentences," Stein explored the relationship between names and other parts of speech, claiming that a noun was not a name and that this difference was "a great discovery." This questioning of the connection between names and nouns is at the heart not only of Stein's drama, but of Surrealist drama as well. Both question the essence of reality: does naming something make it so, or is there a deeper reality that cannot be named but nevertheless exists? These questions are also fundamentally "queer" questions. Does being named a woman make Stein a woman? Does Stein's naming herself "husband" make her a man, if only in her own mind?

This slippery relationship between names and nouns constitutes the central dramatic question in the original Surrealist play, Apollinaire's *Breasts of Tiresias* (1917). In it a woman, tired of her limited role of bearing sons only to lose them to war, changes her gender and on stage becomes a man. Once Thérèse (perhaps an influence on Stein's later name choices?) calls herself a man, she grows a beard and releases her breasts into the sky "like toy balloons" (69). Importantly, the character's transgender transformation is accompanied by her renaming herself Tiresias.[3] Indeed, as a result of naming herself a man, Thérèse promptly becomes one. In response to his wife's transformation, the husband (who, significantly, has no name) joins with a (similarly nameless) policeman to populate the world without women and produces 40,050 children. At the conclusion of the play, Thérèse is reunited with her husband, bringing with her "three influential ladies whose lover I have become" (90). But despite the reconciliation with her husband, Thésèse's identity is never completely resolved. Her husband wants her to give herself breasts again, and he offers her balloons and balls with which to make them. But Thérèse rejects his offer, throwing the would-be breasts into the audience. She declares, "We've both of us done without them/Let's continue," and the husband concurs by saying, "That's true let's not make matters complicated/Let's go and dunk our bread" (91). That Apollinaire chooses gender as the destabilizing force for his Surrealist play reinforces the relationship between the avant-garde and queerness.

In his preface to *The Breasts of Tiresias,* Apollinaire makes clear his intention, stating that "I am in no way undertaking to form a school, but above all to protest against that 'realistic' theater which is the predominating theatrical art today" (60). He names his drama "surrealist":

> To characterize my drama I have used a neologism which, as I rarely use
> them, I hope will be excused: I have invented the adjective *surrealist,* which
> does not at all mean *symbolic*...but defines fairly well a tendency in art
> which, if it is not the newest thing under the sun, at least has never been for-
> mulated as a credo, an artistic and literary faith...And in order to attempt,
> if not a renovation of the theater, at least an original effort, I thought it neces-
> sary to come back to nature itself, but without copying it photographically.
> (emphasis in original, 56)

This division between nature and its copy as filtered through the mind
and language is at the heart of both Surrealist drama and Stein's plays. What
distinguishes the Surrealistic from the "symbolic," according to Apollinaire,
is the number of possible interpretations for a Surrealist drama, as opposed to
the self-evident meaning of a symbolic one. Apollinaire quotes Victor Basch's
definition of symbolic drama as one containing a "relationship between symbol, which is always a sign, and the thing signified [which is] immediately
apparent" (57). Apollinaire actively works against this singular relationship
between symbol and meaning, claiming that "there are notable works in which
the symbolism rightly has numerous interpretations which sometimes contradict each other" (57–58).

Another way of understanding the relationship between nature and its
Surrealistic dramatization is through the language of semiotics. In semiotics
the world and its system of representation are defined through the signifier, the
signified, and the referent. Significantly, Ferdinand de Saussure in *Course in
General Linguistics* (1906–1911) frames his discussion of the linguistic sign
(or signifier) as a challenge to the notion that language is simply a process of
naming. Instead, Saussure argues that "The linguistic sign unites, not a thing
and a name, but a concept and a sound-image" (66). He further argues that
however arbitrary the sign may be, its relationship to the signifier is fixed. "The
signifier, though to all appearances freely chosen with respect to the idea that
it represents, is fixed, not free, with respect to the linguistic community that
uses it" (71). It was this fixed relationship between signifier and signified
that both Stein and the avant-garde theater sought to abolish. For example,
in his "An Introduction to Dada," Tristan Tzara writes that the early Dada
poems "were a part of the general tendency which expressed itself in the form
of an organized struggle against logic. This method presupposed that words
could be stripped of their meaning yet still be effective in a poem by their
simple evocative power" (404). Thus, for both Dada and Surrealism, the goal
in language is to rupture the fixed relationship between the signifier and the
signified, or as Stein put it, names and nouns.

In considering Stein's writing, it is further useful to consider the use
of semiotics in relation to film viewing. According to *New Vocabularies in*

Film Semiotics, "The signifier is the sensible, material, acoustic or visual
signal which triggers a mental concept, the signified. The perceptible aspect
of the sign is the signifier; the absent mental representation evoked by it
is the signified . . ."(8). In a stable semiotic system, the signifier will create
in each audience member a similar, if not identical, mental representation,
which in turn is readily identifiable as an object in reality, the referent: a tree,
a house, etc. But in the Surrealist, Dada, or Steinian system, the corresponding
relationship among signifier, signified, and referent is ruptured. The sign or
signifier is arbitrary and its relationship to the signified is similarly fluid.
The signifier may create any number of different mental representations in an
audience, none of them more or less valid than another. The signified may or
may not have an identifiable referent in reality. In other words, an avant-garde
system of semiotics is a closed system, referring only to itself, rather than
to an objective reality outside its system of representation. Its names refer
only to other names, not nouns. Similarly, in *They Must. Be Wedded. To Their
Wife.* Stein creates a closed system of her own, destabilizing the relationship
between names and nouns.[4]

   In this play, the signifiers or names Stein chose do not have immediately
recognizable signifieds or referents. The names do not necessarily represent
directly corresponding characters, but may in fact represent many characters.
From the beginning Stein challenges the assumption that every name cor-
responds to a single character. The first line of the play (unassigned to any
character) reads, "Any name. Of which. One. Has known. At least two" (161).
Implied in this opening statement are the simultaneous possibilities that for
every name, one knows at least two people with that name, and that a "one"
may have known, or been known by, at least two names. This lack of connection between a single name and a single character may explain Stein's
technique of repeating the same name for every consecutive line of a character's dialogue, as well as her erratic use of punctuation (her overuse of the
period, for example). Unlike most plays, the names in *They Must* do not have
consistently corresponding relationships to characters outside the names; instead, they continually shift, representing first one character, then a part of a
character, and finally no character at all. The names separate from each other
to create the impression of a fragmented identity, but they may also combine
to create an ephemeral sense of unity. By using endlessly evolving names and
characters, Stein creates an environment in which identity exists in a fluid
state and characters operate independently of a fixed body.

   Consider, for example, a passage from one of Stein's Scene IVs:

THERESE.   May she be thought well of, by all who are made clearly in
           their prayers as brother and their brother. She may shut. It.
           Without them. By the time. That they. Are cautious. In this
           case. No. One. Is mentioned.

JULIA.   Julia who has won Guy to be welcome to them. Welcome to them. Julia who has been unwilling to be unwelcome to them. Julia who has been unwilling to be with them unwelcome for them. Julia who has been with them welcome for them. With them. By them.

JULIA AND GUY. One. Two. Three.

ERNEST. And a pause. A pleasure. And a pause.

JOHN.   A pleasure without a pause without them.
              Scene in which they second them. (166)

In this short scene, Stein uses names in a fairly conventional way. But as soon as the characters speak, it is clear that the relationship between the names and the characters is ambiguous at best. Julia, for instance, refers to herself in the third person, creating three simultaneously possible readings: she is talking about herself in the third person; she is talking about another person named Julia; or this is not actually dialogue, but rather a description of Julia or stage directions for her. Given the language and its lack of context, none of these options is more likely than any other, for Stein has left the character of Julia deliberately mysterious. It may be that Stein intends to present only one of the three possibilities, or all of them simultaneously. And the language of the other characters is no clearer. They may refer to themselves, each other, unseen characters, or no one at all. The identities are perpetually in motion, seeming consciously to reject the traditional means for segregating them. Stein admits just such a shifting relationship between characters when she writes in the middle of the play, "They all come together. They have known each other" (167).

Her creation of such flexible character identities reflects both a significant connection with Surrealism and, paradoxically, a major departure from most of her fellow avant-gardists. While, on the one hand, Stein creates the kind of ambiguous dream world without fixed boundaries on which Surrealism based much of its aesthetic, on the other, she explores the limits of gender in relation to the self to a far greater extent than the Surrealists. The attention to gender that Stein exhibits in *They Must* gives her experiments with character names major dramatic (as opposed to merely linguistic) significance, unseen in most other avant-garde drama. Her blending of personalities is not arbitrary, but rather reflects Stein's own ambiguous and shifting gender-identity.

Although characters occasionally blend into one another, they are unable to remain unified as a single character for long. In Chapter 1, I cite "Scene II," in which character names seem to separate and rejoin, culminating in a single unified name and identity. Although the characters do seem to unify, or perhaps distill in Scene II, they do not remain so throughout the play. Indeed, the question of self-identity as expressed through a fixed name is repeated throughout the play both in stage directions and character speech.

Significantly, the character discussions nearly all center on an unnamed "she" and her relationship to the ubiquitous "it." Earlier, I suggested that "it" might be the unified identity for which the characters seem to seek. However, it may also refer to a name. In another Scene II, the combined character of Josephine and Nichole asks "Is it. A name. For a. Woman." (178). In a Scene VI following Josephine and Nichole's question, five male characters (or, at least their names) pursue the multiplicity of the "she's" name. The scene begins with "Could know all," then "They will call./One." (178). If we assume that the progression of names cited in Chapter 1 is indeed focused on a multiple identity, then this text, positioned only a few pages later, seems to follow as a similar meditation on female identity. The outside observer "could know all" the contradictory identities, but could still "call" the person "one" name.

The tension between a fragmented self-identity and the potential for unity is highlighted in the final two lines of the scene. At the end of this scene, Stein offers the possibility that

PAUL.

      and   She may be.

GUY.   They may. Be. As. They. May. Be.

PAUL.   With it. She might. Be united. (179)

Here, Stein distinguishes between the "they," who seem fixed (they may be as they are) and the she who still might be unified. But, of course, although "she" *might* be united, she never is. Constantly poised on the brink of action as expressed through the constructions of "might be" and "may be," "she" does nothing. Thus, Stein creates a world in which the multiple parts of the self cannot be unified, and where individuals lack the ability to connect or communicate with themselves or each other. Taken to its extreme, this is a dramatic world in which all unity is false, even in language. Words cannot form coherent sentences, just as characters cannot unify into single, stable names or identities. In the last few scenes, Stein completely abandons her use of conjunctions to connect character names, instead listing names in isolation. By the end of the play, characters seem to have given up the possibility of unity, connection, or any kind of communion. Listed in isolation and still stuttering, the characters grind the play to a slow halt:

THERESE.   May talk. Of it.

THERESE.   And take. More. Of it.

THERESE.   As they will. Please. Be with it.

THERESE.   Here. With it.

JULIA.   For them. To have no one.

JOSEPHINE.   Or just more. Than ever.

JOSEPHINE.   More than. Alike.

JOHN.   Should.

GUY.   Which they mean.

PAUL.   Maintain.

ERNEST.   One. At one time. (194)

In part because the "it" mentioned is left unidentified, the sense of separateness and isolation in this "dialogue" is overpowering. The totally broken, stuttering sentence structure creates a disturbing distance between the characters. Just as characters cannot find a unified self, their communication has been slowed to a state where punctuation conquers meaning and language cannot congeal into complete sentences. Fragmentation ultimately dominates the self, speech, and the surrounding environment. Everyone is finally "One. At one time," but this is not a cohesive "one." Humanity, once fragmented, is left to exist in total isolation—perhaps individually unified, but separated from every other entity.

Listen to Me (1936)

Whereas *They Must. Be Wedded. To Their Wife.* focuses on individuals in an isolating and unstable world, Stein's next play reduces characters even further—to total anonymity. With the exception of Lillian and Sweet William, whom Stein based on her friend Bertie Abdy, all other characters are referred to as "first character," "second character," etc. Again Stein plays with fluid identity, initially stating that there are three characters and later incorporating fifteen characters coughing. She also "loses" characters, asking no one in particular, "How can they lose the second character" (399). But rather than concentrate on isolation and loss at the individual level, Stein focuses the majority of this play on larger issues of humanity, predominantly the increasingly role of technology and the ultimate futility of all human endeavor. Whereas *Four Saints* and *They Must* both center on language, communication, and the individual, *Listen to Me* depersonalizes the fragmentation of society, concentrating on a more universal state of isolation and despair.

For example, in the first scene of the play, Stein writes:

There is any day not what they say there is a man there and it is well done. If he likes it or not it is well done. They like to know that it is well done ... What is it that a man is a man is that they like to know that it is well done. If it is not well done he is dead and they like to know that he is dead if it is well done. That is the one thing that there is that there is now that he is dead and that it is well done. (387)

Stein announces this passage as "Listen to me/A soliloquy" (387), and in many ways it establishes the major philosophical concerns not only for *Listen,* but also for *Doctor Faustus Lights the Lights,* and *The Mother of Us All.* In *Listen to Me,* Stein critiques the relationship between humankind and knowledge, action, and existence. In advance of existentialist authors such as Jean-Paul Sartre, Albert Camus, and Samuel Beckett, Stein questions what it means to be alive in the modern world. According to this initial passage, being a man is related to something being "well done" and to what is known. Though "it" is never clarified, the importance of its being done, whether one likes it or not, is directly connected to a man's being dead. Like many works of the avant-garde, Stein's breaks apart traditional methods of artistic creation and instead combines creation and destruction into a single work. Like the Dadaists who saw negation as their creative product, Stein implies that an action "well done" is contrary to man's existence, as if an action's not being well done (or perhaps never finished at all) could prevent a man from dying. Yet, at the same time, "If it is not well done he is dead." Both action and inaction lead inevitably to death and in death all that remains is "that it is well done." This circular illogic suggests that existence is equally doomed, whether an action is well done or not. Indeed, perhaps it is only death (the ultimate non action) that can be well done.

Although Stein is interested in humanity's existence, presumably at the individual level, she repeatedly returns to the question of the world as a whole. In *Listen* Stein demonstrates most clearly the historical determinism of her thinking. Throughout the play she alludes to an irrevocable turning point in human history, and she is clearly concerned with the population of the planet, which at first appears comforting and then becomes increasingly threatening. First she asserts that "Nobody denies that the earth is covered with people and since there are no people except on this earth people are people." Then later comes this statement: "All the earth is covered with people and so no one is lost because as the whole earth is covered with people people are people" (394). Finally, Stein asks, "What happened when the earth was covered all over which it is/This happened that there was never any yesterday before to-day and no to-morrow after yesterday" (403).

Thus the comfort that people can give and obtain is limited. "If the earth is covered with people," Stein writes, "and it is and they come to cover which they do the earth altogether which it is then neither one nor another has any bother never to be left to one another where they are" (396). Though the structure of the sentence is confusing, it is clear that the comfort people can get and provide is diminishing as the population increases. The anonymous person can no longer depend on the people of the earth to provide instant companionship, but instead is isolated in a world where people are left alone "where they are." And, eventually, the presence of so many people on the earth seems to force out consideration of everything else. Stein describes an apocalyptic scene that "is the earth all covered over with people and the air and beside that there is not anywhere./Naturally not since there is the air and the earth and all filled with everybody everywhere./So then what can they do they cannot come back to earth too" (401). Though it is not clear what exactly cannot return to earth, the air seems separate from the earth, and water, mentioned earlier in the play, is not included at all. As the "Ninth character" later states, "Everybody has ceased to consider water" (401).

As the play progresses, Stein extends her questioning from whether people cover the earth to their actions. One such action is the creation of artificial light, which prevents dogs from barking at the moon. As "All the characters together" state:

This is so

This we know

Because we wondered why,

Why did the dogs not bay at the

moon.

They did not but why

But of course why

Because there are lights everywhere

anywhere.

And that is what they meant by never

yesterday. (402)

With the increase of artificial light, dogs cannot bay at the moon and the concept of evolving time has also been eliminated, because there is no progression of day into night and thus no more yesterday. Because of the people who cover the earth and the unnatural technologies they use, it "happened that there was never any yesterday before to-day and no to-morrow after yesterday" (403). But if humanity has altered the progression of time and the natural state—dogs barking at the moon—as well as connections between individuals, there is still one more deadly consequence of its having covered the earth: war. Stein would focus on this theme in even greater detail in her later play, *Doctor Faustus Lights the Lights*.

Although Stein weaves the romance of Sweet William and Lillian throughout *Listen to Me*, it is the recurring question of humanity's dominion over the world that is most fascinating to her. She makes room for her protagonist in this rather bleak plot, writing that "there are no characters where there is Sweet William," but then Sweet William himself immediately follows this statement with the announcement, "Suddenly there is a war" (405). And he makes clear the reason for war: the earth is covered with people. Although Sweet William "has his genius" and his love for Lillian, he cannot oppose the war, although he asks himself, "Do I like everywhere if there are people on the earth everywhere" (406). But Stein is ambivalent about the cause of war, and William later claims that "No war is begun again because war is sudden and there is no sudden anywhere because there are people on the earth everywhere" (406). Stein even goes so far as to write that "Sweet William was never troubled by a war" (407).

Thus, Stein asks a question that continues to be relevant today: how is it that with so many people covering the earth, they still remain so isolated from each other as to come into mortal conflict? If the potential for human connection is so great, how is it that war occurs? For a woman who had lived through World War I, only to see its fallen aggressor preparing for yet another war, it may have been perplexing indeed to consider how such a thing as war was possible. Yet Stein does note humanity's limited self-awareness as a probable cause of war, observing that "If the earth is everywhere covered all over with people nobody sees them all" (412). And she finally betrays her utter pessimism by denying William and Lillian their anticipated meeting. In fact, to complement the infrequent appearances of Lillian in the script, Stein frequently ends a scene with the simple "Sweet William was not there" (412) or "Sweet William in nowhere to be seen" (419). By continuing to separate individual characters from each other, she eliminates any possibility that humanity can come together. Although Stein frequently has her characters tantalizingly speak in unison, near the conclusion of the play she writes the following:

> What happens is this none of the characters have met they have not met yet
> if they have not met yet none of the characters have met none of the Acts
> have met none of the Characters and Acts have met yet they have not met
> none of the Characters have met none of the Acts have met and if they have
> not met they have not met yet. (420)

In this short speech, Stein elucidates the very essence of the play as a meditation on humanity's disintegration—"they have not met." Not only are all the characters separate from each other, as are all the people covering the earth, but so too are the parts of the drama—the acts, the scenes, the characters—disconnected and seemingly unaware of each other. If the people/characters have not met, then the very fabric of the play unravels. One might then read this weakness of dramatic structure as a parallel to a world preparing to enter the "theater" of war. Once individuals—characters—separate, then the societies they occupy similarly dissolve. Finally, Stein concludes *Listen to Me* by separating the words on the page and more than implying that humanity is disconnected from itself:

Acts

Curtain

Characters

Characters

Curtain

Acts

There is no one and one

Nobody has met any one

    Curtain Can Come. (421)

She does not even give the audience the satisfaction of letting the curtain come *down.*

Of all three plays treated in this chapter—*Four Saints, They Must,* and *Listen to Me*—the last is most certainly the darkest. Rare in this work is the clever and uplifting wordplay common to *Four Saints,* as in the famous "Pigeons on the grass, alas," and rarer still the shifting personalities of *They Must.* Although the characters of William and Lillian battle against a world full of anonymous and uncaring people, their relationship is unconsummated and William is eventually written out of the play without ceremony. The nameless, numbered characters ultimately reduce William and Lillian to the number of syllables in their names: "the only word in two syllables is William the only word in two syllables is Lillian the only word in three syllables is Characters and the only word in one syllable is Acts" (421). William's and Lillian's names thus become merely another linguistic part of play, depersonalized and empty. The futility of creating a play in which the structure of the text, like the stability of the world, is undermined by the people within it, is perhaps best summarized in Scene V. Stein writes: "There is no scene V" (404).

Although by 1936 much of the avant-garde had disappeared from Europe—Dada had become Surrealism, which itself was fading, and Futurism was no longer tolerated in either Italy or Russia—Stein continued to adopt the techniques of avant-garde drama and performance to express her increasing concern about the fragmentation of the world. It is true that by 1936 she herself had become a well-known figure in the United States, having published *The Autobiography of Alice B. Toklas* to positive reviews, lectured to large crowds, and met with Hollywood celebrities. But despite her success, Stein's view of humanity and its place in the modern world becomes increasingly dark after her 1934 American tour. For she clearly believes that the world has passed some threshold and that modernity, once prized, has emerged as a potentially destructive force. Like avant-gardists before her, she attempted to re-create this twentieth-century world in drama that both represented and challenged it. And this theme—the threat of modern technology to wreak havoc on modern man—would continue to haunt Stein, providing the subject only two years later for her most potent play, *Doctor Faustus Lights the Lights*.

Chapter 4

Atom and Eve: *Doctor Faustus Lights the Lights*

"And God said, 'Let there be light'; and there was light. And God saw that the light was good; and God separated the light from the darkness. God called the light Day, and the darkness he called night. And there was evening and there was morning, one day."

GENESIS, 1.1–1.5, *THE OXFORD ANNOTATED BIBLE*

"The serpent that tempted Eve may be saved, but not Faustus."

CHRISTOPHER MARLOWE, *DOCTOR FAUSTUS*

"And that is the reason why the world is interesting and science which meant progress in the nineteenth century in the twentieth century means simply useful things and now in [World War II] not really that...the discoveries of science are only used for war and destruction..."

GERTRUDE STEIN, *WARS I HAVE SEEN*

Only two years after *Listen to Me* (1936), Stein wrote *Doctor Faustus Lights the Lights* (1938), one of her most often produced plays. More intellectually accessible than much of her early work, *Doctor Faustus* blends Stein's unique approach to language and structure with universal themes, especially feminist ones. This play represents a transition between the two periods in Stein's oeuvre that Donald Sutherland has established: "The Play as Movement and Landscape, 1922–1932" and "The Melodic Drama, Melodrama and Opera, 1932–1946" (207). For the first time in her dramatic career, Stein consistently uses identifiable characters and attributes specific dialogue to them, but the language exhibits all the idiosyncrasies of her earlier drama—lack of punctuation, multiple identities for major characters, disembodied voices,

71

Figure 4 *House/Lights,* The Wooster Group, 1999. Directed by Elizabeth LeCompte. Pictured (L to R): Sheena See, Helen Pickett, Kate Valk, Roy Faudree, Tanya Selvartnam, Suzzy Roche. Used by permission of Paula Court.

punning, non sequiturs, and repetition. As Michael Hoffman has written in *Gertrude Stein* (1976):

> [*Doctor Faustus'*] language now focuses on something other than its own structure; she shifts from its concern to such literary problems as those of moral value and human identity; but she still maintains throughout the play a style readily identifiable as her own. (85)

In *Doctor Faustus* Stein further explored the themes of isolation, chaos, and despair prevalent throughout her dramatic work of the 1930s, even going so far as to repeat nearly verbatim passages from earlier plays. For example, in *Listen to Me* Stein wrote:

FIRST CHARACTER.   No dog barks at the moon.
SECOND CHARACTER.   The moon shines and no dog barks
THIRD CHARACTER.   No not anywhere on this earth.
FOURTH CHARACTER.   Because everywhere anywhere there are lights
many lights and so no dog knows that the moon is there
FIFTH CHARACTER.   And so no dog barks at the moon now no not
                                   anywhere.
FIRST CHARACTER.   And the moon makes no one crazy no not now
                                   anywhere (402)

Then, in *Doctor Faustus,* she writes:

> And then [the dog] says
> Not bright not night dear Doctor Faustus you are right, I am a dog yes I
> am just that I am I am a dog and I bay at the moon, I did yes I did I used to
> do it I used to bay at the moon I always used to do it and now now not any
> more, I cannot, of course I cannot, the electric lights they make it be that
> there is no night and if there is no night then there is no moon and if there
> is no moon I do not see it and if I do not see it I cannot bay at it. (111)

Not only did Stein use technological concerns as the basis for *Doctor Faustus,* but she also used her former title as the closing statement for this play: "Please Mr. Viper listen to me he is he and she is she and we are we please Mr. Viper listen to me" (118). Stein quotes from her nondramatic writings as well, citing both her 1934 lecture "What Are Master-pieces and why are there so few of them" and passages published later in *Wars I Have Seen* (1945). The similarities between *Doctor Faustus* and Stein's other writings demonstrate the endurance of her preoccupation with technology, communication, and identity. *Doctor Faustus* incorporates themes and techniques gleaned from Stein's more than forty years of writing and draws from nearly every genre in her oeuvre, including drama, poetry, essays, novels, and screenplays. As such, *Doctor Faustus* represents the culmination of Stein's thinking about the modern world: its wars, its technology, and its humanity.

Moreover, Stein presents these themes or subjects in uniquely theatrical ways. For example, she elaborates upon her earlier consideration of identity in *Four Saints* by making the fragmentation of an individual more explicit than before. In *Four Saints,* Saint Therese's multiplicity—represented through the repetition of her name—needed to be inferred by the reader and was, arguably, invisible to the opera's 1934 audience. Conversely, Marguerite Ida-and-Helena Annabel of *Doctor Faustus* (the central female character whose dual names and fluctuating identity mark her as a kind of conflated womankind) cannot go unnoticed either on the page or in performance. Her four-part name is re-peated throughout the play both by her and the other characters. Marguerite Ida-and-Helena Annabel's name draws attention to her divided identity by complicating verb tenses throughout the play: "Of course her names is [*sic*] Marguerite Ida too and Helena Annabel as well" (104). The linguistic chal-lenge of the name not only distracts the attention of the reader/audience, it also isolates Marguerite Ida-and-Helena Annabel from other characters and may, in fact, be the reason why she was bitten by a snake. As an unidentified character muses, "Would a viper have stung her if she only had one name ... " (104).

The language of *Doctor Faustus* itself echoes the frustrated communica-tion of *They Must. Be Wedded. To Their Wife.* (1931). The staccato rhythms of *They Must*—with its abundant punctuation and pauses—saturate *Doctor*

Faustus. However, Stein again adapts her earlier use of language specifically for the stage and writes *Doctor Faustus's* speeches as distinctly theatrical monologues. In *They Must,* Stein interrupted the flow of her characters' language visually with periods and short, choppy sentences. Conversely, *Doctor Faustus* seems to suffer from a dearth of punctuation. For example, many of Faust's monologues are interrupted not by "literary," internal punctuation, but by his "theatrical" dog, who repeatedly says "Thank you." Language in *Doctor Faustus* is further marked by endless repetitions contained within a single speech. The circular monologue conveys a struggle to communicate, but instead of characters' fighting full stops imposed on their speech, they suffer from their own overabundance of language. Ironically, Faust cannot communicate because he seemingly cannot stop talking. As a result of this shift in obstacle from external punctuation to internal profusion, the language of *Doctor Faustus* becomes much more dynamic than it was in Stein's earlier drama.

This newfound theatricality in *Doctor Faustus* is not surprising considering the play's origins. Stein first began writing this play as a novel called *Ida* (later published as *Ida, A Novel* [1941]), which told the story of a young woman bitten by a viper.[1] In addition to the basic plot, Stein also incorporated the name Ida (as part of Maguerite Ida-and-Helena Annabel) into *Doctor Faustus.*[2] Apparently, Stein decided to shift from novel to drama during the performance of Mozart's *Don Giovanni* on February 23, 1938, at the Académie Nationale de Musique et de Danse. Among the notes she scribbled in her production program that evening were an opening stage direction for *Doctor Faustus*—"Doctor Faustus sitting alone surrounded by electric light" (Figure 5)—and a line of dialogue for Faust (omitted from the final version of the play): "What kind of light".[3] In the same program, Stein also wrote the first repetitive phrases that would find their way into the completed play:

> If I do it,
>
> If I do it,
>
> What is it.
>
> Bathe me
>
> Will it
>
> Will it
>
> Will it be
>
> Will it be it. (YCAL)

The program notes themselves for *Don Giovanni* may have also influenced Stein's decision to combine the woman from *Ida* with the Faust myth. An announcement of upcoming productions listed the performance of

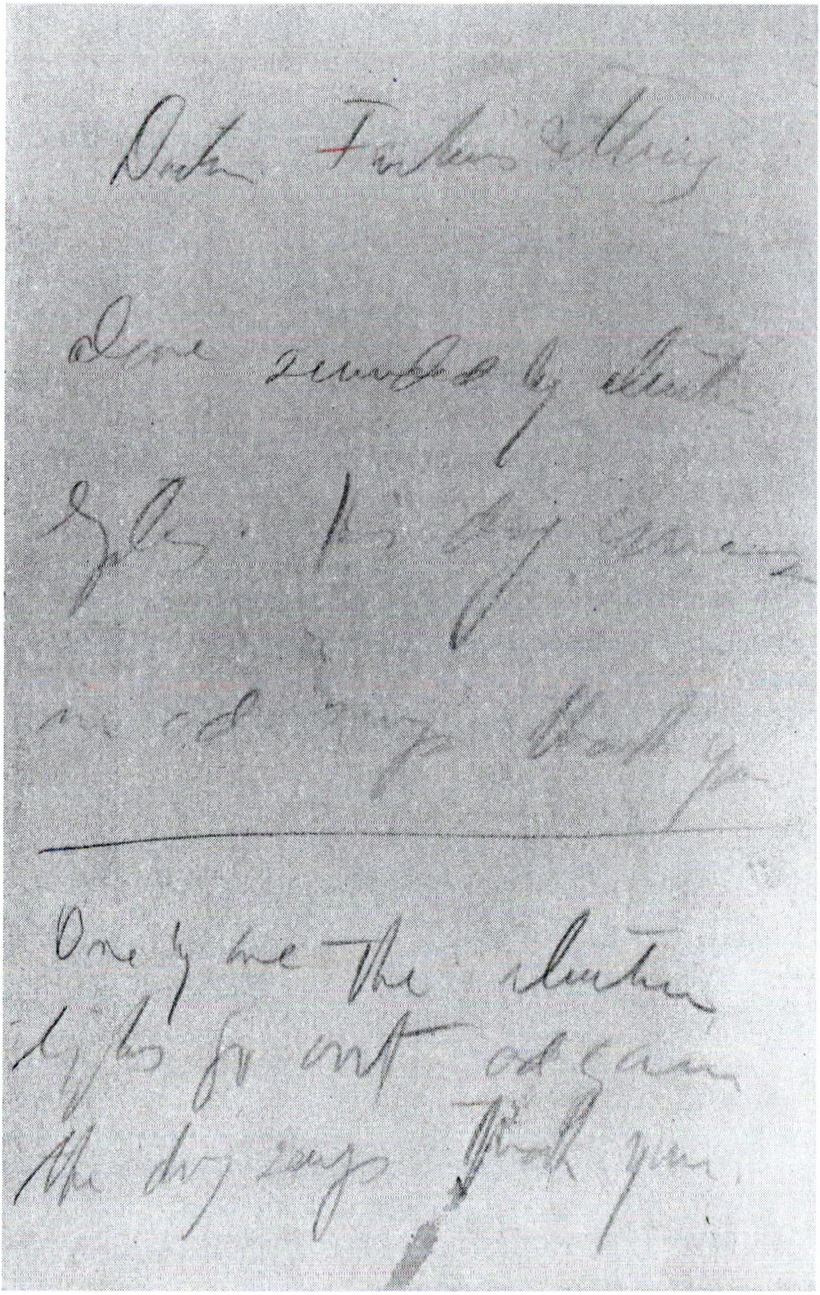

Figure 5 Gertrude Stein's notes for the beginning of *Doctor Faustus Lights the Lights,* written in her program for Mozart's *Don Giovanni* at the Académie Nationale de Musique et de Danse, Paris, France, February 23, 1938. Used by permission of the Estate of Gertrude Stein.

Figure 6 Production of Hector Berlioz's *The Damnation of Faust* at the Académie Nationale de Musique et de Danse, Paris, France, January 1938. The photograph appears in Gertrude Stein's program for Mozart's *Don Giovanni*. Used by permission of the Estate of Gertrude Stein.

Charles-François Gounod's *Faust* (1859) for the following Saturday at the Académie. Also included in the program was a photograph from the Académie's production of Hector Berlioz's *The Damnation of Faust* (1846) presented earlier in 1938, which bears a striking resemblance to Stein's visual opening to *Doctor Faustus* (Figure 6). Like the photograph of the Berlioz set, which shows a large cross upstage in silhouette, the opening to Stein's play describes Faust himself as the image of a cross: "Faust standing at the door of his room, with his arms upon the door lintel looking out, behind him a blaze of electric light" (89). Thus, it is not difficult, based on the conclusion of *Don Giovanni*—in which the title character descends into Hell—and the program's references to previous productions of Faustian operas, to see how Stein began combining the elements that would eventually become *Doctor Faustus Lights the Lights*.[4]

Whatever the initial inspiration for the play, the theatricality of *Doctor Faustus's* character-driven language perfectly complements its apocalyptic themes—namely, the elimination of God, the irreversibility of technological progress, women's fragmented identities, and the impossibility of meaningful human communication. Stein presents a world in which humanity is ultimately responsible for its own condition. For example, because Stein uses Faust's own language as the obstacle to his communication with others, he becomes ultimately responsible for his own isolation. In *They Must*, characters had difficulty forming complete sentences because they were ungrammatically broken up by periods. External forces in the form of punctuation slowed these characters' articulations of even the simplest ideas to a frustrating crawl. In

Doctor Faustus, however, the obstacle to communication is not an inability to speak, but an inability to listen. At the beginning of the play Mephistopheles attempts to answer Faust, who has inquired whether he ever had a soul to sell. But Faust refuses to listen to the answer to his own question. Instead he rebukes Mephistopheles: "You fool you devil how can you know, how can you tell me so, if I am the only one who can know what I know then no devil can know what I know and no devil can tell me so..." (90).

This arrogance of Faust's introduces a new twist in Stein's depiction of character. For the first time in her dramatic career, characters speak predominantly in the first person.[5] For example, when Marguerite Ida-and-Helena Annabel first appears, she states, "I am I and my name is Marguerite Ida and Helena Annabel" (95). Faust similarly introduces himself by declaring, "What am I. I am Doctor Faustus who knows everything can do everything..." (89). For these newly self-involved characters, Stein writes sweeping, almost operatic monologues (not surprising, considering the play's origins) that isolate these figures from each other and the world around them.[6] For example, Faust's greatest despair comes not from the realization that he ("I") cannot control the electric lights, which now torment him, but from the solipsistic realization that he did not create them by himself:

[I]f I had not

been in a hurry and if I had taken my time I

would have known how to make white electric

light and day-light and night light and what

did I do I saw you miserable devil I saw you

and I was deceived and I believed miserable

devil I thought I needed you... (89)

Because of their individualistic monologues, Stein's two central characters constantly push all others away. Following the opening monologue Faustus kicks Mephistopheles away and Faustus repeatedly tells his companions to "Let me be alone/Little boy and dog let me be alone, Marguerite Ida and Helena Annabel let me be alone..." (100). Whereas the characters in *They Must* and *Listen to Me* struggle to come together, to find some unity, the characters of *Doctor Faustus* fight against such communion. Marguerite Ida-and-Helena Annabel tells Faust not to look at her, even while he attempts to cure her snake bite, and when the man from over the seas arrives, she turns her back on him. Even the devil embraces a state of isolation and determined individualism. Mephistopheles says, "I have a will of iron yes a will to do what I do. I do what I do what I do, I do I do" (109). In fact, the only characters who reach out to others are the little boy and little girl, who, at the conclusion of the play, stand pleading "listen to me" (118). Not surprisingly, their pleas for communication or attention go unanswered.

Thus, while themes of existential isolation, overwhelming technology, and frustrated communication are present throughout many of Stein's plays of the late 1920s and the 1930s, her formal manipulations of these themes change dramatically in *Doctor Faustus Lights the Lights*. Faust, unlike previous Stein characters, controls his own fate. He begins the play by choosing not to believe Mephistopheles and he ends the play by choosing to kill his companions. The play itself begins in the aftermath of his earlier and most significant decision to sell his soul in order to create electric light. In fact, in her notes on the play, Stein describes Faust's condition as being alone in "his electric lighted cell" (YCAL). Her ideational shift further distinguishes *Doctor Faustus* not only from Stein's previous drama, but also from all previous Faust tales. In her version of the Faust myth, Stein adapts the form of the play to communicate her belief that humanity had passed an irrevocable turning point. Whereas the turning point of Goethe's or Marlowe's Faustian dramas is Faust's decision to sell his soul to the devil, Stein begins her play *after* his decision has been made:

> What do I care there is no here nor there.
>
> What am I. I am Doctor Faustus who knows
>
> everything can do everything and you say it
>
> was through you but not at all, if I had not
>
> been in a hurry and if I had taken my time
>
> I would have known how to make white electric
>
> light and day-light and night light and what
>
> did I do I saw you miserable devil I saw you
>
> and I was deceived and I believed miserable
>
> devil I thought I needed you, and I thought
>
> I was tempted by the devil and I know no
>
> temptation is tempting unless the devil tells
>
> you so. (89)

Critics have interpreted this style of speech in a variety of ways. In one of the earliest analyses of *Doctor Faustus,* Allegra Stewart argued for a Jungian interpretation of the text. To her, Faust's apparently scattered ramblings actually represent three separate aspects of one human psyche; in reading the play, "One should remember that it is an interior action, and that all the characters are functions or complexes within [that] one human psyche" (159). According to Stewart, Stein's use of three different names for Faust—Faust, Faustus, and Doctor Faustus—is additional evidence that, in Jungian terminology, this character's psyche consists of the subordinate self, the ego, and the persona, respectively. In a later examination of *Doctor Faustus,* James F. Schaefer, Jr., similarly argued that there are two Fausts engaged in a "psychological duet." In Schaefer's interpretation, "[Faust]1 has been used to designate an aging Faustus who questions the value of his life's work and is uncertain whether or not he ever had a soul, while F2 designates an arrogant Faustus who is cock-sure of himself and his invention, and who is convinced that he can outwit the devil who has come for his due . . . " (5).

Both these interpretations are plausible, as is the belief that Faust's dis-enchantment with his invention can be traced to Stein's anxiety following the publication of *The Autobiography of Alice B. Toklas* (1933), her first commer-cial and critical success. As Betsy Alayne Ryan notes:

> After writing her widely disseminated *Autobiography of Alice B. Toklas* and *Everybody's Autobiography* in the early thirties, she wrote often about the consequences of fame for a writer, wondering openly in plays and theoretical writings whether it was possible to retain any sense of self in the glare of publicity and with ever-present awareness of audience expectation. (128)

Richard Bridgman extends this analysis further, beyond Stein's concern with her own identity to her anxiety over an emerging American technology:

> American technology and the threat of success to her personal identity coa-lesced for her in the phenomenon of electric lights to make Doctor Faustus a disgruntled Edison. Electric lights stood for the sometimes useful but never ultimately satisfying, true, or illuminating function of reason. (209)

What all these interpretations ignore, however, are the blatant similarities between Stein's response to twentieth-century experience in *Doctor Faustus* and the responses of the Dadaists and Surrealists. Though her own experiences undoubtedly influenced her dramatic choices, it is limiting to view the play solely as a product of Stein's brushes with fame. Rather than being merely an extension of her psyche, Stein's Faust exhibits the same frustrations, desires, and creative impulses as her fellow avant-garde artists in Europe. To wit, Faust had been enchanted enough with electric light to agree to sell his soul for it, yet when he first appears in Stein's text, he has nothing but contempt for the light he has created:

I keep on having so much

light that light is not bright and what after

all is the use of light, you can see just as well

without it, you can go around just as well

without it, you can get up and go to bed just

as well without it, and I I wanted to make it

and the devil take it yes devil you do

not even want it and I sold my soul to make

it. (90)

Compare Faust's complaints, then, with sentiments expressed by Dada artists, such as Hans Arp. In his "Notes from a Dada Diary" (1932) Arp writes, "time and space no longer exist for modern man. with [*sic*] a can of gasoline under his behind man whizzes faster and faster around the earth so that soon he will be back again before he leaves" (221). The Dada dilemma is Faust's—"the light of day is beautiful but poisonous and rustic life even creates hexameters and madness" (Arp 223)—just as their solution is Stein's—"through language too can man grow into real life" (Arp 225). Like the Dadaists, Faustus exhibits an early fascination with the technology of the modern world, but he eventually rejects the light he has created. Written several years after the demise of Dada and on the eve of Hitler's invasion of France, Stein's *Doctor Faustus* incorporates not only the Surrealists' interest in the unconscious, then, but also the Futurist fascination with technology—particularly the technological art of cinema—as well as the Dada distrust of technology clearly warranted by the horrors of mechanized warfare already exhibited during World War I.

In *Doctor Faustus* Stein again uses formal techniques similar to those employed by Dada. In her lecture "Composition as Explanation" (1926), she describes the "continuous present" as "a beginning again and again and again, it was a list it was a similarity and everything different it was a distribution and an equilibration" (29). Often referred to as repetition, this "continuous present" might also be understood as a form of simultaneity, originally a performance technique borrowed from the Italian Futurists by Dada. In *Dada Performance,* Mel Gordon describes Francis Picabia's Dadaist play, *Relâche* (1924), as an example of such a performance:

Relâche began with a film prologue by a young René Clair and music by Erik Satie. After one minute, hundreds of lights in photographic metallic reflectors blinded the audience. These formed the backdrop. On the stage, dozens of disconnected activities were enacted. A fireman for the theatre smoked cigarettes and poured water from one pail to another. Man Ray, the American artist, sat on the side of the stage, occasionally marking off space with his shoes. Figures from Cranach's "Adam and Eve" appeared. Tuxedoed playboys disrobed. And an automobile brought on a young couple in evening clothes. (24)

While *Doctor Faustus* does not contain such simultaneous, layered activity, the lack of progression in the plot does create a kind of "continuous present." There is no cause and effect, no evolving plot line. Rather, the events that occur in *Doctor Faustus* embody the simultaneous present that Donald Sutherland associates with twentieth-century life in Stein's writing: "It has been, in a way, the mission of the twentieth century to destroy progressive history and create a single time in which everything in the past and possibly the future would be simultaneous" (133). As Stein herself writes in her 1934 lecture, "Plays," "The business of Art as I tried to explain in Composition as Explanation is to live in the actual present, that is the complete actual present, and to completely express that complete actual present" (104–105). By opening her play after Faust's fatal decision has been made, Stein creates that "complete actual" or continuous present, for she has effectively robbed the drama of its potential suspense. Without it, the tempo of the play is flattened, for suspense by its very nature is dependent on time. Although Marc Robinson oddly describes *Doctor Faustus* as "taut with anticipation" (24), the audience has most of its questions answered from the opening moment. There is no question as to whether Faustus will or will not sell his soul, or as to whether he made the right decision; from the start, Doctor Faustus admits both his decision to sell his soul and his dissatisfaction with that decision. By so diffusing the suspense, Stein disrupts not only her drama's timeline, but also its causal progression.

Similarly, Stein uses rapid shifts of location to create a sense that various activities take place simultaneously, even if they do not actually do so. As suggested in Chapter 2, this attempt at "editing" or "montage" is a technique Stein borrowed from the cinema. It is clear that she believed film had fundamentally changed people's ways of viewing and hearing. To return to Stein's mention of cinema in "Plays":

> I suppose one might have gotten to know a good deal about these things from the cinema and how it changed from sight to sound, and how much before there was real sound how much of the sight was sound or how much it was not. In other words the cinema undoubtedly had a new way of understanding sight and sound in relation to emotion and time. (103–104)

For Stein, the cinema made clear that what one sees and what one thinks one sees are two disjointed perceptions. Because cinema controls perception, it not only records reality, but *creates* it. Thus, in her efforts to capture a modern world, riddled with miscommunication, misrecognition, and irreparable mistakes, Stein uses cinematic conventions to convey the dangers of the modern world. Aside from its formal similarities to the European avant-garde and that avant-garde's much smaller dramatic offshoot in the United States, *Doctor Faustus Lights the Lights* is important for its explicit violations of the fundamental elements of conventional or traditional drama, including divinity, causality, psychology, and a clear semiotic relationship between words and meaning. Rather than merely mimic the techniques of the Dadaists or Surrealists, Stein disrupts the conventions of the well-made play even further than either E. E. Cummings in *Him* or Thornton Wilder in his allegedly avant-garde *Our Town* (1938), thereby establishing herself as the foremost dramatist of the American avant-garde.

It is noteworthy that *Our Town,* published in the same year as *Doctor Faustus* and written by her close friend, deals with the same issues as Stein's play—namely, the individual's place in the world, the individual's relationship to a higher power, and the longing, if not for a better world, then for a greater appreciation of the world-in-itself, in all its mundane dailiness. Considering that both Stein and Wilder were writing in Europe (she in Paris and he in Switzerland) on the eve of World War II, it is not surprising that both were preoccupied with the question of where the world was headed. Although the two were friends and corresponded during this time, their dramatic results could hardly be more different.[7] Whereas Wilder in *Our Town* clearly advocates a retreat from modernist technology and a return to simple living in the small towns of late nineteenth-to-early-twentieth-century America, Stein seems to believe that there can be no retreat and that the consequences of this technology must be faced in the present as well as in the future. To repeat, Doctor Faustus begins his journey not before or even with the decision to sell his soul, but after its sale. And further, Stein sees the creation of the electric lights as a dissatisfying conclusion. As she writes in an earlier unpublished version of the play, "Doctor Faustus having sold his soul . . . has invented electric lights and now has nothing further to do" (YCAL). Earlier in the twentieth century, the Dadaists emerged into a world that had already rejected divine absolutes and individual action, and as a result, they too rejected faith in both the divine and the self. In nearly all avant-garde drama, the individual had been reduced to a kind of puppet figure, at the mercy of his own unconscious drives as well as the victim of an uncaring and increasingly technological world.[8] So too did Gertrude Stein emerge and so was she confronted with the result that a patriarchal God had to disappear from her drama, to be replaced by a humanity in conflict with itself and with an industrial-technological environment of humankind's own creation.

The Faust legend itself is a kind of retelling of the biblical myth of the Garden of Eden. Eve is tempted by the devil, in the form of a serpent, to taste fruit from the tree of knowledge and to share that fruit with Adam—an action that banishes all humanity from paradise. Similarly, the Faust of legend is tempted to sell his soul to the devil (and, consequently, his right to paradise in heaven—the only Eden humankind can ever know) in exchange for omniscience, even omnipotence. Throughout Stein's play, central characters themselves usurp or reject power typically associated with God. Faustus claims the power to create light, as does Marguerite Ida-and-Helena Annabel, although she seems less interested in this power than Faust.[9] Instead, Marguerite Ida-and-Helena Annabel rejects all deities, turning her back on both the sun (which could be interpreted as a natural god) and the electric light (the new technological god). Like the biblical Eve, however, Marguerite Ida-and-Helena Annabel is bitten by a viper. Initially, Marguerite Ida-and-Helena Annabel appears to triumph over the bite. Faustus successfully cures her, despite his repeated assertions that he cannot see her, and consequently Marguerite Ida-and-Helena Annabel becomes immune to the viper's poison. As Stein's Chorus intones, "See how the viper there,/Cannot hurt her" (106). At first glance, this seems to be a triumph of science over God, but Marguerite Ida-and-Helena Annabel rejects both the natural light of the sun and the science of Faust. And for the first time in the play she gains a unity of identity: "With her back to the sun/One sun/And she is one/Marguerite Ida and Helena Annabel as well" (107).

With both unity and duality thus present in her main female character, Stein focuses attention on the multiple identities of women. Like the avant-garde dramatists who rejected the unity of character on stage, Stein creates a character who in name alone evokes both the good and evil depictions of women in history and literature. Half of the four-part name, Marguerite Ida, contains positive connotations of motherhood—Margaret the faithful wife and mother of multiple Faust legends, and Ida the mother of the gods—while the second half, Helena Annabel, suggests images of sexual temptation and demonic, anti-familial sentiment, aside from its possible (ironic?) reference to the mother of the Virgin Mary (see note 9). In creating such a fractured, complex identity, Stein, in my view, is contradicting one-dimensional representations of women and illuminating the absurdity of the longstanding Madonna-Whore dichotomy. In fact, Stein first wrote the character as only Ida-and-Anabel, but eventually expanded the name beyond the binary to encompass four names and, consequently, more aspects of identity than just the two names create. A reader or viewer must constantly reconcile the manifold nature of Marguerite Ida-and-Helena Annabel with the singular pronoun "she." The stubbornness of Stein's technique is evident in criticism of the play, where scholars almost always shorten the character's name to "Marguerite Ida" or her initials, MIHA, rather than confuse their own readers' sense of grammar and logic.

The duality (or "quadality") of Marguerite Ida-and-Helena Annabel's character is visible not only in her name, but also in the events that surround her. She is at once an agent of action and the passive victim or recipient of others' actions. As an embodiment of Eve, she survives the bite of the snake to become as powerful as Doctor Faustus in her ability to create light (candlelight). Nevertheless, she still succumbs to "the man from the sea" (107), who appears as another embodiment of the same viper and seduces her, exclaiming that "I am the only he and you are the only she and we are the only we" (108). His language, of course, recalls Adam and Eve, the first he and she. But through Marguerite Ida-and-Helena Annabel, Stein inverts the story of Adam and Eve in the Garden of Eden. For this Eve is not only *not* responsible for her own temptation (she is unwittingly bitten by the serpent and even fails to realize it was a serpent that had bitten her), she is also relieved of the responsibility for the fall of humanity. It is the Adam figure, in fact ("the only he"), who is linked to both the devil and the serpent: "And indeed behind the man of the seas is Mephistopheles ... " (108). This Adam is born from the sea, an image often equated with female sexuality, whereas the Eve of the Bible is born of Adam's rib. When the man from the seas arrives with Mephistopheles, moreover, two children repeatedly call the (maternal?) man from the seas "Mr. Viper." Indeed, the only figure from the first three books of Genesis who does not appear is God himself.

Despite the inversion of the Eve character and the absence of a Judeo-Christian God in *Doctor Faustus,* humanity suffers a spiritual fate equivalent to Adam and Eve's banishment from the Garden of Eden. Even as Stein dismantles traditional theology, humans seem to impose a similar fate on themselves as they choose to reject God and face their difficult lives alone. This rejection of God by humanity culminates in Faust's damnation, not as the result of an act of God or seduction by a woman, but rather of his own free will. Considering her dismissal of traditional theology, it is not surprising, then, that Stein opens the play after the central religious crisis—Faust's decision to sell his soul to the devil for knowledge—which in other dramatizations of the Faust legend serves as the turning point. For Stein, like the Dadaists and Surrealists, the religious crisis—whether to believe in or turn from a higher being, whether to accept or reject organized religion—is past history and no longer relevant to her "continuous present."

Rather than concern himself with his relationship to, or the repercussions of the existence of, a godlike figure, Stein's Doctor Faustus begins the play by lamenting his own foolishness at allowing another (the devil) to wield influence over him. Like that of previous Fausts, his egotism is central to his character, as we see at the start of the play when this Faustus vents his frustration on Mephistopheles:

I am Doctor Faustus who knows

everything can do everything and you say it

was through you but not at all, if I had not

been in a hurry and if I had taken my time

I would have known how to make white electric

light and day-light and night light and what

did I do I saw you miserable devil I saw you

and I was deceived and I believed miserable

devil I thought I needed you, and I thought

I was tempted by the devil and I know no

temptation is tempting unless the devil tells

you so. (89)

While Faust immediately regrets his decision to sell his soul for electric light, his remorse is motivated not by fear of an almighty creator or a crisis of conscience, but rather by his immediate *physical* discomfort—caused by the relentless glare of the lights. "I keep on having so much light that light is not bright" (89), he complains. As I have implied, the spiritual wrath of God is systematically replaced by the secular wrath of technology, as represented by electric light, in *Doctor Faustus Lights the Lights.*

That God is replaced by the modern technology of electricity may be Stein's punning reference to Goethe's criticism of the Enlightenment in his *Faust.* Despite its centrality to the play, the "spirituality" of the electric lights has so far been ignored in criticism of this play. In recent scholarship about *Doctor Faustus,* in fact, Faust is frequently compared to so secular a figure as Thomas Edison. In an early consideration of the play, Richard Bridgman sums up Faust's—and Gertrude Stein's—conflict quite simply, or rather simplistically. To repeat:

> Doctor Faustus' problem is that he is the dissatisfied inventor of the electric light, which, since the American trip, had been on Gertrude Stein's mind . . . American technology and the threat of success to her personal identity coalesced for her in the phenomenon of electric lights to make Doctor Faustus a disgruntled Edison. (209)

In his review of Robert Wilson's 1992 Lincoln Center production of Stein's *Doctor Faustus Lights the Lights,* David Savran suggests a similar interpretation of Faustus's obsession with electric light:

> In Stein's text Enlightenment is at once liberalized and subtly degraded. Reconceptualized for a technological age, it means little more than flicking on a switch. And the good Doctor in search of illumination is less the sorcerer of yore than a second-rate Edison completing an electric circuit. (26)

James F. Schaefer, Jr., articulates much the same point with his comparison between the morality of the play and economics:

> Stein's play depicts Faustus as an embittered Thomas Edison who has sold his soul for the secret of electric light. Tired of technological accomplishment, the aging inventor now wants the freedom of a dark and solitary hell. But

this twentieth-century Faustus is a businessman as well as a scientist, and
his bargain with Mephisto has an odd capitalist twist: since he has sold his
soul, he no longer has a soul, and without a soul he cannot go to hell. (3)

But these interpretations ignore the tremendous theological or ontological
weight placed on the electric lights in the absence of a god figure. Faust is not an
inventor grown tired of his invention; rather, he has ceased to be able to control
it. He cannot escape the very lights he has created and they torment him. In
her notes on the play, Stein refers to events in the Marguerite Ida-and-Helena
Anabel subplot as, "While all this happens Faustus remains in his electric
lighted cell" and she later states quite plainly "the electric lights they won't go
out" (YCAL). Furthermore, these electric lights communicate with Faustus,
an issue not addressed by the Edison analogy. Early in the play, for example,
Faust sings a duet with his dog—and the lights—about the electric lights:

Bathe me

>   says Doctor Faustus

Bathe me

In the electric lights

>   During this time the electric lights come and go

What is it

>   says Doctor Faustus

Thank you

>   says the dog.

>   Just this moment the electric lights get brighter and nothing

>   comes

Was it it

>   says Doctor Faustus

>   Faustus meditates he does not see the dog.

Will it

Will it

Will it be

Will it be it.

>   Faustus sighs and repeats

Will it be it.

A duet between the dog and Faustus

Will it be it.

Just it.

At that moment the electric light gets pale again and in that moment
Faustus shocked says

It is it... (92)

The above "duet" between Faust, the dog, and the lights clearly indicates
a superior role for the lights as well as their ability to convey information
to Faustus. Indeed, just before his repetitious questioning of the lights, Faust
meditates so deeply that he seems to forget the dog, with whom he has sung
the duet until now. This meditation then culminates in an unnamed or unde-
cipherable revelation by the lights: "It is it... " Clearly this relationship is
more complicated than that between an inventor and his object, and, although
Faustus does usurp a godlike power in creating the light, it is the light that
ultimately controls him.

Further articulated through this relationship between Doctor Faustus and
the lights is the play's singular moral design. Faust may be able to create
electric light, but he cannot control it; he has produced a never-ending day,
but no corresponding night. Stein has thus returned, via Faust's creation,
to a godless and disordered world by undoing God's first act of creation.
According to the Oxford edition of *The Holy Bible,* the first book of Genesis
reads:

> And God said, "Let there be light"; and there was light. And God saw that the
> light was good; and God separated the light from the darkness. God called
> the light Day, and the darkness he called Night. And there was evening and
> morning, one day. (Genesis 1.3–5)

God's first act is to separate light from darkness, thereby creating day
and night, evening and morning. But Faust's creation of the electric light does
away with this distinction, and Stein equates this merging of day and night,
light and dark, with the disappearance of moral order from the universe. After
Doctor Faustus has acknowledged that he foolishly traded his soul for the
lights, he articulates the new "moral order" of the play:

> Who cares if you lie if you steal, there is no
>
> snake to grind under one's heel, there is no

hope there is no death there is no life there is

no breath, there just is every day all day and

when there is no day there is no day (90)

The cycle of day into night has been broken and with it the moral certainty of the separation of light from dark, good from evil. When Faustus questions, "Who cares if you lie if you steal," it is clear that God might have cared, but He is now absent. In the absence of God, the natural world suffers, as do all living beings who are dependent upon it. Not only is Faust tormented by the unrelenting lights, for example, but so is his dog. To repeat the dog's lament:

> I am a dog and I bay at the moon, I did yes I used to do it I used to bay at the moon I always used to do it and now now not any more, I cannot, of course I cannot, the electric lights they make it be that there is no night and if there is no night then there is no moon and if there is no moon I do not see it and if I do not see it I cannot bay at all. (111)

From the human angle, Faust's boy companion notes that without a moon, "no one is crazy any more" (111). Given the events of the play, however, the boy's observation begs the question, what is "crazy" in the context of this play? Given the talking dog who says "thank you," multiple identities, a day without end, a devil who appears to have little direct power over humanity, and a society without moral order, it seems that the lack of a moon has actually made the world crazier. Of course, what Stein implies through her dismantling of theological assumptions is that the craziness of humanity is the result of neither a natural aberration nor the absence of God. Humanity is innately prone to maddening self-destructiveness, and the lifting of moral sanctions merely reveals the true nature of the beings underneath.

Stein posits the inability of humanity to advance or improve itself in her essay "What Are Master-Pieces and why are there so few of them." In a piece that seems to gloss *Doctor Faustus,* she questions anyone's ability to create art—to create timeless *master*-pieces—when human development seems less to support Charles Darwin's theory of evolution than to be trapped in its own vicious cycle or re-volution:

> What is the use of being a boy if you are going to grow up to be a man. And what is the use there is no use from the standpoint of master-pieces there is no use. Anybody can really know that.
>
> There is really no use in being a boy if you are going to grow up to be a man and boy you can be certain that that is continuing and a master-piece does not continue it is as it is but it does not continue. It is very interesting that no one is content with being a man and boy but he must also be a son and a father and the fact that they all die has something to do with time but it has nothing to do with a master-piece. (153)

Written in 1936, just two years before *Doctor Faustus,* the above text finds its way into Faust's musing about himself and his role in the universe: "I go where I go, where is there there is where and all the day and all the night too it grew and grew and there is no way to say I and a dog and a boy, if a boy is to grow to be a man am I a boy am I a dog is a dog a boy is a boy a dog and what am I I cannot cry what am I oh what am I" (98). In what might be construed as a dream sequence—"Doctor Faustus the dog and the boy all sleeping" (98)—Faustus repeatedly sees himself here as interchangeable with the dog and the boy and consequently lacking a definite identity of his own:

> Man and dog dog and man each one can tell it all like a ball with a caress no tenderness, man and dog just the same each one can take the blame each one can well as well tell it all as they can, man and dog, well well man and dog what is the difference between a man and a dog when I say none (98)

Toward the end of the play, Faust even responds to his dog with the very same line that has been repeated by the animal throughout the play: "Yes thank you" (111).

Stein may create multiple identities for Marguerite Ida-and-Helena Annabel, but Faust's ongoing questioning of himself does not result in even a temporary unity or oneness of identity. Doctor Faustus thus appears to be incapable of fulfillment through God or even the devil, who is unable to convince Faustus that he has a soul. Faust's self-querying actually begins with his questioning of the devil: "I have made it but have I a soul to pay for it" (90). His question, "what am I" (89), made to appear a declaration, is repeated frequently throughout the play; yet Faustus does not find an answer. In fact, after his final action—the killing of the boy and the dog so as to gain entrance into hell—Marguerite Ida-and-Helena Annabel's failure to recognize him denies Faust his identity. Before falling helplessly into the arms of the man from the seas, Marguerite Ida-and-Helena Annabel says, "you are not Doctor Faustus no not ever never never" (118). Faust's quest to understand himself may be as unrelenting as the glare of the electric lights, but it is also just as unfulfilling. As the circularity of Faust's musings suggests, the attempt to know oneself— in the hope of bettering, renewing, or redeeming oneself—is essentially futile.

Not only has Gertrude Stein replaced the spiritual certainty of God with the secular amorality of modern technology, but she has also replaced the psycho-scientific certainty of integrated yet developing personality with the inability of humanity either to comprehend itself or to evolve. In this play, all the characters are reduced to the same frustrating inability to understand the world or act upon it. Marguerite Ida-and-Helena Annabel cannot defend herself against the man from the seas; the devil cannot control Doctor Faustus (not even long enough to convince him that he has a soul); Faust cannot regulate the lights once he has created them, and at the end of the play he fails to convince Marguerite Ida-and-Helena Annabel to accompany him to hell; and both the boy and the dog have no power over their own lives—manipulated as they are by Faust—and are ultimately killed by him.

Like Wilder's *Our Town, Doctor Faustus Lights the Lights* investigates the triumph of modern technology and the role of God in the contemporary life. But rather than offer romantic nostalgia and spiritual redemption to a Depression-weary and war-wary American public, through isolation—and isolationism—in a quaint New Hampshire town of the turn of the century, Stein accepts the impotence of humanity without a god, without morals, and without a real sense of itself. Indeed, in an almost absurdist fashion, Stein's characters revel in their own frustration and ignorance. As a final gesture of this frustration, Stein ends the play with a little boy and little girl calling for the man from the sea, whom they call Mr. Viper: "Please Mr. Viper listen to me he is he and she is she and we are we please Mr. Viper listen to me" (118). The end for Doctor Faustus is a similarly fruitless gesture. Faust's frustrations with the world culminate in his desire to "go to hell,"[10] which neatly returns the play to its theological question—does Doctor Faustus have a soul? Ironically, Mephistopheles informs Faustus that he cannot enter hell without a soul, which Faust has sold. In order to enter hell, Doctor Faustus is told, he must commit a sin. When he asks, "What sin, how can I without a soul commit a sin," Mephisto peremptorily replies, "Kill anything" (116). Faust then kills his companions, the boy and the dog, and descends into hell.

In light of Faust's damnation, we may usefully consider the doctrinal distinction between venial sin and mortal sin as articulated by the Catholic Church. In her essay "Faustus and the Apple," Ceri Sullivan articulates this distinction: "Damnation occurs where the sin is mortal, not venial. For sin to be mortal the act must be of grave matter and involve a deliberate turning away from God. This, say the catechisms, asks for as full a knowledge of the consequences as the sinner is able to comprehend" (49–50). Such a distinction may explain why Doctor Faustus can turn away from God initially (through the pact he makes with Mephisto before Stein's play begins) with no obvious consequences, but must again turn from God at the conclusion of the play, through murder, to enter hell. Significantly, the word "sin" is used only in this final scene. Faust's initial turning away from God is motivated by his desire for knowledge, not by any desire to repudiate or "kill" the deity. For this reason we may regard his first sin as venial. At the end of the play, however, Faustus consciously turns from God by committing the mortal sin of murder—i.e., by killing a human being made in God's image.

I believe that Stein uses the majority of the play as a build, undramatic as it may seem, to this final moment. Faust desires to go to hell to escape the reality that he himself has created through his rejection of God in favor of technology. But, for Stein, the term "hell" describes this very technological reality (or nightmare): "Any light is just a light and now there is nothing more either by day or by night just a light" (91). The unrelenting light can be read as a modern analogue to the eternal fires of hell. This technological light has the capacity, with its heat and radiance (neither warm and nourishing like the sun, nor gently haloed like candlelight), to overwhelm all other forms of light and, like the hell of theology, every type of faith. Living in Europe during the 1930s, Stein thus reflects the anxiety of a continent only recently recovered from the first mechanized world war, yet now poised on the brink of a second—one whose technological devastation and human waste would beggar the imagination. Unlike the retrogressive Emily in *Our Town,* Stein could not advocate that humans simply and happily "realize [this] life while they live it—every, every minute" (100). Rather she suggests, like other avant-garde writers of her time, that life cannot be totally realized or understood, and she avers, unlike the comforting Stage Manager in Wilder's *Our Town,* that no God exists to create moral order or to prevent humankind from technological self-extinction. The question remains, did Gertrude Stein reject faith in God or is she warning others against the abandonment of such faith? Clearly, Stein demonstrates a fascination with religion, Catholicism in particular. In *Everybody's Autobiography,* Stein claimed to have read the Old Testament at the age of eight and religion as an (usually oppressive) institution is prominent in early writings such *Quod Erat Demonstrandum* (1903), and *The Making of Americans* (1925). If one compares her characterization of Marguerite Ida-and-Helena Annabel as a self-contained, candlelit entity to her essentialization of Faust in the amorphous "what am I," Stein appears to argue for a feminine version of spirituality. And yet, Marguerite Ida-and-Helena Annabel falls helplessly into the arms of Mr. Viper at the conclusion of the play, a final action that indicates nihilistic hopelessness for humanity rather than religious salvation.

Like the Dadaists, to name only one avant-garde group, Stein has lost faith in the traditional patriarchal God, but she has also lost faith both in unconventional feminine spirituality and, paradoxically, in the potential of any individual *without* absolute faith. Faust's individual quest, after all, ends in murder, despair, and chaos: Mephisto declares himself deceived; Faust himself sinks into darkness still rejecting the now-dead boy and dog; Marguerite Ida-and-Helena Annabel lies helpless, perhaps even lifeless in the arms of the man from the sea; and the children, who might represent an optimistic future for humanity, can only repetitiously plead with an unresponsive Mr. Viper. In this final scene, Stein systematically breaks apart all human connection, while simultaneously preventing closure. Faust has achieved his ultimate goal, but the world he leaves behind has not resolved the torment of the electric lights and the fate of Marguerite Ida-and-Helena Annabel is far from certain. The repetitions of the children's plea in the final lines of the play suggest that they will continue to plead, never to be answered. They endlessly ask that Mr. Viper "listen to me," but we do not know what they want to say, or even to whom it is addressed. Mr. Viper may be Mephistopheles, but the lack of any answer precludes our ultimate knowing.

This dramatic representation of a technologically tormented modern world without end prefigures the major dramatic themes to follow World War II in the works of such writers as Sartre, Camus, Beckett, and Eugène Ionesco, who saw humankind's trust in a higher power betrayed by the human folly—the hellfire of the Holocaust and atomic obliteration—of the last great war. Like Beckett's *Endgame* (1957), which begins "Finished, it's nearly finished, it must be nearly finished" (1), but ends without resolution, Stein's *Doctor Faustus* suggests that while the end may be near, it is not near enough.

Chapter 5

"My Long Life": Final Works

"The end of the movement of absurdity, of rebellion, etc. . . . is compassion . . . that is to say, in the last analysis, love . . ."

ALBERT CAMUS, *CARNETS 1942–1951*

Following *Doctor Faustus Lights the Lights,* Stein would write only two more major works: a surprisingly simple melodrama, *Yes Is for a Very Young Man, or In Savoy* (1944–45); and a second, final opera with Virgil Thomson, *The Mother of Us All* (1945–46). As I have demonstrated in the previous chapters, Stein's dramatic technique developed gradually and in relatively distinct stages. First influenced by cinema and avant-garde performance, Stein continuously refined her drama so that she could more effectively treat the themes of gender, sexuality, and spirituality, while reflecting the growing chaos of a war-torn and technologically overwhelmed twentieth-century. But if the path to *Doctor Faustus* was a process of gradually integrating fragments of the avant-garde, cinema, and queerness into a cohesive whole, then the last two plays of Stein's career split this unity into two utterly distinct directions. One play expands upon Stein's previous experiments in language and dramatic structure, while the other reaches into the previously unexplored world (for Stein) of representational drama. It is as if Stein's ambivalence about her gender, the effects of modernity and war, and the influence of the avant-garde finally fractured her drama into two oppositional parts.

Consequently, *Yes Is for a Very Young Man* and *The Mother of Us All* could hardly be more different. On the one hand, Stein writes her most representational work: a rather simple and, arguably, over-romanticized well-made play about the occupation and liberation of France during World War II. On the other, Stein concludes her career much as one would expect, with a great modernist opera about feminism, complete with self-reference and agonizing

Figure 7   *The Mother of Us All.* Columbia University, 1947. Photograph by Carl Van Vechten.
Used by permission of the Van Vechten Trust.

language. *Yes Is for a Very Young Man* follows a French family as they struggle
under the Nazis in occupied France. The dramatic tension of the play centers
around Henry, a devoted family man whose family has become radically divided. On the one side is his wife, Denise, a member of the French upper-class
and an ardent supporter of Maréchal Pétain's army and the Vichy government.
Throughout the play, Denise is portrayed as a selfish nag, who brags endlessly
about her "hero" brother Achille, a member of Pétain's army. On the other,
is Henry's brother Ferdinand, the young man of the title, who is obsessed

with liberating France from German occupation. Indeed, Ferdinand's hatred of the Germans is matched only by his love for the American Constance, the unrequiting object of his affection. But despite this developing romance, Ferdinand leaves for Germany to liberate his countrymen imprisoned, including his own brothers. Similarly, although Henry remains devoted to his wife, if not her principles, he joins Constance in supporting the Resistance and moves dynamite smuggled into the country by Americans to the Resistance fighters.[1] The climax of the play comes when Henry learns of his father's murder at the hands of Germans and, perhaps even more painful, his mother's anxiety that Denise's family will blame the murder on the Resistance. Finally pushed to action, Henry avenges his father's death and openly opposes Denise and her family. Significantly, both actions occur off stage. In the final scene, Ferdinand is reunited with his brother and Constance, only to announce that he is returning to Germany to continue liberating the oppressed, both French and Germans. Henry, newly liberated himself, opts to remain with his family, if only as "the most unpopular son-in-law" (50). The play ends with nearly all characters, except Denise, saying "yes" to the future.

If *Yes Is for a Very Young Man* looks to the future, *The Mother of Us All* draws its material almost exclusively from the past. Loosely based on the suffragette Susan B. Anthony (1820–1906), Stein weaves together figures from American history—John Adams (1735–1826), Daniel Webster (1782–1852), Thaddeus Stevens (1792–1868), Andrew Johnson (1808–1875), Ulysses S. Grant (1822–1885)—with invented characters, including her ubiquitous Contstance Fletcher, and Stein's contemporary Americans, including Virgil Thomson, Donald Gallup (the long-time curator of the Stein and Toklas papers at Yale University), early twentieth-century stage performer Lillian Russell (1861–1922), and even Stein herself. The play pits the character of Susan B. anachronistically against the political figures, most of whom led contentious political lives themselves, in her struggle to achieve the right of a woman to vote. The structure of the play foregrounds the antagonism between Susan B. and the rest of the characters, repeatedly casting dialogue as debate and monologue as stump speech. Despite the play's deliberate attempts at conflict (for example, casting the radical Republican Thaddeus Stevens opposite Andrew Johnson, whom the Republicans impeached in 1868) there is relatively little action. Susan B. debates Daniel Webster on several occasions, fictional characters Jo the Loiterer and Indiana Elliot attempt to get married, and John Adams and Constance Fletcher endlessly flirt, but little else happens. (Reading the program synopses for several productions of the opera reinforces this point.) Instead, the characters talk, mostly about themselves. Indeed, Susan B. grows increasingly frustrated with her intended audience as they repeatedly fixate so intently on the absurd minutia of their own lives that they are unable to hear her words. By the end of the play, Susan B. returns from the grave to witness not only the success of her demand for the right to vote, but also recognition for her efforts in a memorial statue erected in her honor. However, despite this recognition (not unlike the kind Stein herself craved), Susan B. concludes the play questioning her life's work.

For this final work, Stein reunited with her first major theatrical collaborator, Virgil Thomson, nearly twenty years after their first endeavor and the resulting project is grand in scale. Whereas *Yes* focuses on a small family in the French countryside, *Mother* depicts Susan B. among major political figures spanning more than one hundred years of American history. Although *Yes* takes place against the backdrop of World War II, both the Nazi occupation and France's liberation occur largely off stage. Unlike most of Stein's drama as well as that of the avant-garde, *Yes* focuses almost exclusively on representational human relationships and individual journeys instead of addressing political, artistic, or philosophical questions. In fact, a major irony of this play is that, despite the momentous changes in France, the world of these country people and the people themselves remain remarkably unchanged, as if they are somehow immune to the effects of the world outside their lives. Despite Henry's profound emotional journey, for example, he concludes the play in the same position as he began it. Conversely, *Mother,* which seems at first to focus on profound political and philosophical issues quickly devolves into petty disagreements and the characters, with the exception of Susan B., never seem to be able to escape their own egotism. These characters remain flat, two-dimensional stand-ins for deliberately simplistic political views.

Perhaps most noticeable, however, is the difference in tone between the two plays. One need only consider their respective endings to see the vast emotional distance between them. For example, *Yes* concludes with the liberation of France and the young protagonist's enthusiastic return to Germany to organize French workers there. As Ferdinand tells his former love Constance:

> Yes, Constance, this is our war, you have done your share, your countrymen will fight some more, but this is our war, our war, and we will fight it and we will win. . . . Yes, look facts in the face, Constance, for you it is all over, for Henry it is all over, but for me it is just beginning, yes is for a very young man. (51)

The "yes" here echoes the title and reflects the profound optimism of the characters in Stein's play and their ability not only to survive the adversity of the occupation, but also to triumph over it. The phrase is first introduced in Act One, Scene I, when Constance seemingly mocks Ferdinand's optimistic affection for her, but by this conclusion Constance has joined him in his progressive outlook and Ferdinand claims his role as a very young man of the future. Throughout the play Stein pounds the text with "yes," but it is particularly salient in this final scene. Through its sheer repetition of the affirmative, *Yes* ends with a courageous look forward to the future. The young male protagonist has persuaded his former love, and indeed himself, to say "yes" to love, to duty, to life. Significantly, although Stein begins *Yes* after the critical moment has been decided (not unlike the structure of *Doctor Faustus Lights the Lights*), the future is not predetermined. As the play's protagonist, Ferdinand observes, no one can return to an ordinary life, but the life of the future is by no means unpleasant and, indeed, it is the past that holds the only darkness of the plot. The events unfolding within the play embody unification, survival, and, ultimately, point to the triumph of the future.

The conclusion to *The Mother of Us All* is decidedly darker. At the conclusion of the opera, Susan B. Anthony returns from the dead to witness the realization of women's right to vote. Yet, despite witnessing the fulfillment of her lifelong dream, Susan B (as she is named in the text) is disillusioned and despondent. *The Mother of Us All* ends with her alone on stage. Although productions of the opera usually have Susan B. appear from behind the statue or have the actor playing Susan B. stand as the statue (see Figure 7), in the text a voice emerges from behind the statue. This disembodied voice of Susan B. Anthony concludes the opera by observing her own memorial statue and reflecting on her life:

> We cannot retrace our steps, going forward may be the same as going backwards. We cannot retrace our steps, retrace our steps. All my long life, all my life, we do not retrace our steps, all my long life, but.
>
> (A silence a long silence)
>
> But—we do not retrace our steps, all my long life, and here, here we are here, in marble and gold, did I say gold, yes I said gold, in marble and gold and where—
>
> (A silence)
>
> Where is where. In my long life of effort and strife, dear life, life is strife, in my long life, it will not come and go, I tell you so, it will stay it will pay but
>
> (A long silence)
>
> But do I want what we have got, has it not gone, what made it live, has it not gone because now it is had, in my long life in my long life
>
> (Silence)
>
> Life is strife, I was a martyr all my life not to what I won but to what was done.
>
> (Silence)
>
> Do you know because I tell you so, or do you know, do you know.
>
> (Silence)
>
> My long life, my long life. (87–88)

In addition to the image of an immoveable statue and the disembodied voice, the punctuation of this text with silences, the repetition of a "long life," the rhyming of "life" and "strife," and Susan B.'s disbelief in genuine progress further emphasize the desolation of this character's final speech. Susan B. sees the goal achieved but feels compelled to ask herself, "But do I want what we have got." As has been noted by numerous critics, it is difficult not to imagine the character of Susan B. in this final speech as the embodiment of Stein and her seemingly empty search for fame and literary recognition.

But even as she is writing *Mother,* Stein is finishing *Yes* for production in Pasadena. As often as Stein repeats "strife" in *Mother,* she repeats "yes" in *Yes.* One protagonist laments her life from the grave, while the other embraces his future. Furthermore, Stein leaves Susan B. utterly alone at the conclusion of the play; yet at the end of *Yes* she brings together the former lovers Ferdinand and Constance, who, though they do not reunite, do peacefully say their good-byes. The resolution of this relationship is in stark contrast to Susan B.'s stated opinion of heterosexual relationships, which she plainly calls "horrible": "if there are men and women, it is rather horrible, and if it is horrible, then there are children . . . " (85). If only on the basis of her work in *Yes,* Stein clearly did not universally condemn all heterosexual relationships, but she was ambivalent about them. While this sexual ambivalence drives many of her plays, it is not until her two final works that the extent of Stein's own divided nature becomes apparent.[2]

Nearly all her dramatic work is the product of a divided sensibility, frequently between a male and female sense of self. Although previously contained in a single play, such as *Four Saints* or *Doctor Faustus,* in these two final plays Stein's divided sense of self separates into distinct parts. Together *Yes* and *Mother* form virtually perfect dichotomies: male and female; youth and age; optimism and pessimism; beginning and ending; life and death. In the final year of her life Stein identified with both the young soldiers who surrounded her during World War II and the deceased suffragette Susan B. Anthony. In these two concluding plays Stein captures her optimism about the possibilities of America post-World War II, as well as her own anxiety about her place in history, the role of women in society, and the future of humanity. Her ambivalence about these subjects so critical to her work emerges in their clearest realization, for Stein herself is both masculine and feminine, optimistic and pessimistic about the future, a young spirit and an aging body, at the relative beginning of widespread professional recognition and at the end of her life. This reading may appear at first to contradict dominant interpretations of Stein's writing as explicit violations of such discreet dichotomies. Dinnah Pladott, for example, argues that Stein's *The Mother of Us All* "achieves a deconstruction of a whole system of oppositions, beginning with the antimony 'reality-illusion'" (121). However, it is my contention that Stein's final two works, written almost simultaneously, cannot be read as two individual texts, but must be read against each other. Thus, the violations that Pladott sees within *The Mother of Us All* can be viewed in direct opposition to the conformity of structure in *Yes Is for a Very Young Man.* At the risk of over-personalizing these two final plays, I would further suggest that the root of their radical differences can be found in Stein's own life during her last years.

Perhaps the best way of understanding Stein's dramatic indecisiveness is through the work of the psychoanalyst Erik Erikson. He divided the life cycle into eight distinct stages, each of which had what Erikson called a "psychoso-cial crisis." The crisis of the eighth and final stage is that of integrity versus despair. According to Erikson, this crisis is resolved either in *wisdom,* the "in-formed and detached concern with life itself in the face of death itself" (61), or in *disdain,* "a reaction to feeling (and seeing others) in an increasing state of being finished, confused, helpless" (61). Stein's final two plays represent her own final crisis, in which she dramatically pursues both wisdom and dis-dain. From this foundation, it is possible to understand why Stein would write almost simultaneously an optimistic romantic drama about the liberation of France and a pessimistic avant-garde opera about the struggle of women in America.

In *Yes,* Stein may create a drama in which her characters face the future with optimism, but they also face it without naïveté. In this play, Stein seems to accept with calm reflection her past and perhaps her own literary rebellion through the lens of France's liberation at the end of World War II. It is sig-nificant that Stein began writing *Yes* in 1944 before she began experiencing the intestinal problems that would eventually develop into fatal colon cancer. Although she lived in almost total obscurity during the war, following the liberation of France, Stein was once again a popular figure in Paris. In the spring of 1945, she published her account of World War II, *Wars I Have Seen,* which would follow *The Autobiography of Alice B. Toklas* (1933) as a popular success in the United States. At this time she frequently entertained and fed young and adoring American GIs. One need only consider the numerous let-ters, photographs, and mementos that fill her papers to understand the extent of Stein's relationship with the American GIs, and in June of 1945, Stein also published an essay in the *New York Times Magazine* (3 June), in which she reciprocated their affections. Stein titled her essay "The New Hope in Our 'Sad Young Men,'" and she explained the difference between this group of young soldiers and the "lost generation" she had identified after World War I:

After the last World War there was the lost generation, they were very suc-cessful but I called them sad young men because their life was finished at 30, they dreaded their thirtieth birthday, that was the end of life for them, life began early, success was great and after 30 what was there to do, noth-ing. . . . And now I have been asked are the young men of this war after the war is over, are they going to be sad young men. No I do not think so. And I

do not think so for a most excellent reason, they were sad young men already,
if you are sad young men then there is a fair chance that life will begin at
30 instead of ending at 30 and I think more or less that is what is going to
happen to this generation. (5)

Stein's sympathy for and identification with the young men she writes
about is unmistakable. Not only does she romanticize and idealize their collective future, she sees herself as a part of it because of their mutual identities
as Americans. She concludes the *New York Times* essay with the following
prayer:

God bless them, innocence and a kind heart, yes they will go on, innocence
and a kind heart, it worries them, they are troubled, so am I, life will begin at
30 for them, so really did mine, I like them, they like me, we are American.
Bless them. (38)

Clearly, much about this essay and her play *Yes* seems inconsistent with
Stein's previous writing and worldview. The God she so systematically excised
from *Doctor Faustus* reappears without irony in her simple prayer for the
young soldiers. And although she had always liked having a stable of young
men around her—Hemingway, Thomson, and Fitzgerald, among others—
these young men of the war are different in that they are largely unremarkable,
unlike Stein's earlier protégés. Furthermore, Stein seems less interested in
teaching and mentoring these young soldiers than in identifying with them.
Her attitude toward them is, of her own admission, quite the opposite of her
earlier perspective on the "lost generation" from World War I. If World War I
left a lost, directionless, and world-weary generation behind, then, from Stein's
astute perspective, World War II reinvigorated the generation that survived it.
    Unlike the pessimistic *Doctor Faustus,* which seems much more in line
with postwar existentialism, *Yes* drastically departs from other European writing of the time and adopts what can only be considered a uniquely American
perspective—a fact Stein herself seemed to recognize. She writes repeatedly
about her native land in *Wars I Have Seen,* demonstrating an enthusiastic national identification with the American soldiers arriving in southern France.
With perhaps typically American optimism, Stein seems largely unaffected
by the devastating potential of the atomic bomb. As she writes in her "Reflection on the Atomic Bomb" (1946), "What is the use, if [atomic bombs]
are really as destructive as all that there is nothing left and if there is nothing
there is nobody to be interested and nothing to be interested about" (179).
Thus, unlike her contemporaries in postwar Europe, Stein deliberately turns
away from humanity's concern for its own survival in the wake of the most
devastating of all wars, and instead focuses her attention in *Yes* on the details
of simple life in the French countryside. As she writes in *Wars I Have Seen,*

"A long war like this makes you realise the society you really prefer, the home, goats chickens and dogs and casual acquaintances" (161).

Stein writes *Yes* as a play in which she employs few of the avant-garde techniques outlined in Chapters 1 and 3. In direct contradiction to nearly all of her previous dramatic writings, she obeys numerous conventions of late nineteenth-century drama. In addition to numerous "My God" statements throughout the script, several characters invoke His name in the simple plea, "God bless him" (33). While there is no monarchial figure to take God's place, there is a crisis in government that divides the characters in *Yes*. The government is split between the acquiescing, collaborationist forces and the resistance movement. But unlike Stein's stance in her earlier works, where she surely would have condemned both sides as futile, here her position is to champion the Resistance. In fact, she structures the play according to the evolution of the Resistance, titling the five scenes, "The Armistice," "The Departure," "The German," "The Return," and "The Liberation," respectively.

Each of these five scenes represents a different stage in the characters' collective attempt to come to terms with the power of the Germans in France and their nation's inability to resist. In the opening scene, Denise, a member of the fallen French aristocracy, attempts to persuade her husband Henry to join the army, so that she will no longer be poor. This self-centered pragmatism is directly contrasted with Henry's brother, Ferdinand's idealist desire to fight the Germans. Ferdinand eventually goes to Germany to fight and possibly rescue two other brothers caught in German prisons, but Henry remains, restrained both by his shrewish wife and his own inability to act. During Ferdinand's absence, Constance, Ferdinand's American lover, joins the local resistance movement with Henry, smuggling dynamite. The play ends with the "rightful" government restored to power in France, an event that is celebrated by all the characters in the play regardless of previous alliances.

Perhaps most distinct from Stein's early work is the role of human motivation and psychology in *Yes*. In this play each character understands his or her own actions and motivations, as well as those of the other characters. Constance can explain quite clearly to Ferdinand why she will not say "yes" to him and, although he challenges her reasoning, he eventually accepts her explanation. Henry understands his own ambivalence about the war and the Resistance as the product of his feeling pulled between opposing views of himself and his family and of his wife and her family. In fact, Henry's acute understanding of his divided allegiances brings him the greatest despair. Whereas Stein's early works portrayed humanity as fundamentally unable to understand its own conflicts, let alone its own psychology, here she develops motivations for her characters that are perhaps too clear. So clear, in fact, that she eliminates suspense from the action of the play. The characters do exactly what they say they will do, for reasons that are more than apparent both to themselves and to the audience.

Not only do Stein's themes and characters here deviate profoundly from the avant-garde model, so too does her use of dramatic form. Her writing in *Yes* is clear and individual words deviate very little, if at all, from their intended meaning. Language is an effective form of communication, and characters do not struggle to express themselves. In fact, Stein appears at times to mock the confused speech of her previous characters. Constance repeats Faust's formative question, "Is it it?" but the context makes the question immediately understandable as a reference to the train bringing Ferdinand home. Often, the dialogue is often so simple as to be trite. Gone is the overwhelming presence of rhyme, repetition, and skewed syntax. Characters may repeat themselves, but such repetition is almost always related to extreme emotion. As, for example, when Henry announces his killing of his father's murderers: "My father is avenged. My knuckles are broken but my father is avenged" (43). The words in *Yes* have no double meanings, and the language carefully contributes to the building of the story, rather than detracting from it. Not only has Stein turned to a representational environment and realistic dialogue, but she has also done so without any intent to satirize. There is nothing satirical or ironic about *Yes*. Stein has produced a completely sincere representation of simple life in a French village during World War II. She evidently cares deeply for these characters as people, not symbols, and she works to protect their image as such—going so far as to dispense with "deep" character psychology, with mysterious action or motivation of the kind one will later find in David Hare's play on a similar theme, *Plenty* (1978).

Perhaps out of further adoration for these characters, Stein does not pursue her interests in cinema and queerness in *Yes*. None of the fragmentation or simultaneity of film appears in this play, and is instead replaced by cinematic melodrama. Stein embraces unity of time, place, and action with nearly textbook-like devotion. Absent is her continuous present. Stage time is fixed and linear, without interruption or deviation. The action on stage is driven by the characters' conversation, and the striking visual images that she executed so beautifully in *Doctor Faustus*—for example, through the manipulation of light on stage—are gone. So too is queerness. There is no overt duality to these characters; they fulfill perfectly unified gender roles without comment or irony. There is no fracturing of character, no hesitation in action, and, to repeat, their psychology is self-evident. Unlike *The Mother of Us All*, with its scathing critique of heterosexuality and procreation, *Yes* allows its characters to couple without obstacle or reproof. Stein seems quite devoted to the possibility of an enduring marriage for Denise and Henry, and, although Constance and Ferdinand are unable ever to unite completely, this couple ends their relationship and the play on a hopeful, optimistic note. Thus, in this play Stein seems openly and uncritically to have embraced everything she had been dramatically working against since her first play in 1913. *Yes Is for a Very Young*

Man is clearly a work of unfettered love and compassion, an anomaly among her major plays and, as a result, probably the weakest of them.

This apparent change in attitude may be attributed to numerous changes in Stein's life during and after the war. While living in the French countryside, she for the first time in her life had to work to get food. The woman who once employed one of the best known private chefs in Paris was walking long distances simply to obtain bread. Hidden away in the French countryside, this once famous figure was no longer the center of the social elite and instead spent most of her time with Toklas and her rural neighbors. In fact, these neighbors would become the inspiration for the characters in *Yes,* perhaps resulting in Stein's reluctance to criticize, distort, or simply "use" them. Drawing the plot and characters from the common people around her, Stein implicitly connects the events in these people's lives with her mother's stories of life during the Civil War. As she wrote in the program notes for the 1946 production of *Yes:*

> I was in France during the occupation, knowing intimately all the people around me, I was struck with the resemblance to the stories my mother used to tell me, the divided families, the bitterness, the quarrels and sometimes the denunciations, and yet the natural necessity of their all continuing to live their daily life together, because after all that was all the life they had, besides they were after all the same family or their neighbors, and in the country neighbors are neighbors. (Van Vechten, Introduction xv)

While Stein compares the politically divided families of the Civil War to the divided familial loyalties during the Nazi occupation of France, she represents the French people as a resilient community to be unified faster than were the American North and South. (Perhaps too fast, given the continuing debate in France today about what constituted a Nazi collaborationist as opposed to a French loyalist.)

Why Stein pursued such a new direction in her work, though only for one play, is somewhat of a mystery, and to date there has been little explanation or analysis of *Yes.* It is possible that by 1944 the avant-garde was a luxury she felt she could no longer afford, or perhaps to a woman who had lived so simply in the country, modernism seemed trivial next to the daily need to hunt for food. Ryan attributes this shift in Stein's dramatic writing to her increasing concern for the staging of her plays: "as her plays received more attention in the theater, she began to think more in terms of production, and wrote some texts, particularly during the thirties and forties, which display some knowledge of theatrical conventions" (35). Though possible, it seems unlikely that Stein would deviate from the writing style that had made her famous simply to make her plays more likely to be produced. While still completing *Yes,* she writes a thoroughly avant-garde opera, *The Mother of*

Us All. In justification of her avant-garde drama, Stein had even opined that "Anybody can understand that there is no point in being realistic about here and now, no use at all not any, and so it is not the nineteenth century but the twentieth century, there is no realism now, life is not real it is not earnest, it is strange which is an entirely different matter" (*Wars I Have Seen* 44). Hence the question remains unanswered: why late in her career does Stein write this one simple, clear, almost formulaic, even nineteenth-century play?

In keeping with Erikson's theory of a psychosocial crisis, I believe that *Yes* is one of Stein's final ruminations on her own life and the lives of "little" people against the backdrop of larger historical events—the twin subject of both her final plays. In her final days part of Stein is clearly still optimistic about the future, despite the war, despite the Holocaust,[3] despite her own poverty, and despite her illness. Her interest in country people and their daily lives, portrayed here with loving simplicity, is not merely an instance of superficial sentimentality; in fact, this interest reflects an optimism about the future and a belief in the ultimate triumph of human goodness over evil. In the wake of World War II—with its atomic bombs and Holocaust—Stein creates a simple story whose intention, in part, is to illustrate the seemingly meaningless, yet infinitely precious, details known only to those living through the Nazi occupation of France. As Stein writes in her notes for the play:

> I think we could use a lot more detail, little stuff about daily life under the Nazi occupation...all the things that are really interesting to people who have not been occupied. All the stories that came out of France during the occupation were of great personal heroism, daring exploits, open and covert flouting of the Nazis. To see the other side, which was lived by most of the ordinary people, will be most interesting and effective. (YCAL)

Unfortunately, the effect of Stein's attempt at realistic theatre was perceived as neither effective nor interesting. Although there were reportedly eight curtain calls at one Pasadena Playhouse production, reviews of the play were decidedly mixed. As Burns Mantle writes in *Best Plays of 1945–1946:*

> The Pasadena Playhouse premiere of "Yes" by Gertrude Stein was inordinately dull. One went expecting at least some of that fantastic alleged originality of the author as a fillip, but aside from a few early sorties in that direction, the play seemed shortly to settle down to a kind of pseudo-conventionality, and very little vitality was discernible either in plot or characters, while most of the situations even with the French wartime background carried little or no impact. The play can be written off as amateurish. (26)

Recent critics have held similar point of view. According to Richard Bridgman, "*Yes Is for a Very Young Man* is poor, crude theater. Its language is often ludicrously stiff... The action is loose, often improbable and insufficiently developed, and rarely dramatic" (334–335). Evidence in support of Bridgman's argument is scattered throughout the play. For example, Henry's announcement of his killing of the Germans sounds awkward and forced. He states, "We fought, we killed, we made prisoners and I beat the prisoners up. I did not shoot them, I beat them up, my knuckles are broken and my father is avenged" (43). Bridgman is not alone in his criticism. Both books previously devoted to Stein's drama all but ignore the play completely. Ryan mentions the play only a few times, focusing primarily on what she calls its "naturalist" style, and Bowers refers to *Yes* only in a footnote.

While I do not question these authors' evaluations of the play's objective worth, I do contend that *Yes* is an important part of Stein's oeuvre precisely because of its somewhat clumsy, heavy-handed attempt at sentimental drama. On the basis of this play alone, one could perhaps argue that Stein is truly an avant-garde playwright, if only because she writes so poor a realistic play. But Stein's failures in *Yes* are as important to understanding her drama as her successes elsewhere. It is significant, for example, that Stein shows in *Yes* that she was aware of the melodramatic play structure, although she studiously avoided it for most of her career. She clearly understood conventional dramatic form much better than has previously been acknowledged. It was not out of ignorance that Stein wrote such works as *They Must. Be Wedded. To Their Wife.* or *Listen to Me,* but out of a desire to represent a new age to which the old rules of dramatic form no longer applied. The atrocities of World War II, however, could turn even mama dada into a sentimental melodramatist, if only temporarily. Her optimism in *Yes,* her belief in the ability of people to face the future with full knowledge, yet without self-defeating bitterness, and her emphasis on the primacy of familial relationships indicate a fundamentally different perspective from the one exhibited in *The Mother of Us All.* This perspective, in Erikson's words, combines wisdom with the affirmation of life even in the face of death.

It is likely, in fact, that Stein recognizes her own mutual and competing views on the world at the end of her life. In one of the more touching scenes in *Yes,* she expresses the difference between these perspectives by placing them in the mouths, respectively, of a young man and an older woman. Her young protagonist Ferdinand attempts to woo Constance by repeatedly saying "yes." He deliberately connects the global tensions to his own romantic intentions and encourages Constance to see their love as the means to a brighter sociopolitical future. It is to this somewhat selfish idealism that Constance in this titular scene replies, "very slowly":

> Yes, yes is for a very young man, and you Ferdinand, you are a very young boy, yes you are, yes is for a young one, a young man, but I am not so young, no I am not, and so I say no. I always say no. You know, Ferdinand, yes you know that I always say no. (9)

Constance and Ferdinand thus represent the two opposing forces of "yes" and "no," and as such they embody the moral dilemma Stein outlines in *Wars I Have Seen:*

> [William James] said he always said there is the will to live without the will to live there is destruction, but there is also the will to destroy, and the two like everything are in opposition . . . and now in 1943 the thing that we know most about is the opposition between the will to live and the will to destroy . . . (63–64)

It is possible, then, to recognize yet another set of oppositional binaries in Stein's play: the will to live versus the will to destroy. Although Constance and Ferdinand are not directly connected to this binary, their opposition to each other in the language of "yes" and "no" can be seen as similarly irreconcilable.

In his critique, Richard Bridgman found it odd that the two potential lovers of this scene do not reunite at the conclusion of the play. He writes that "This must be one of the rarest situations in stage history: a lovers' disagreement in the first act that fails to be resolved in the last" (334). But if, as I have suggested elsewhere in this study, Stein often writes from a dual perspective, the reconciliation of these two lovers who embody her own ambivalence would be impossible within the context of the play. Stein can no more unify these two opposite characters than she can meld her own split identity into one or unify the opposing forces of World War II. Though intended as independent and autonomous people, these characters can be read as emblems of Stein's own psyche or even of the psyche of war-ravaged Europe. However, it is significant that even though the lovers do not fully unite at the conclusion, Ferdinand does ultimately sway Constance to his optimistic perspective. During Ferdinand's absence, Constance clearly misses him, and in their final meeting it is Ferdinand who tells Constance that he must go on without her. If Constance sees Ferdinand as a little boy in the first act, by this final encounter, through grief, courage, and optimism, he has become a man with a future. It is precisely because Ferdinand says no to Constance that he accomplishes his ultimate goal of liberating his countrymen.

Even their names suggest Stein's belief in these figures' perspectives. She names her male character Ferdinand, perhaps in memory of the bullfights she loved so much in Spain. (Not surprisingly, Stein often wrote that she considered bullfights and circuses to be the most engaging forms of theater.) For her American female character, she recycles the name Constance, one that appears in much of her writing and in both her final plays. Stein had an enduring interest in the name of her friend, the novelist Constance Fletcher— a character included in *Mother* and written about exclusively in "A Portrait of Constance Fletcher" (1911)—perhaps because "Constance" sounded like "constants." Certainly the Constance of *Yes* is a "constant" or unwavering character. In accordance with their names, the character of this Constance is an older woman who prefers to remain in one place, whereas Ferdinand is a man who travels a great deal throughout the play, always bullishly seeking out new fights. However, the name that carries the greatest weight in the play is that of the unseen Achille.

Undeniably named for the great warrior Achilles of Greek mythology and Homer's *Iliad,* Stein references the Greek name ironically. Whereas the Greek warrior Achilles proved to be almost unbeatable in battle (with the exception of his famous heel), the Achille of *Yes* is highly touted by his sister Denise, but dismissed and derided by nearly everyone else. Henry attacks him for abandoning his fellow countrymen by joining the complicit French army and accuses Achille of licking at the heels of the Germans. Constance openly mocks Denise's claim that Achille shot down six enemy planes and in their final confrontation attacks Denise's final attempt to justify her brother's (non)action during the occupation: "So Achille is just like a dog, when you tell him to heel he comes to heel and when you tell him to fight, he fights. What's the use of being a man if you are going to be like that, what's the use?" (47). Achille further becomes the object of attack when it is revealed that he has killed the family's high-priced pig by feeding it a diseased rabbit. As Henry complaing, "Achille just takes it modestly, he doesn't mind. Six planes, one pig, what the hell" (23). In short, the off stage Achille becomes the embodiment of a complacent and compliant France, arrogant and ignorant in his rush to German acquiescence. At the conclusion of the play, Achille unsuccessfully attempts to reenter the army, but his lack of participation in the Resistance ultimately prevents his return to military life and instead condemns him to a life of incompetent farming.

By displacing the sins of the French government onto the unseen and ironically titled character, Achille, Stein humanizes and personalizes the highly political decisions of the French occupation during World War II. Here the mythic warrior has been reduced to a foolish farmer, while the humble farmers, like Ferdinand have become symbols of freedom and action on the world stage. Although *Yes* has been called a play about the French occupation and liberation, it is clear from the intimacy of its scenes and the role of characters like Achille that Stein was far more interested in describing human relationships rooted in the love of family rather than the enmity of war. Stein writes people, not soldiers cast in a play about the occupation in which both the enemy and the hero are largely unseen and, perhaps even more importantly, are virtually indistinguishable from each other. Like Achille as the representative for French complicity, the German occupying army appears only as a single German soldier who says the following on behalf of the Resistance: "tell the maquis that they need not be afraid. I admire them and I would never let anybody do them any harm, not anybody, I admire them, they are good citizens, I admire them" (34). Even the Germans appear on stage in the context of interpersonal relationships.

Although the events of the war occasionally intersect with the lives of this family in the country, then, their personal relationships dominate the action of the play. As in Chekhov's *Three Sisters* (1901), which Stein compares to *Yes* in her early notes on the play, nearly all of the major events—Achille's leaving the Resistance, Ferdinand's visit to his brother in Germany, and Henry's vengeance for his father's murder—occur offstage. Although Stein does not fulfill her original intention to confine the entire play to Constance's living room, the setting nearly always creates intimacy between the characters and keeps the larger political or military events in the distance, beyond the frame of the stage. Stein sets her play in a garden, a park, a train station, and a parlor, and she rarely has more than three or four characters together at the same time. Thus does she create a family drama that places maximum importance on human relationships, not on the historical forces that to some extent determine the characters' lives. The effect of this political and social distancing is an overwhelming emphasis on character relationships and emotions and ultimately undermines the potential power of the play. Stein's dramatic power is rooted in her master manipulations of complexity and contradiction. Absent these, her simple characters and terse family relationships, even when cast against the backdrop of the French Resistance, fail to compel either an audience or a reader to sympathy. If in this play Stein does pursue her own youthful optimism, it is clear that such a "yes" is not the fullest expression of her voice.

Immediately following *Yes,* Stein began work on a very different play that coincided with the most despairing period of her life. The end of World War II occurs almost simultaneously with the onset of Stein's eventually fatal cancer. By 1945, at seventy-one, the cancer, and life in the country had taken their toll. Photographs from this time reveal the formerly robust, "monumental" Stein to be a frail old woman, a mere shadow of her former self. By the time she returned to Paris in December 1944, she would have only a year and a half to live. Toklas and she sold much of their famed art collection in order to buy food during the war, and Stein regretted not being able to return to her fabled 27 Rue de Fleurus address. The GIs with whom Stein had spent so many days after the war were slowly returning to America. Increasingly, they became familiar to her only through their subsequent letters from America and a collection of photographs. As they began to disappear, the underlying darkness of the time reappeared in Stein's writing, as in *Wars I Have Seen:* "Any day and in everyway this can be seen, eating and vomiting and war" (25).

As she adjusted to postwar life in Paris, Stein's dramatic focus understandably turned inward. Whereas *Yes* depicted the world around Gertrude Stein during the war—primarily her rural neighbors and their daily lives under the Nazi occupation—*The Mother of Us All* dramatized her growing inner turmoil. Not all of this turmoil was physical, for in the midst of her physical decline, Stein worried about her artistic legacy. Throughout her career, she had expressed the desire to be remembered. She had concluded her collection *Geography and Plays* (1922), for example, with the plea, "When this you see remember me. FINIS" (419), and she repeated the phrase in *The Mother of Us All* in a private moment between Susan B. Anthony and her companion, Anne. Stein wrote in the opening to her *Selected Writings* (1946), "I always wanted to be historical," and frequently asserted her role as a genius in history, claiming in *Everybody's Autobiography* (1937) that "Einstein was the creative philosophic mind of the century, and I have been the creative literary mind of the century" (22). But as her health deteriorated, the confidence that had previously caused Stein to compare herself—without irony—to Shakespeare, Homer, and the Bible, as well as Einstein, disappeared from much of her writing. Unlike her previous productions—*Four Saints* (1934) and *A Wedding Bouquet* (1937)—in which she took no interest in the process of performance, Stein appears to have obsessed over the details of an upcoming production of *Yes Is for a Very Young Man* in Pasadena, California. While writing *The Mother of Us All,* Stein was simultaneously making numerous corrections to drafts of *Yes* and writing detailed notes regarding its staging.

It is only logical then, to assume that as she neared the end of her life, Stein's literary and dramatic legacy preoccupied her thinking. For this reason, *Mother* is paradoxically a deeply personal, perhaps even narcissistic, work in comparison with every other play Stein wrote. Stein writes herself and Virgil Thomson into the prologue of the play, and she writes the cast of diverse characters as a collective portrayal of herself. For instance, Stein gives "All the characters" the following line: "Daniel was my father's name,/My father's name was Daniel" (53), which, of course, was the name of Stein's (and Susan B. Anthony's) father. She readily acknowledges what she is doing by having the character G. S. respond, "My father's name was Daniel, Daniel/and a bear, a bearded Daniel,/not Daniel in the lion's den no/Daniel, yes Daniel my father had/a beard my father's name was Daniel" (53). By having the entire cast name "Daniel" as its father, she makes clear that, collectively, the characters are actually Stein herself, or at least varying dimensions of her. Whereas previous plays such as *They Must* merely suggested that the various characters were fragments of a single person, *Mother* unambiguously presents "all the characters" as the collective embodiment of Stein herself.

The self-absorption of *Mother* is most likely the result of Stein's belief that this would be her last play, perhaps her last writing altogether. Her fear of death and concern for her literary legacy both appear in *Mother,* and the play seems specifically to reflect Stein's feelings about her long, mostly ignored, dramatic career. This, in part, explains the difference between the mood in *Yes* and *The Mother of Us All,* Stein's final major play and a decidedly pessimistic work. *Mother* is everything that *Yes* is not. Here the protagonist is an older woman. Stein shifts her focus (and identity) from the "young man" full of "yes" to the "mother" who can feel only despair even about her greatest accomplishments.

All the major action of the play occurs on the stage, never off it. Unlike the unseen German enemy in *Yes,* Susan B. Anthony's enemies surround and frequently taunt her, the greatest being Daniel Webster the prosecutor. Not even Susan B.'s companion, Anne, can reassure her. Thus the optimism that drives the narrative of *Yes* has by *Mother* completely evaporated.

It is significant that *Yes* was written as melodrama—a nonmusical dramatic form (at least by the time Stein writes one) in which evil is punished and order is ultimately restored—while *Mother* was composed as an opera. Although *Four Saints in Three Acts,* Stein's first collaboration with Virgil Thomson, was clearly a play to which Thomson added music (and for which Grosser supplied a "scenario"), *The Mother of Us All* was originally conceived as an opera, and, as previously mentioned, Stein wrote having already seen what Thomson could do with her words. As in none of her previous dramatic work, Stein here writes large crowd scenes, extended speeches (or arias), and numerous characters speaking/singing in unison. She does not eliminate the small intimate scenes that characterized much of her earlier work, but such scenes are few and far between. And the grand scale or heightened reality of the majority of this opera makes its less grandiose moments appear equally riveting. Whereas Susan B. displays power in public, as in her debates with Daniel Webster, in private she is anxious and doubtful as she confesses to Anne her regrets and doubts. Because of the contrast between the extremes of public bravado and private turmoil, the emotional isolation of Susan B. is even more poignant. To return once again to Erikson's analysis, *The Mother of Us All* is clearly Gertrude Stein's embodiment of despair, a work in which she looks back at her life with regret, disillusionment, and pain.

Take, for example, Susan B.'s lines at the opening of Act II, Scene 2. She asks Anne, "Shall I regret having been born, will I regret having been born, shall and will, will and shall, I regret having been born" (64). Later, Susan B. tells Anne, "A life is never given for a life, when a life is given a life is gone, if no life is gone there is no room for more life, life and strife, I give my life, that is to say, I live my life everyday" (64–65). But despite Susan B.'s pleading that Anne understand the depths of her despair, Anne can only respond with non sequitur questions such as, "And Isabel Wentworth, is she older or younger than she was it is very important very important that I should know just how old she is" (65). Even in this closest of relationships between Susan B. and Anne, probably a parallel to Stein and Toklas's own relationship, the dialogue does not progress. In fact, Anne appears either to ignore or to misunderstand Susan B.'s frustrations. Yet again in this final work, Stein returns to dialogue that reflects people's inability both to communicate with each other and to understand the world around them.

In her articulation of Susan B.'s frustration and despair, Stein returns to the dramatic techniques of the avant-garde. Although the drama of the historical avant-garde had already given way to postwar absurdism in Europe (which signaled both the culmination and exhaustion of the avant-garde), Stein recycles the techniques she perfected in *Doctor Faustus Lights the Lights*. Repetition and rhyme dominate much of the play, for example. In addition to non sequitur dialogue, we find simplistic patterns chosen primarily for their rhythmic and rhyming qualities, as in Susan B.'s line, "No, this the cause, and a cause is a pause" (70). Similarly, the form of the play returns to Stein's previous formal experiments. Although *Mother* is loosely structured as an historical pageant, its scenes, characters, and individual lines of dialogue are most often simply juxtaposed against each other without necessarily developing according to logic or reason. Instead of a plot, Stein writes "events," such as Daniel Webster's speeches, Susan B. pleas for voting rights, or Jo the Loiterer and Indiana Elliot's marriage, among others. Although she treats an historical theme, Stein breaks down or telescopes the linear progression of history by combining historical figures from more than one hundred years of American history to create her "continuous present" in nearly every scene.

Within this form or framework, Stein revisits her earlier critiques of religion, government, and social institutions by condemning Jo the Loiterer and Indiana Elliot's marriage. First, she links the religious to the civil in her line, "We are all here to celebrate the civil and religious marriage of Jo the Loiterer and Indiana Elliot" (74). Susan B. then questions the purpose of marriage as it applies to women, suggesting that marriage serves the patriarchy of government and religion more than it does individual women. She asks, "What is marriage, is marriage protection or religion, is marriage renunciation or abundance, is marriage a stepping-stone or an end. What is marriage" (74). In other words, do women choose marriage for protection or to fulfill religious obligations? Do they renounce their independence and ambition in marriage, or is marriage a means to a higher end? Stein then extends this critique of marriage to all human institutions, attacking them as institutions of law rather than of humanity. Just as the religious sacrament of marriage has come under the dominion of the state, so too has basic humanity or human dealings become subservient to the rule of law. Susan B. argues that "there is no humanity in humans, there is only law, and you will not because you know so well that there is no humanity there are only laws, you know it so well that you will not you will not vote my laws" (77–78). Stein locates the increased mechanization of human life even in the realms of law and governance, institutions that in Stein's view oppress women. The idea of women as human-reproduction machines is addressed more explicitly in this final work than in earlier dramatic and cinematic works such as *Photograph* and *Film*. In *Mother*, Stein connects her larger existential questions about humanity in the modern era to women in particular. It is as if Gertrude Stein has taken her entire life to acknowledge feminism and to speak against the oppression of women in her native land.[4]

Stein's queerness, thus, becomes overtly political for the first time in *The Mother of Us All*. Her criticism of heterosexuality, her emphasis on the

romantic relationship between Susan B. and Anne, and the grotesque depictions of men combine to create her most cynical and politically subversive
drama. In few of Stein's writings is her hostility to men and the patriarchal
order as expressly stated as it is in *Mother.* For example, Susan B. plainly
describes the difference she perceives between men and women: "Ah women
often have not any sense of danger, after all a hen screams pitifully when
she sees an eagle but she is only afraid for her children, men are afraid for
themselves, that is the real difference between men and women" (80). Moreover, Stein knows the impossibility of a feminist position, one in which even
to achieve victory is simultaneously to realize defeat and yet still to struggle
onward in the face of futility. As Susan B. tells Anne of the time when women
will vote:

> By that time it will do [women] no good because having the vote they will
> become like men, they will be afraid, having the vote will make them afraid,
> oh I know it, but I will fight for the right, for the right to vote for them
> even though they become like men, become afraid like men, become like
> men. (81)

On the basis of such dialogue, some critics have argued that Stein did not
have faith in the women's movement or in Susan B. Anthony's struggle. As
Bowers points out, "Gertrude Stein felt that suffrage was a dead end without a
corresponding education in what Stein called in *Fernhurst,* the 'fundamental
facts of sex,' and without, as she says, a remaking of women, so that they would
be willing to adopt male standards in their struggle" (125). The acceptance
of male values by women may be more effective in achieving equality, as
Stein seems to acknowledge, but she also realized that women's adoption of
the male standard was hardly an ideal solution, since women would also be
embracing the faults of men in their desire to become men's equals. Thus
Stein implies, through the character of Susan B., that all attempts at achieving
equality will be futile. Even as humanity has entered an irreversibly destructive
technological age, Stein pessimistically appears to believe that the inequalities
between men and women are insurmountable. She offers no solutions here
and no hope. By the end of the play, the vital turning point for the possible
reconciliation between men and women has passed, and Susan B. states quite
plainly that "we cannot retrace our steps" (87).

Others, however, have seen this play in a much more positive light.
Franziska Gygax, for instance, in *Gender and Genre in Gertrude Stein*
writes that, in the final scene, "Anthony's voice permeates both the temporal
and spatial realms, and opens them for women" (57). Bowers herself reads
Susan B.'s final monologue as one of relative triumph, writing that "Through
art, Susan B. Anthony will survive the final curtain, and Gertrude Stein with
her. That is Stein's consolation, that is her triumph" (127). Robert K. Martin,

for his part, criticizes Bridgman's assessment of this final scene, stating that Bridgman's conclusion "that the opera ends bleakly in the recognition of Anthony's sterility is outrageously misguided" (213). Martin claims instead that "What Anthony recognises at the end is not her failure, but the need to measure [the] success or failure of the endeavour in the creation of new, free individuals rather than in particular material accomplishments" (213).

Still, it is difficult to read Stein's conclusion, punctuated with silences and ending with Susan B.'s final line, "My long life, my long life," as anything but a final lament, if not for Stein herself then for humanity in general. Susan B.'s final scene leaves one with the impression that Stein saw humanity in a downward spiral from which she could not imagine its escape, a perspective found in much of her writing in the last two years of life. In *Wars I Have Seen,* for example, there is more than a hint of sadness in her description of children at the end of World War II:

> It's wonderful in the evening hearing the voices of the children playing, for such a long time they played quietly they were afraid to play in the streets or on the sidewalk but now they are let loose and the elders smile indulgently and all of a sudden you hear a childish voice cry pomm pomm pomm, pomm pomm pomm, pomm pomm pomm that's that, of course that, is a mitraillette killing the Boches . . . (241)

This observation about the children is echoed in Susan B.'s statement that "it will do [women] no good because having the vote they will become like men" (81). Stein seems to recognize the unending cycle of violence, already beginning again in child's play amid the rubble of a war only just ended. She thus resigns herself to a kind of historical inevitability that is difficult to read as anything but despair.

Stein clearly believed that the modern world had profoundly changed as a result of two mechanized and devastating wars as well as the burgeoning of technology, industry, and commerce. She wrote drama that reflected and criticized these changes, often employing the techniques of other theater and film artists yet always writing in her own unique style and voice. Although superficially there is something alienating, inaccessible, and cold about much of Stein's drama, underneath her calculating prose can be found an emotional significance that emerges fully in *Yes* and most profoundly in *Mother.* Her simultaneous joy and despair, at the end of her life and at the end of a war, break apart, respectively, into two final works of theater that would be performed following her death in 1946. These two plays are, each in its own way, Stein's dramatic and emotional legacy, written not only to be experienced by an audience, but also as a means through which she could reexperience her own remarkable life in her final days. As she herself wrote in 1945, "remembering back is not only remembering but might be being."[5]

Chapter 6
"America Is My Country": Gertrude Stein and the American Avant-Garde

"To live in the USA was to be avant-garde."

ARNOLD ARONSON, *AMERICAN AVANT-GARDE THEATRE: A HISTORY*

"When we [The Wooster Group] read *Doctor Faustus Lights the Lights* aloud, we said 'Ah, this is it! This is what we want to do."

KATE VALK, INTERVIEW, *AMERICAN THEATRE*

"I always wanted to be historical...."

GERTRUDE STEIN, "A MESSAGE FROM GERTRUDE STEIN"

Gertrude Stein passed away on July 23, 1946, but her drama has experienced a more fruitful life after her death than perhaps even she would have thought possible. In her seventy-two years, Stein witnessed only two performances of her work: *Four Saints in Three Acts* on Broadway in 1934 and a ballet adaptation of *They Must. Be Wedded. To Their Wife.,* titled *A Wedding Bouquet,* by Lord Gerald Berners in London in 1937. (A third production, *Identity* [1935] was staged in 1936 by Donald Vestal with puppets, but Stein did not attend either of its two performances in Chicago and Detroit, respectively.) In the years immediately following her death, both *Yes Is for a Very Young Man* and *The Mother of Us All* were produced, but for the first half of the twentieth century Stein's drama went largely unperformed and was for the most part unknown.[1] And yet, although Stein herself was rarely considered a playwright during her life and has rarely been treated as one since her death, perhaps her most enduring legacy resides in the theater, most especially in America. Stein's operas and drama are frequently found on American college campuses and professional productions of her plays and adaptations of her

Figure 8 *Doctor Faustus Lights the Lights.* Directed by Richard Foreman. Festival d'Automne, Paris, France, 1982. Used by permission of Enguerand.

nondramatic writing have steadily increased in the latter half of the twentieth century. As recently as the spring of 2003, two new theatrical adaptations of Stein's *The Making of Americans* (1925) have appeared: The first, *Hashirigaki,* (Japanese for "the act of walking, thinking, and talking at the same time") combined Stein's text with Brian Wilson's music in its American premiere at the Brooklyn Academy of Music while, simultaneously, the Gertrude Stein Repertory Theatre continued preparations for its major four-part digital theater adaptation of the same novel. If one surveys what has been called avant-garde, or experimental, or alternative theater over the second half of the twentieth century, it is impossible to ignore the continuous presence of Gertrude Stein.

Even a cursory look at the history of avant-garde theater in America demonstrates the pervasiveness of Stein's dramatic ideals. Her plays are scattered throughout the production histories of many of the most recognized experimental theater companies and artists, including the Living Theatre, the Judson Church Poets' Theater, Richard Foreman, Robert Wilson, Peter Sellars, the Wooster Group, and Anne Bogart. As Peter Sellars notes, "Gertrude Stein is a wonderful sort of return to Shakespeare in our century because she breaks up those sentence patterns and inverts them the way that Shakespeare did. And the inversions are very, very dramatic" (Bartow 274). Anne Bogart, concurs, reading Stein as a significant and uniquely American playwright: "Stein emerged out of the evangelical tradition which is hyper-American. The sounds of the words are more important than anything else. So she seems to be a quintessential American artist."[2] In addition to those who have produced Stein's plays or created theater and film in admitted accordance with her dramatic principles, there are many more instances of avant-garde drama and cinema that have seemingly emerged from the same sources as Stein's dramaturgy without ever claiming such roots. While a playwright such as Suzan-Lori Parks readily invites comparisons with Stein's dramaturgy, less obvious, though no less compelling, playwrights include Tina Howe, Elizabeth Wong, and Mac Wellman. The performance artists Laurie Anderson and Karen Finley, the filmmakers Jack Smith and Nick Zedd, and the visual artists Cindy Sherman and Andy Warhol also seem to have borrowed themes and techniques from the drama of Gertrude Stein.

This is not to imply that Stein had a direct and demonstrable effect on each of these artists. In many cases, no evidence exists that would definitively prove that these artists had any interest in or knowledge of Stein's work. Nonetheless, the work of all of them—and many more—has much in common with that of Stein. Andy Warhol's silk-screened "Marilyn," for example, combines both the art of the fragment with the identical repetition of the photograph to create a haunting image of a woman reproduced in four nearly identical squares.[3] Similarly, Laurie Anderson's integration of technology into performance and her oddly disjointed delivery of lines—creating punctuation where none would ordinarily exist—exemplify a kind of Steinian exploration of the spoken word and the breakdown of human communication. Indeed, the carefully interrupted language of a play like *Listen to Me* forces the speaker to adopt a staccato rhythm nearly identical to the rhythms of language articulated in Anderson's spoken work.[4] Listening to recordings of Stein reading her own work further reinforces her aural similarities to Anderson.

Throughout multiple genres, these artists share with Stein the exploration of the limits of language; attention to the fragment as an instance of larger societal fragmentation; deliberate rejection of realistic representation, even in photography and film; repetition or reproduction of identities and events; and, often, inclusion of queer or deviant sexualities. Through even a cursory examination of American experimental theater, film, and art, the prophetic quality of Stein's dramaturgy becomes clear. Her drama not only borrows from the historical European avant-garde, but it also transforms the elements of that avant-garde into a uniquely American art. Acting as a kind of artistic *Zeitgeist* for the twentieth century, Stein's drama emerges as a major influence on experimental American art throughout the second half of the twentieth century and into the twenty-first. So much so that she must be considered one of this century's most important dramatists. As Judith Malina states,

> Everything in the modern theater has been touched by Stein's recognition of the English language. She freed the theater in every dimension. She simply plowed everything under and allowed us a wide field to experiment with new forms. And the seeds she planted have continued to grow. (Watson 304)

Yet, despite her importance and influence, Stein has been marginalized in studies of the American theater, even those concentrated on the avant-garde. Michael Vanden Heuvel comments in *Performing Drama/Dramatizing Performance* (1993) that "Stein's influence on [Robert] Wilson and other elements of the contemporary avant-garde has been largely neglected" (245). It was not until quite recently that Stein has been considered a significant influence on American avant-garde theater, and despite essays such as Kate Davy's "Richard Foreman's Ontological-Hysteric Theatre: The Influence of Gertrude Stein" and Randi Koppen's "Formalism and the Return to the Body: Stein and Fornes's Aesthetic of Significant Form," Stein has been predominantly represented as a personality to be adapted and replayed in American theater, rather than as a significant dramatic predecessor. (This prominence of her personality over her writing bothered her throughout her life as well.) Even recent considerations place a lopsided emphasis on Stein as the personality. In the title to her article in *American Theatre,* for example, Celia Wren asks the question "Why Has Gertrude Stein Become a Recurrent Character on America's Stages?" (30). Despite numerous recent productions of Stein's plays (over 20 professional productions since 1992), Wren focuses primarily on productions in which the character of Gertrude Stein appears, but largely ignores the presence of Stein's own work in American theater.

Undoubtedly, part of this critical neglect can be attributed to the marginal position of drama within the Stein canon. However, the complexity of Stein's influence also prohibits a clear path of reaction in American theater. For example, Stein is a key influence for John Cage, who in turn collaborated with Merce Cunningham, the Living Theater, the Judson Church Dance Theater, and the educational experiment known as Black Mountain College. But while Stein was certainly an influence on these artists, Antonin Artaud's newly translated *The Theater and Its Double* (1938; translated 1958) also emerged a key

reference for new performances. At the same time, Stein was also a major influence in the work of the New York underground cinema in 1960s, including
Jack Smith, Michael Snow, and Stan Brakhage. As the divisions between the
different genres of theater, music, art, and cinema blurred, so too did the path
of Stein's influence. When one then turns to the work of Richard Foreman,
for example, multiple influences converge. Foreman was introduced to Stein
through the underground cinema of the 1960s and he has written extensively
of Jack Smith's work. He has written repeatedly of Stein's dramatic principles
as an influence on his work, but it is impossible either while reading his plays
or while viewing his productions to separate the influence of Stein from other
influences of film, literature, and art.

What becomes immediately clear from even a preliminary consideration
of Stein's drama and the avant-garde is that while Stein's is undoubtedly a
major influence on the American avant-garde, the path of her influence is
hazy and fragmented. For this reason, among others, the temptation to treat
the history of the avant-garde as linear and evolutionary is misleading at best.
Rather, the history of the avant-garde is perhaps best evaluated as an intricate
web of overlapping and conflated influences, Stein being only one of them.
She is probably best considered as a kind of cultural prism through which the
European avant-garde theater and film of the 1920s was filtered, to become
the American avant-garde of the 1960s. Heavily influenced by film, Stein
produced drama that directly influenced the American avant-garde film and
drama, each of which further influenced each other.

While it is beyond the scope of this chapter to examine in detail the en-
tirety of Stein's complex influence on American theater and film, I intend
to demonstrate the pervasiveness of her presence in the avant-garde of the
twentieth century and beyond by considering representative works from the
areas of American playwriting, cinema, and performance. Furthermore, I pro-
pose that the theoretical foundation for understanding Stein's dramaturgy as
a conflation of avant-garde drama and performance, cinema, and queerness,
can be used to examine the multiple influences on the development of the
American avant-garde in general. Of course, separating the impact of cinema
from European avant-garde drama and performance is difficult, and in the
case of some, impossible. Nearly all the works discussed here blend genres
and styles and they interpret and reflect Stein very differently. However, it
is precisely these generic and stylistic blends that best demonstrate the ubiquitous influence of Gertrude Stein and her unique dramatic vision and what
further encourages a queer reading. As Eve Sedgwick argues in *Tendencies,*
"'queer' can refer to: the mesh of possibilities, gaps, overlaps, dissonances
and resonances, lapses and excesses of meaning when the constituent elements of anyone's gender, of anyone's sexuality aren't made (or *can't* be
made) to signify monolithically" (emphasis in original, 8–9). If one considers the following artists, companies, and performances in terms of their

polyvalent significations, their deconstructions of gender and sexuality, and their radical disruptions of dramatic, cinematic, and theatrical form, then the relevance of Stein to the American avant-garde becomes not only visible, but defining.

Stein and American Drama

When Stein has been considered in light of avant-garde theater, it is almost always in terms of her effect on playwriting, most obviously with regard to her use of language and form. In *The Other American Drama,* one of the first major studies to consider Stein as a playwright, Marc Robinson "attempts to tell the story of American drama in a new way, with the acute sensitivity to form that Stein encouraged" (3). Arnold Aronson, in his more general overview *American Avant-Garde Theatre: A History,* similarly argues that Stein "devoted much of her writing to finding an alternative foundation for twentieth-century theater and literature, a *structure* that would accommodate twentieth-century sensibilities" (my emphasis, 26). I have argued throughout this study that Stein created a new forms of drama that echoed her own experiences of the twentieth century, both in the world around her—two world wars, film, and the rise of avant-garde theater—and as an internal response to her own gender ambivalence and queer identity. Such considerations of dramatic form follow broader assessments of Stein's writing as examples of Cubist syntax,[5] and *l'écriture féminine,* which emphasizes the structure of language as a means of rejecting patriarchal language. Dinnah Pladott brings this second aspect to bear on Stein's drama in her essay, "Gertrude Stein: Exile, Feminism, Avant-Garde in the American Theater." Pladott argues that Stein's writing cannot be viewed as exclusively feminine, but instead functions as both a theatrical and a gendered dialectic: "Stein's [writing] in particular, is the repudiation of more than just 'patriarchal, conventional speech.' It questions all so-called 'stable and traditional' dichotomies on which the mainstream constructs its norms and values, including gender dichotomy" (125).[6]

This emphasis on structure and linguistic form offers clear comparisons with American playwrights Adrienne Kennedy, Maria Irene Fornes, and Suzan-Lori Parks, among others. Though in many ways very different from Stein, each uses language, particularly its sound, as a means of representing a fractured sensibility similar to the one Stein was so intent on representing on the stage. Kennedy, for example, uses techniques similar to Stein's in constructing gender and racial identities. In *Funnyhouse of a Negro* (1964), Kennedy lists character names as different identities of the central character. She surrounds protagonist Negro-Sarah with a collection of characters—the Duchess of Hapsburg, Queen Victoria Regina, Jesus, and Patrice Lumumba— each described as one of Negro-Sarah's "herselves" (1) In the *dramatis personae* at the beginning of the play, Kennedy lists these characters under the name of her protagonist, thereby suggesting that all are derivative of the central character. This simultaneous presence of multiple selves directly compares to Stein's multiple Thereses in *Four Saints,* and it constructs a representation of fractured femininity similar to that of Marguerite Ida-and-Helena Annabel in *Doctor Faustus Lights the Lights.* As the play evolves, these shifting identities continually redefine the central character, creating a fractured image not unlike the kind one sees in the funhouse mirror suggested in the title.

Kennedy's *A Movie Star Has to Star in Black and White* (1976), contains further similarities to Stein, including not only the fragmentation of the central female character, Clara, but also projecting the fragmented pieces of this central self onto a collection of recognizable movie stars, who then "play" the protagonist in Clara's life story. As the title clearly conveys, Kennedy's play is deeply rooted in questions of filmic representation and she juxtaposes the black and white of race against the black and white of the classic movie screen. Like Stein's saints, the story is not told by its author, Clara, but is recreated (in "romantic" shades of black and white) by a coterie of movie stars in the style of *Now, Voyager* (dir. Irving Rapper, 1942), *Viva Zapata!* (dir. Elia Kazan, 1952), and *A Place in the Sun* (dir. George Stevens, 1951). In fact, Clara herself occupies only "a bit role" in the play (81). Just as Stein's St. Therese evolved from a series of photographs, so too does narrative of Kennedy's Clara's unfold as a series of film clips, gleaned from films of the 1940s and 1950s. In a pun worthy of Gertrude Stein, several of these films are examples of film noir: Kennedy displaces the experiences of a black woman, Clara, onto white movie stars in so-called "black" films.

Kennedy, like Stein, foregrounds the process of writing a play (Clara both writes a play on stage and refers to her writing process throughout), not only by making the process visible, but also by making the act of representing, or creating, the only action we see. All other events (Clara's husband Eddie's time in Korea and her father's suicide, for example) are described in retrospect. Critics have argued that what we see are Clara's thoughts about these events. However, more potently, we not only see Clara's thoughts, we also see her transform these thoughts into representation. Through Kennedy's juxtaposition of Clara's intimate thoughts against the hyper-visible movie stars, this process of creation cum representation feels both personal and public, intimate and grandiose. Like Stein, who attempted to create first portraits, then characters that could reflect the simultaneous processes of representation, so too does Kennedy explicate her own process of theatrical representation until, as Stein said, she has not one thing, but many things.

Maria Irene Fornes, for her part, uses language structurally as a frame in ways strongly reminiscent of Stein. As Randi Koppen writes, "Fornes's aesthetic practice works on the principle of framing . . . Examining gesture, movement, and utterance in a particularly controlled aesthetic space in which everything is differently charged, thus more resonant and expressive"

(797–798). This framing is readily apparent in *The Danube* (1982), in which Fornes uses the structure of recorded language lessons in Hungarian and English to contain her characters' dialogue. Like Stein's use of punctuation in *They Must. Be Wedded. To Their Wife.* or the words "thank you" in *Doctor Faustus Lights the Lights,* Fornes uses the bilingual language tapes to interrupt her characters' speech. For example, in the following monologue, Fornes use the symbol "//" to indicate where the recorded voices of the Hungarian language tape are heard:

> //This may be the last time I come here.// Here is where I first kissed you.//I kissed you that day, you know.// I kissed you because I could not help myself.// Now again I try to exert control over myself// and I cant.// I try to appear content and I can't.// I know I look distressed.// I feel how my face quivers. And my blood feels thin.// And I can hardly breathe. And my skin feels dry.// I have no power to show something other than what I feel.// I am destroyed. And even if I try,// my lips will not smile.// Instead I cling to you and make it harder for you.// Leave now.// Leave me here looking at the leaves.// Good bye.// If I don't look at you it may be that I can let you go. (53)

What might otherwise be a free flowing, emotionally driven monologue becomes, due to Fornes's linguistic interruptions, a stilted, hesitant speech that draws attention to the difficulty of communication much like Stein's *They Must. Be Wedded. To Their Wife.* did more than forty years earlier.

Perhaps the strongest connection to Stein is the drama of Suzan-Lori Parks, who breaks language apart in ways that directly echo Stein's most radical experiments. Like Stein, Parks uses language to fragment perception and history and she uses repetition more prolifically (and I would argue, more successfully) than any other contemporary playwright. Drawing explicitly from the structure of jazz as well as Stein, Parks uses repetition of language and action to critique history in plays such as *Venus* (1990) and, most profoundly, in *The America Play* (1990–93). Just as Stein argued that there was no such thing as actual repetition, Parks argues for "repetition and revision." In her explanatory essay "From Elements of Style," Parks writes:

> What about all those words over and over? We all want to get to the CLIMAX. Where does repetition fit? First, it's not just repetition but repetition with *revision*. And in drama change, revision, is the thing. Characters refigure their words and through a refiguring of language show us that they are experiencing their situation anew. (emphasis in original, 9)

This emphasis on repetition is evident not only in Parks's dialogue, but also in the form of her plays. For example, in *The America Play* Parks tells the story of a man—"The Foundling Father, as Abraham Lincoln"—who finds meaning in life by replaying the President's final moments at the performance of *Our American Cousin* (1859). The Foundling Father performs the role of Lincoln so that his "audience" can enact the character of Booth, who "shoots" the President and yells Booth's final words, either "Thus to the tyrants!" or "The South is avenged!" (165). The play's structure, which flashes backward and forward in time, revolves around the repetition of this single historical moment, complicated by the image of both Lincoln and Booth as African American. As Shawn-Marie Garrett writes, "[Parks's] theater of history . . . is a space of simultaneity. History for Parks is not necessarily a progressive experience, or even a finished set of events that can be divided and dramatized by decade" (26). This "simultaneity" of history runs throughout Stein's work, but has its strongest presence in her *Mother of Us All*. Just as Lincoln's final moments are replayed endlessly in Parks's *The America Play*, Stein's portrayal of Susan B. Anthony replays itself without forward progress. Both plays conclude without accomplishment and with a profound sense of emptiness and regret. Parks includes a "spell," what she defines as "An elongated and heightened (rest). Denoted by repetition of figures' names with no dialogue. Has a sort of architectural look" ("Elements of Style" 16), while Stein punctuates Susan B. Anthony's final speech with a repetition of silences.

Stein and American Cinema

Stein's influence on American playwriting remains central to considerations of her plays, and her dramatic principles are not only relevant to dramatic literature, but also to cinema. Although Stein is less frequently cited in considerations of American avant-garde film than theater, her dramatic techniques are no less visible. The films and performances of Jack Smith, for example, provide numerous examples of Steinian interruption and discontinuity. His infamous *Flaming Creatures* (1962) presents oddly juxtaposed shots of naked or nearly naked bodies, fragmented by the choice of canted angles, confusing framing, and by the costumes of the performers. Nearly every frame of the film is filled with body parts, but these parts are rarely integrated into a larger whole. Although the film has been regarded as explicitly "gay" (most particularly, by the Senate committee investigating the film in 1968), the film itself does not follow present integrated sexual or personal identities, but rather dismisses any individual identity (sexual or otherwise) in favor of fragmented and disjointed erotic action. Juan A. Suárez best articulates the queerness of Smith's film when he writes, "while earlier depictions of gay subjectivity in experimental cinema tended to advance toward some sort of subjective closure . . . Smith's film forbears such trajectory, emphasizing instead the recurrence of fragmentation and dissolution" (191). Given their similarities, one can easily extend this comparison between Smith and Stein, noting not only the structural parallels between them, but also the dominant themes of queer sexuality, transgression of gender roles, and their mutual rejection of psychological motivation and linear plot. These points of comparison can be further traced back to the avant-garde film of 1920s Europe, which were undoubtedly an influence on the new underground cinema of which Smith was a central figure.[7] To bring this influence full circle, these European avant-garde films were themselves influenced by avant-garde theater performances and American film comedy. And, of course, these are the same films and performances that had such a profound impact on Stein's playwriting in the 1930s and 1940s.

But Smith is not the only filmmaker to reflect Stein's dramaturgy. Like their European forerunners in Paris, numerous films of the American avant-garde have much in common with Stein's playwriting aesthetic. For instance, Maya Deren's films include multiple, simultaneous embodiments of women—as in *Meshes in the Afternoon* (1943)—as well as continuous references to the act of looking in the form of mirrors (frequently broken or distorted), eyes displaced onto other parts of the body, and windows that offer unpredictable and disorienting views. Stan Brakhage has openly acknowledged his debt to Stein. Brakhage attributes much of his film aesthetic to the writings of Gertrude Stein and has produced numerous films in response to her ideas and writings. In 1993, Brakhage finished his *Visions in Meditation* as a visual response to Stein's *Stanzas in Meditation* (1935). Consequently, critics have devoted a great deal of time and attention to the many connections between Stein and Brakhage. But even more than the films of Deren and Brakhage, what P. Adams Sitney has identified as "trance films," the structural films of the 1960s seem to draw directly from Stein's dramatic theory.

For example, in comparison with Michael Snow's film *Wavelength* (1967)—which is composed of one long, slow zoom into a room in which little happens—even the most static Gertrude Stein play seems positively brimming with activity and excitement. Just as Stein draws attention to the act of writing by exposing the writing process, so Snow foregrounds the cinematic apparatus. What happens is largely irrelevant. To reinforce this point, Snow includes a few moments of action, but isolates them from each other and the expectant viewer. By disconnecting the seemingly random events, he precludes even a hint of narrative. However, the actions themselves are worth considering, precisely for their lack of drama. Near the beginning of the film, when the frame still includes most of the loft in its view, two people enter the room and turn on a radio. After hearing part of a verse and an incomplete chorus of the Beatles's "Strawberry Fields Forever," one of the two listening promptly turns the radio off and both leave. The interruption of the familiar song and the seemingly vast distance between the camera position and the action, create a profound impression of isolation. Because the camera is positioned at a high angle, as if the viewer were a fly in the highest, furthest corner of the loft, the perspective of the spectator is vaguely inhuman. This emotional distance is not softened as the zoom glides (and bumps and jerks) the viewer through the space. Approximately midway through the 45-minute film, an unidentified man enters the frame briefly, only to immediately collapse and fall unseen, but heard, to the floor. Later, near the end of the film, a woman enters the room, gasps at the man on the floor, and calls another man, Richard, to tell him about the dead body. We hear her leave and the slow zoom continues into a final image of a postcard (nearly invisible from the original camera position) of ocean waves.

Significantly, these few moments of action (Snow identifies four in all) happen away from the viewer. In her analysis of the film Annette Michelson reads the film as a metaphor for consciousness: "We are proceeding from uncertainty to certainty, as our camera narrows its field, arousing and then resolving our tension of puzzlement as to its ultimate destination, describing in the splendid purity of its one slow movement, the notion of the 'horizon' . . ." (31). However, the end of the film is by no means certain. We go deeper into a room, seeing greater detail, but less space, and by no means understanding more. In his response to Michelson and the film, Sitney suggests that the film "also summons up the empty rooms of Mallarmé's most ambitious writing" as a symbolist work of art (417). But even more than Edward Husserl (whom Michelson cites) and Stéphané Mallarmé, the lack of overt action and attention to exaggerated time seems closely akin to Gertrude Stein. Most importantly, Snow seems to echo Stein's desire to thwart the expectation of dramatic action. As Stein attempted to make painfully clear in "What Happened. A Play," the "plot" of such works follows the technique of artistic creation, not the story of events. By including actions that are apparently meaningless (two people carry in an armoire for no apparent reason), interrupted (the Beatles' song), inexplicable (the man's death), and unseen (the woman's phone call), Snow effectively isolates his audience from dramatic action and expectation. In the absence of such action, the viewer concentrates on the minutia of the zoom. The changes in film quality (Snow used different types of film stock, including some that had expired and therefore look rather green), the shifts between reels, and the tiniest scratches, glitches, and pops of the images capture the attention of the viewer. One studies the room obsessively with an attention to structure and form that Stein surely would have appreciated.

Stein and Avant-Garde Performance

Although Stein clearly played a critical role in the development of experimental playwriting and cinema it is in performance that Stein's influence is most visible and most enduring. Nearly every year for the past decade, another new Stein play or adaptation has appeared on American stages. The operas *Four Saints in Three Acts* and *The Mother of Us All* are regularly performed and her work has been consistently adapted for performance. Indeed it is the theater, not merely the dramatic text, that most powerfully marries Stein's experiments in dramatic literature and her thinking about film. This section will, then, necessarily blur divisions between the dramatic text and the theatrical event, between cinematic influences on Stein and the theater artists who followed her example. However, these blurrings and complications find common origins in Gertrude Stein, despite the vastly different spectacles that grow from her.

Despite the argument that American avant-garde performance has been and continues to be largely antitextual, Stein's influence has been an enduring presence. In fact, it is precisely this apparent incongruity that makes Stein's presence in avant-garde performance so compelling. One might question how a director such as Robert Wilson can baldly state that, "You don't have to listen to the words, because words don't mean anything" (Shyer xv), and yet still claim the word-fixated Stein as a major influence; or why a theater ensemble as visceral and revolutionary as the Living Theater would begin its inaugural season with a playwright as cerebral as Gertrude Stein. Or, how two artists as radically different as Judith Malina and Robert Wilson could both find their origins in Gertrude Stein. It is in response to such queries that Stein emerges as more than a great playwright. Stein's writing not only transformed dramatic literature, but her sense of theatricality and her interest in film, expressed both in her drama and in lectures, also profoundly affected American avant-garde performance.

The Living Theater

Founded in 1947 by Julian Beck and Judith Malina, the Living Theater broke ground as America's first truly avant-garde production company—one that would collaborate with numerous the avant-garde theater artists and companies of the 1960s and 1970s, including John Cage, Merce Cunningham, the Open Theater, Richard Schechner and the Performance Group, Amiri Baraka, Eric Bentley, Jean Cocteau, and William Carlos Williams. Although hardly a "cinematic" theater company, the Living Theater was intimately related to the underground of American film (Maya Deren was a frequent visitor), and several of their productions were reproduced as films, most notably Shirley Clarke's film version of *The Connection* (1961). If the American avant-garde of the 1960s was a community, the Living Theater was most probably its center. Although perhaps best known for its extreme physicality in such works as *Paradise Now* (1968), which eschewed any fixed text and included the nearly nude "Rite of Universal Intercourse," the company's founders, Beck and Malina, began their joint venture in theater and drama by investigating the works of modernist writers such as Ezra Pound, E. E. Cummings, James Joyce, T. S. Eliot, and Gertrude Stein. Turning to Stein for inspiration, Beck refers to her in a journal dated October 17, 1952, as "the best playwright."

Following this early fascination with Stein, Beck and Malina inaugurated their new company in 1951 with a selection of short plays including Stein's "Ladies Voices" (1916) performed in their living room. In December that same year they opened their first season at the Cherry Lane Theater with Stein's *Doctor Faustus Lights the Lights* (1938).

Sadly, little was documented from these early productions, other than a few production notes and the original programs. In the program for the evening of one-act plays, Malina includes brief notes on the other two plays—Pablo Picasso's "Desire (Trapped by the Tail)" (1941), and T. S. Eliot's "Sweeney Agonistes" (1932)—but says nothing of the Stein play selection. More is known of *Doctor Faustus Lights the Lights* both through production notes (the production copy of the script is available in the New York Public Library's Billy Rose Theater Collection) and critical reviews. According to its reviews, the Living Theater production focused on the technological aspects of the play, equating the irrevocable passage of Faustus, as Stein did, with the horrors of war. As described by *The New York Times* on December 3, 1951, "The set, consisting largely of flashing lights, suggests a gigantic angry pinball machine (tilted)." However, photographs taken by Carl van Vechten in 1952 convey a rougher and more primitively styled performance than the one evoked by the *New York Times* review (Figure 9). To be sure, Van Vechten's photographs are clearly posed for publicity purposes and, as such, demonstrate little of the production as it appears in performance. However, the image of the rough costumes in the photographs juxtaposed against the excessively lit stage described in the review, suggests that even in this early work, the Living Theater was building its theatrical aesthetic out of a clash between the technologically advancing modern civilization and the primal forces underneath it.

Although *Doctor Faustus Lights the Lights* has been described as part of an early and forgettable stage in the history of the Living Theater,[8] the incongruent juxtaposition of the mystical against the technological is a theme that continued throughout their production history (although admittedly, the troupe would increasingly embody the mystical and leave the technological to the world around them). Most importantly, however, is the fact that this dichotomy is at the heart of Stein's plays, most especially *Doctor Faustus*. While directing his own version of *Doctor Fautus Lights the Lights* in 1982, Richard Foreman made a similar observation of Stein. In an article written for the German periodical *Theater Heute,* Foreman writes, "The accuracy of today's science has lead to a fragmentation and dissolution of the object . . . while the mystical speaks to the eternity of the inexpressible. One learns both from Stein" (37).[9]

In addition to their Steinian negotiations between the primitive and the modern, the Living Theater continually approached language with the same destabilizing impulse that for so many years caused Stein to be branded a literary imbecile. Even their most physical performances embraced language

Figure 9   Publicity photograph of Mephisto from *Doctor Faustus Lights the Lights*. Directed
by Judith Malina. Designed by Julian Beck. The Living Theater, 1951. Pictured: Robert King
Moody. Photograph by Carl Van Vechten. Used by permission of the Van Vechten Trust.

as a central point of connection between the performers and the audience-cum-participants. (What good, after all, is a protest without chanting?) And, as numerous critics have noted, they frequently found ways to reinscribe language onto the body as, for example, the moment in *Paradise Now* when the performers position themselves to spell first "Anarchism" and then "Paradise." It was precisely this fragmented and overtly corporal use of language that repelled nearly all of the Living Theater's critics. As John Simon writes of the Living Theater in 1968, "The essence of the act is repetition. Some forty or fifty lines of dialogue . . . are reiterated over and over again, accompanied by assorted leaps, tumbles, fits, collapses, gyrations, crawling, strutting, and running around" (54). Just as Stein sought to take apart language, using words for their sonic quality rather than for their inherent meaning, so too did the Living Theater see language and the violation of its rules as integral to their revolutionary purpose. As Beck writes in his *Theandric,* "The reformation of language is one of our testaments to fundamental and often unconscious desire to overthrow the untenable conditions of deliberate lies" (157).

Although it seems somewhat odd that a blueblood such as Stein should inspire such revolutionary fervor in a radical group like the Living Theater, this incongruity only serves to underscore Stein's importance not only to dramatic literature, but also to performance. Stein's attitude toward language continues to be one of the most radical in the history of drama. She took the fundamental tenets of written and aural communication and rewrote their rules according to her evolving vision of modern life. Similarly, the Living Theater violated and reformed the rules and conventions of performance—the intellectual separation of actor and character, the physical separation of audience and performer, and the practical separation of life and art—to suit their aesthetic and political agenda. Like Stein, who recognized that the world—in the wake of two world wars and the creation of atomic energy, the invention of cinema, and the emergence of modern art—had fundamentally changed the way it looked at itself, so too could Julian Beck and Judith Malina produce theater that reflected not only society's changing structure, but also their own idealized version of what that structure should be.

Finally, it is important to note that, even as the Living Theater created a lifestyle and theater aesthetic that led away from the technologically fascinated modernism of the early twentieth century, this group fulfills nearly all the previously mentioned criteria for avant-garde theater. Their productions reject the image of a patriarchal God, replacing this singular entity with spiritual icons and ideas gleaned from around the world and reformulated into a symbolist-inspired diversity of beliefs. Human psychology remains a sacred mystery. The greater truth of "primitive" existence is repeatedly celebrated in their plays, even as critiques are offered of social systems that isolate humanity from its "natural" existence. Like their European forerunners, Beck and Malina eliminate logic and causality from their performances, just as the

Dadaists and Surrealists did in their drama. Moreover, the Living Theater, like Stein, produced their avant-garde work with an awareness of cinema. Though Beck and Malina's theater can hardly be called "cinematic," Julian Beck was keenly aware of the increasing effect of cinema on theater and film's effect on audiences. As Beck and Malina state in Rostagno's *We, The Living Theatre,* "If you start doing things in the aisle or near the audience, it's just like doing a movie with a big close-up. The audience, instead of having to see things at a distance, is seeing a close face like in the movies" (23). Significantly, Beck saw the Living Theater as part of an American tradition in the avant-garde that began with Stein and the European avant-garde and immigrated to the American stage through the work of the Living Theater. In his last notebooks shortly before his death, he wrote, "Just as the work of Stein, Kandinsky, Joyce has not been surpassed in our time—surpassed in the sense of experiment—so *Mysteries, Paradise, Six Public Acts,* the work of [Robert] Wilson and [Richard] Foreman have no need to be surpassed" (189). That Beck should include Wilson and Foreman with himself in the genealogy of Stein is as revelatory as it is also accurate.

Richard Foreman

Of all the theater artists discussed here, Richard Foreman has perhaps the strongest and best-documented connection to Gertrude Stein. Not only has Foreman himself written of his artistic debt to Stein, but Kate Davy, Marc Robinson, and Arnold Aronson among others, have also written extensively about the influence of Stein on Foreman's Ontological-Hysteric Theatre. Indeed, Davy's essay "Richard Foreman's Ontological-Hysteric Theatre: The Influence of Gertrude Stein" was one of first essays to address the relationship between Stein and American avant-garde theater.[10] In her essay Davy asserts that there are three Steinian influences on Foreman's theater: the use of the "continuous present," the act of "beginning again and again," and the pressure put on the mind of the reader/viewer to create meaning out of the work—Stein in the form of non-punctuated sentences and Foreman through complex stage imagery. Davy attributes the similarities in Stein's and Foreman's respective dramas to their mutual interest in the mind, arguing that both attempted to make their art a record of their own internal states. Finally, she argues that both Stein and Foreman articulated a unique relationship between "being" and "existence,"[11] and concludes that, for both Foreman and Stein, their own interiority was paramount to their theater. She writes that:

> Rather than imitate life as it was known and lived during the first half of the twentieth century, Stein focused on the timeless qualities of the human mind, relentlessly documenting through her work the progressive stages in the evolution of consciousness, always concerned with the "next" evolutionary phase. (124)

Davy is not alone in her comparison of these two figures. In *The Other American Drama,* Robinson writes that:

> In several crucial respects, the correspondences between [Foreman's] approach and Gertrude Stein's are manifold. Stein's landscape plays, preeminently *Four Saints in Three Acts,* also are much obsessed with the placement and proximities of figures in space; the simplest movement of one character toward another sets psychological and emotional ripples throughout her world . . . And her notion of the "continuous present" finds new demonstration in Foreman's determined (and often repetitive) assertion of his characters' "being there." (159)

More recently, in *The Death of Character,* Elinor Fuchs draws comparisons not only between Stein and Foreman, but also between Stein and Robert Wilson, the Wooster Group, and Reza Abdoh. Fuchs additionally finds Stein's use of the "pastoral," or landscape, in the work of Peter Schumann of the Bread and Puppet Theatre, Meredith Monk, Ping Chong, Anne Bogart, Tina Landau, JoAnne Akalaitis, and Lee Breuer. In relating these artists to Stein, Fuchs writes:

> What I had not previously noticed was that many works which have non-linear spatial structures, and are concerned not with individual character or a temporal progression but with a total state or condition, also draw important moments of imagery from natural *landscape,* and even hint at the thematics of pastoral. (my emphasis, 96–97)

In addition to Foreman's use of the Steinian landscape, Fuchs cites his use of repetition: "while the Voice grandly instructs his actors to, in effect, 'repeat after me'—robbing them of their (already inauthentic) voices—he too is at some level engaged in repetition" (84).

While the above studies do lay the foundation for the recognition of Stein as a seminal influence on Foreman, the similarities between these two artists go beyond their mutual use of repetition, dramatic "landscape," and mental interiority in drama. As I have previously argued, the avant-garde cannot be totally isolated from either the history of cinema or the evolution of queerness. And the relationship among these three is as relevant to the work of Richard Foreman as it is to the drama of Gertrude Stein. This is not at all to say that repetition, linguistic wordplay, and the deployment of static landscape in drama are unrelated to these larger historical strands. However, it may be useful to document the similarities between the work of Foreman and Stein in the areas of film and sexuality.

Like many of the avant-garde playwrights who came before him, Richard Foreman was fascinated by film. Recalling his early years in New York to

Charles Bernstein, Foreman states that:

> In that period from 1962 through the early 1970s there is no question that the only person who saw more film, who had a wider view of the whole scene was Jonas Mekas.[12] Every night, literally—I would be looking at films, other times I would go to Jonas's loft and I would look at *more* films. I saw everything. (129)

In fact, Foreman's first production for his Ontological-Hysteric Theater was performed in Mekas's Cinemateque, which Foreman helped found. If Stein had Man Ray's films to capture her dramatic imagination, then Foreman had Jack Smith's. Interestingly, Foreman seems to have gleaned some of the same principles of temporal and dramatic progression from Smith's work as he did from Stein's. As Foreman writes in *Unbalancing Acts: Foundations for a Theatre*, "I was also influenced by the early events staged by Jack Smith and the particular acting style he encouraged in his performers, which was based upon having very little happen, stretched out over long, long periods of time" (33). And in an essay included in the retrospective on Smith in *Artforum*, Foreman wrote, "In his films and performances, Jack twisted each new moment of frustration into the baroque complex of a torture machine that, step by step, made consciousness more and more alive" (74). Foreman's observations about Smith's productions could just as easily be made of Stein's plays, which stretch out time without overt action and create a series of moments of frustrated audience impulse. Both Stein's and Smith's manipulations of time, duration, and suspense ultimately find expression in Foreman's work.

But Foreman's debt to cinema is not limited to the elongated time of Jack Smith's films. Foreman's plays echo not only the static, elongated quality of Smith's films, but also the fragmented structure of avant-garde films such as those of Bruce Conner and Kenneth Anger, who used quick cuts and ambiguous juxtaposition to create alternately humorous and haunting images. Foreman even uses cinematic techniques to mediate between actors and audience. For example, many of his works contain an unseen character called simply "Voice." This character is nearly always played by Foreman himself and offers obscure commentary on the work in progress. In *What Did He See?* (1988) the Voice addresses the audience, while the characters on stage slow to a stop: "Try thinking of it like this: if the earth does revolve, who's best at accompanying those revolutions? He who does revolve, or he who revolves not, or he who revolves definitively, and therefore productively, though at great cost?" (280). Though more obtuse than most films can accommodate, the "Voice" is nothing if not a theatricalized version of a cinematic voice-over.

Foreman himself has credited underground cinema for moving his playwriting away from narrative. In response to an interview question, Foreman stated that he turned away from the well-made play "for one reason. Because I encountered the underground filmmaking movement and Jonas Mekas. While I was still at Yale, maybe the last year, I happened upon one of the earliest showings of their films—at the Living Theater's loft, as a matter of fact. And I was just amazed. It was like nothing I'd ever seen."[13] For this and other reasons, Foreman's work is frequently referred to as "cinematic," and watching a Foreman play is often akin to watching a quickly edited montage by Stan Vanderbeek. Foreman's dramatic language often jumps around like a rapid series of film cuts or a speedy remote-control, zapping through endless cable stations. Even a short excerpt will demonstrate this dramatic effect in Foreman's work. Here is one from *Symphony of Rats* (1987):

PEYTON:　Dizzy, Mr. President?
PRESIDENT:　Not at all. I call this my watch!
KATE:　What's that on your wrist?
PRESIDENT:　(*Glances at his wrist, disoriented*) What time is it?
KATE:　(*Coy*) You will have a bad effect on me, don't you think?
PRESIDENT:　What I think should certainly take precedence over...
KATE:　You're not getting the satisfaction that you seek, Mr. President.
PRESIDENT:　Somebody just made sense!
JEFF:　What a foolish concern, Mr. President.
PRESIDENT:　Ah, you know who I am—
JEFF:　Was that an issue?
PRESIDENT:　One or two wheels in my head—
JEFF:　(*Interrupting*) It would be foolish for me to repeat myself. (226)

Finally, Foreman's habit of beginning again and again and including all his false starts in the finished play is itself a filmic technique. In fact, when describing his writing process, Foreman refers to it as "not editing." This particular technique is directly analogous to that of a filmmaker who shoots several consecutive takes of a single scene and then, rather than select one, includes each take, however flawed, in the final product. In his recent production, *Maria del Bosco: A Sound Opera (Sex & Racing Cars)* (2001), Foreman fills the stage with people behaving like automatons, spinning, thrusting, or bending mechanically. Suddenly, the music starts and the figures dance in similarly mechanically gestures. The music stops and the dancing halts. A voice-over plays. Much of the hour-long performance repeats this pattern, twisting the performers into increasingly bizarre postures with a halting, interrupting rhythm that jolts the audience.

The other major area of connection or overlap between Foreman and Stein is sexuality. The thread of deviant sexuality runs throughout many of Foreman's plays—at times, in far more explicit ways than in Stein's work. This is perhaps most notable in his *Paradise Hotel* (1999), which, as an anonymous announcer informs the audience at the start of the play, "is not in fact *Paradise*

Hotel, but is in truth a much more disturbing and possible illegal play entitled *Hotel Fuck.*" The characters of *Hotel Fuck* are in fact in search of nothing less than sexual satisfaction, which is endlessly denied them; and *Hotel Fuck* must itself fight off the threat of a third play, *Hotel Beautiful Roses.* This dramatic duel between the two hotels/plays juxtaposes the deviant with the sentimental, clearly promoting the deviant even as the romantic threatens to overtake it. In a neat twist of logic, the perverse is in danger of being corrupted by the sublime, and it may in fact no longer be possible to distinguish between the two.

Although Foreman's plays may not specifically address homosexuality, his characterization of sexuality as potentially subversive, dangerous, and deviant recurs throughout his plays. This should, of course, come as no surprise, given Foreman's interest in dreams and the unconscious (part of his playwriting technique is to take naps and quickly write the first things that come into his mind upon waking) and the influence of Jack Smith, whose infamous *Flaming Creatures* (1962), was banned for depicting according to one description, "a grotesque cunnilingual rape committed on a lone undefended woman by a man (not in feminine costume), aided and abetted by a bevy of transvestite males who, disheveled and naked, handle each other's limp genitals" (Tyler 19). Like Stein, Foreman uses sexuality as a weapon against the status quo. The characters of *Paradise Hotel* use "fuck" as their defense against the threatening "Hotel Beautiful Roses," until the word is drained of any meaning. Foreman's language echoes Stein's "continuous present," her repetitions, and the "automatic" quality in writing, but he also responds to film much as Stein did, and, following not only Stein but also the Living Theater and Jack Smith, he incorporates perverse sexuality into his work as a disruptive device. Foreman is perhaps most like Stein, however, in his devotion to text—a devotion that is considered by many to be anathema to the agenda of the avant-garde. But just as Tristan Tzara devoted his drama to "words, just words" and Stein "plunged into a water of words," Foreman concludes in *Plays and Manifestos* (1976) that "There are many things that distract from the text but the text is at the center" (ix).

Robert Wilson

Although usually considered to be primarily a visual artist, one might also argue that the text is at the center for Robert Wilson, as well. As he says, "I don't believe in talking back to a masterpiece. I let it talk to me" (Holmberg 30). That Wilson has returned to Stein so frequently suggests his interest in language, if only as the foundation on which to build his visual universe. Whereas Richard Foreman is considered to be the artist most directly influenced by Stein, Robert Wilson's work is often regarded as the theatrical embodiment of her dramatic ideals. As Michael Feingold writes in his review of Wilson's 1992 production of *Doctor Faustus Lights the Lights,* "in a sense [Robert Wilson's] whole theater is a physicalization of the [premise] Stein seems to envision in her plays: a meditative, visionary theater in which images and conditions, not people, are the active agents; one in which events, like words, repeat, multiply, and interpenetrate one another instead of coming in sequence; a spiritual banquet at which tales are evoked rather than told, and dramas adumbrated rather than acted out" (99). Certainly, Wilson's elongation of time—what he called "natural time"—seems deliberately to imitate the Steinian theatrical experience in which the audience would *not* experience the syncopation between "the thing seen and the thing felt," which Stein felt made one "nervous." As she writes in "Plays":

> No matter how well you know the end of the stage story it is nevertheless not within your control as the memory of an exciting thing is or as the written story of an exciting thing is or even in a curious way the heard story of an exciting thing is. And what is the reason for this difference and what does it do to the stage. It makes for nervousness that of course, and the cause of nervousness is the fact that the emotion of the one seeing the play is always ahead or behind the play. (98–99)

As I have noted earlier in this study, Stein's concern for the "nervousness" of the theater viewer has been cited as evidence that she was not an avant-garde playwright. However, in the work of Robert Wilson, widely recognized as one of America's foremost avant-garde theater artists, one finds the realization of Stein's concern—plays that do not race ahead of the viewer, but rather slow down to accommodate (even lag behind) the spectator's own time frame. Like the Stein who responded "nervously" to the melodrama of her childhood, Wilson felt similarly affected by the theater he saw in New York as a student in the 1960s. According to Laurence Shyer, "Wilson found that most of the theater he attended moved so quickly he had difficulty focusing and processing all the information he was being given" (xvi). Wilson's dramatic response was virtually identical to Stein's. Both disliked the speed of conventional theater and worried about the ability of the audience to keep up with the story as it unfolded on stage: both these artists responded by slowing the pace of a play. Whereas Stein did this through repetition, fighting to maintain a single moment on stage through her manipulation of language, Wilson visually elongated each moment, claiming that he was not working in slow motion, but rather re-creating "natural time." He writes that "We are not dealing with slow motion, but with *natural time*. The scene is aided by accelerated time, but I use the natural time that helps the sun to set, a cloud to change, a day to dawn. I allow the audience time to reflect, to meditate on other things besides those which are happening on stage; I allow them time and space to think" (emphasis in original, Quadri 12).

But their unusual treatment of time is only the first of several important connections between Wilson and Stein. There is also Stein's famous theory of the "landscape play," which Wilson readily embraced and incorporated into his own work. As he writes in his "Director's Notes" for his production of *Four Saints in Three Acts:*

> In the early sixties I began to read Gertrude Stein's work and I also heard the recordings of her speaking. That was actually before I began to work in the theater and it changed my way of thinking forever. The mental space she created was something foreign and at the same time quite familiar. I felt a creative dialogue with her, especially her notion of seeing a play as a landscape. The architecture, the structure, the rhythms, the humor—they invited mental pictures.

Watching a Robert Wilson production, especially of a Stein play, one can easily imagine her satisfaction. With a style that has often been called "painterly," Wilson creates his plays literally as landscapes in (very slow) motion, using language as music and image as emotion. If Stein wondered what a play would look like without plot, characters, personalities, and suspense, then Wilson provides an answer. In fact, his instructions to his audiences are remarkably similar to Carl Van Vechten's instructions to those who see productions of a work by Gertrude Stein. Wilson instructs his audience to:

> Go [to the play] like you would go to a museum, like you would look at a painting. Appreciate the color of the apple, the line of the dress, the glow of the light.... My opera is easier than *Butterfly*. You don't have to think about the story, because there isn't any. You don't have to listen to words, because words don't mean anything. (Shyer xv)

Similarly, Van Vechten advises the first audience of *Four Saints in Three Acts* that:

> [O]n the whole, it is better to take your seat in the theater where *Four Saints* is being performed with nothing in mind, in fact, but curiosity to discover what this firm may be that the author and composer, choreographer and decorator, have worked so consciously to create. (YCAL)

Each man advises the audience simply to listen and watch. No interpretation is required or even advisable.

However, in the cases of both Stein and Wilson, it is erroneous to assume that their theater is completely nonnarrative. Rather, each creates theater out of narrative fragments that are also fragments of image, language, and time. Just as Stein borrowed such fragments from Dada and film to create a unique kind of dramatic tension or narrative suspense in her plays, Wilson uses the fragment as a tool in his productions. As Arthur Holmberg rightly points out, "one characteristic of a Wilson production like *Einstein on the Beach* is the profusion of narrative fragments that cross, crash, and collide on stage" (11). Like Stein, Wilson often conceives even his "traditional" productions in discrete parts that will eventually combine into a whole work. As Wilson instructed his actors in his 1992 production of *Danton's Death* (1835):

> I separate the text and the blocking to create tension, but it should never seem arbitrary. Eventually, the elements are not separate, they form a complete whole. In a formal theater, the actors *do* have characters and ideas and emotions, but they have to structure it for themselves and they can't force an audience to accept this structure. (emphasis in original, Baker 101)

Wilson takes his inspiration for this approach partly from film, specifically film as a collection of subtly distinct fragments. Wilson explains his interest in film as the result of the work of Daniel Stern, a professor of psychology at Columbia University. In a 1971 interview with *The New Yorker,* Wilson said that:

> [Stern] is working on a study of babies from the time of birth to the age of three weeks, with camera and stopped-action films. The baby cries, the mother leans down to pick him up. What we see with our eye is the big movement, the mother loving the baby. But you film it, and look at the isolated first frame of the film, and nine times out of ten what you see is the mother *lunging* at the child. So many different things are going on, and the baby is picking them up. I'd like to deal with these things in the theater, if that's possible. (emphasis in original, 30)

Viewing a Wilson production creates the impression of watching a film in slow motion. The scale of his works greatly exceeds that of most other theater, finding closer proximity to the oversized film screen. Wilson's cinematically inspired structure extends not only to his use of time, but also dictates the progression of scenes. Like much of the theater of the avant-garde, Wilson builds scenes according to a kind of theatrical montage, foregrounding juxtaposition and contrast, repeating moments with slight variation, and, in his more recent work, accompanied by strikingly cinematic scores that create emotional and thematic connection between visually disparate scenes. Indeed, many of his original productions have been close collaborations with contemporary musicians, many of whom (Philip Glass, Lou Reed, and Tom Waits) have also written numerous film scores. Though most often treated as opera because of the overt presence of music, the music in these productions more closely resembles the cinematic scores that accompany most movies. What distinguishes Wilson's use of cinematic time, montage, and filmic score from conventional film, however, is the attention drawn to each of these elements. His is a dialectic similar to the Russian formalists, but it is it not a pure synthesis. Wilson's scenes may be arranged in a kind of montage, but the results lack the thematic (and political) clarity that a filmmaker like Sergei Einsenstein sought to achieve. Instead, Wilson follows the Steinian precedent of discordant collision between elements, a montage of violence, not synthesis.

Even Wilson's sets seem to channel Stein's presence, such as that for *A Letter for Queen Victoria* (1974) in which a white wall is painted with columns of words: "ok," "SPUPS," and, in proper Steinian fashion, seemingly endless rows of "THERE." Shyer maintains that this set is best seen as a dam through which words are bursting, akin to Wilson's own "burst" into language when he conquered his stutter as a child.[14] However one chooses to interpret this "linguistic" set, it is clear that both Stein and Wilson treat individual words as objects, divested of their meaning, "played" for their musical qualities, and subject to whimsical reorganization. Wilson's interest in Christopher Knowles seems to mirror his interest in Gertrude Stein and her deracination of language. Knowles, a brain-damaged fourteen-year-old boy with whom Wilson created a number of works in the early 1970s, created and played with language in ways similar to both Stein and the Dadaists. For example, a section of Knowles text used in *Queen Victoria* reads:

THE SUNDANCE KID WAS BEAUTIFUL

THE SUNDANCE KID DANCED A LOT

THE SUNDANCE KID DANCED AROUND THE ROOM

RAISING RAISING

RAISE RACE RACING

THE SUNDANCE KID RAISED DANCE RACE

DANCE DANCING

RAISE RAISING

RACE RACING

YEAH THE SUNDANCE KID COULD DANCE A LOT
(Fairbrother 118)

If one recalls the way Stein uses verbs to structure her "Portrait of Constance Fletcher," the parallels in writing are readily apparent. The forcing of language into the present tense, particularly the present progressive implies the kind of action within stasis that is the defining feature of Stein's sense of character. Character for both Stein and Wilson is not devoid of activity, but the action is so constrained, so fixed, as to become almost catatonic.

In addition to his interest in theatricalizing fragmented and repetitive language, Wilson also creates theater out of "found" words and sounds. Just as Stein thought that drama could be made out of advertisements and newspaper clippings, Wilson has incorporated television talk into his texts as a kind of "automatic writing" of his own. In an essay for *The Drama Review,* Wilson explains his process for creating *I was sitting on my patio this guy appeared I thought I was hallucinating* (1977):

> The language I wrote was more a reflection of the way we think than of the way we normally speak. My head became like a TV, switching from thought to thought (and in writing from phrase to phrase) like flipping a dial from channel to channel. I write best when I am alone and there are no interruptions. I sometimes keep a television on at low volume and incorporate phrases I hear into my text, which I write quickly, usually leaving it untouched and in its original order once the words are on the page. (76)

From even a cursory glance at the work of Robert Wilson, the influence of Gertrude Stein becomes apparent. Incorporating film and technology, Wilson, like Stein, creates imaginative theater that transcends the bounds of language and grammar. Perhaps the connection between Stein and Wilson is best articulated in the opening statement to a 1992 review of Wilson's *Doctor Faustus Lights the Lights* in *Variety.* Greg Evans writes, "Robert Robert Robert Wilson is back back back. And in an expatriate marriage made in Modernist heaven, he's brought Gertrude Stein with him" (68). If Stein's is the theater of the ontological word, Wilson's is that of the primal image.

Conclusion

As the American avant-garde moves into the twenty-first century, Stein continues to be an integral part of its theater. Since Robert Wilson's production of *Doctor Faustus Lights the Lights* in 1992, he has directed two other works by Stein: *Four Saints in Three Acts* in 1996, and *Saints and Singing* in 1998. In 1998 the Wooster Group produced a (literally) brilliant adaptation of *Doctor Faustus Lights the Lights,* that combined Stein's text with Joseph Mawra's 1964 sexploitation film *Olga's House of Shame.* Making the relationship among Stein and film and queerness explicit, the resulting production, *House/Lights* perhaps best embodied the essence of Stein's drama as fragmented, technologically-driven, and queer. Directed by Elizabeth LeCompte, the structure of the production accentuates its fusion of film and theater, including violent collisions between the two.[15] Presented on a stage littered with video monitors, electrical cables, and oppressively blinding lights, the actors transition violently between scenes on stage and the black and white movie playing on monitors. Further playing on the technological implications of the text, the Wooster Group production fragments the character of Faust, both visually and conceptually. The use of real time video (often superimposing live actors into the *mise-en-scéne* of the Mawra film) visually creates multiple versions of Faust, while the casting of a single actor (Kate Valk) to play both Faust and Mawra's character Elaine, creates a single character fundamentally degendered and divided. The double casting of Mephistopheles as an overtly sexual and feminized Olga creates an overtly queer reading of the play, the highlight of which comes in an ingenious moment when Mephistopheles portrays Stein's "country woman" and sings Johnny Cash's "Ring of Fire" to a supine Faust who repeats, "it burns burns burns."

In 2000 Mark Morris and his dance troupe presented an abbreviated version of *Four Saints in Three Acts* at the Brooklyn Academy of Music. Morris's version of Stein's text with Thomson's music is in many ways the most faithful of all the recent productions of Stein's drama, despite the production's abbreviated nature. The major obstacle to staging an early work like *Four Saints* is its ambiguous relationship between text and character. Make the text too neatly fit specific characters and the production loses the suggestive fluidity of Stein's text. Leave the text too amorphous and the clarity or meaning of the words is completely lost. Morris solves this fundamental problem by adapting the opera to dance, thus freeing the language from the bodies of the performers. The singers stand in the orchestra pit alongside the musicians, and with the exception of St. Therese and St. Ignatius, the identities of the dancers and saints are not matched. Many more saints exist than dancers and the visual similarities between dancers, both in costume and movement, prevent the consistent identification of a single dancer with a single character. Thus, much as Stein intended, the identities of the saints shift and change, never becoming associated with one physical body. Criticisms by audience members following the performance included the complaint that "You couldn't tell who was talking," which is precisely what Stein intended for her written text. By separating language from the body, Morris achieves in performance what Stein imagined on paper, and he expresses in dance what Stein might have envisioned for her all her plays' productions in the theater. While there is certainly no one best method to produce Stein's drama, dance, with its abstract and heightened reality, may be the most faithful to her intent.

Despite the myriad of Stein productions—both those of her drama and those based on her life—Stein's influence on twentieth-to-twenty-first-century American theater may be even greater in the area of criticism, changing not only the theater that critics watch, but also the *way* they watch. Many of the theater critics and scholars who write about Robert Wilson, Richard Foreman, the Wooster Group, Suzan-Lori Parks, Maria Irene Fornes, Reza Abdoh, and others, also write about Gertrude Stein. Although few studies explicitly mark the relationship between Stein and the theatrical avant-garde, numerous critics weave artifacts of Stein into their studies of experimental drama, if only through the use of such terms as "continuous present" and "landscape plays." Elinor Fuchs in her *Death of Character* uses Stein as the impetus for examining the pastoral in the works of Wilson, Heiner Müller, Foreman, Elizabeth LeCompte, Abdoh, Meredith Monk, Parks, and Charles Mee. In *The Theatre of Images,* Bonnie Marranca cites Stein in her introduction to the plays of Foreman, Wilson, and Lee Breuer, as well as devoting a number of essays published elsewhere exclusively to Stein's own drama. And Michael Vanden Heuvel refers to Stein in his study of avant-garde drama titled *Performing Drama/Dramatizing Performance*. In fact, Heuvel concludes his study with an observation about the last forty years of American avant-garde theater that could just as easily apply to Stein. He writes:

> [I]f one common denominator exists among the few works mentioned here and the many related theater projects left out, it is that all have been motivated by a desire to expose the entrenched workings of traditional literary drama. Instead of representing what is perceived in contemporary culture through the simplified and naturalized topography of the classic dramatic text, these artists have recognized the need to break up that seemingly objective relief map and to scan the landscape in other ways. (231)

Such investigations of Stein's use of landscape have led to new directions in theater studies, as evident in Elinor Fuchs and Una Chaudhuri's recent collection, *Land/Scape/Theater* (2002).

It is clear from her plays that Stein is the first American playwright to "scan the landscape in other ways," yet her attempts to do so brought her derision during her lifetime—and theatrical idolization after it. She is perhaps America's greatest unread dramatist: ironically, one whose ideas and theories are quoted far more than the plays she wrote. Yet her ideas and theories are almost meaningless without the accompanying texts she composed in embodiment of her artistic principles. Moreover, it is in production that her works best incarnates her dramatic vision. Richard Foreman writes in his *Unbalancing Acts* that, "I like to think of my plays as an hour and a half in which you see the world through a special pair of eyeglasses" (5). Through her drama, Gertrude Stein has given the American theater just such a pair of eyeglasses for the last fifty years and promises to do so for many more years to come. Ever in the vanguard, she is truly "the mother of us all."

Appendix A

A Chronological List of Gertrude Stein's Plays

In order to analyze Stein's drama one must first identify which of her numerous writings are plays, as opposed to poems, "portraits," essays, or simply notes and writing exercises. In this study I have focused on eight of the texts that, I believe, Stein wrote specifically as dramas or scenarios—texts that she referred to as plays or screenplays in notes and letters, that she attempted to have produced, and in which she demonstrated her awareness of form (even as she worked against this form). Beyond the six major plays and two screenplays examined here, there are many more texts that have previously been analyzed as drama.

At present there are two separate lists cataloging Stein's complete drama: Betsy Alayne Ryan's Appendix A in *Gertrude Stein's Theatre of the Absolute* (1984), and Jane Palatini Bowers's Appendix to *"They Watch Me as They Watch This": Gertrude Stein's Metadrama* (1991). Although the majority of both lists consists of the same plays, each appendix includes a number of plays that the other excludes. Not surprisingly, each author uses somewhat different criteria for distinguishing a Stein play from other writing by her. Ryan bases her criteria for a Stein play on the presence of the following characteristics: juxtaposition, time, character, repetition, modification, rhyme, and text divisions (69). Based upon these criteria Ryan arrives at a list of seventy-seven plays. Bowers, for her part, assesses the plays according to Stein's designation of the writing as a "play," its inclusion in *Operas and Plays,* the presence of dialogue, divisions between main text and side text describing characters, or the text's function as "metadrama," which indicates that it was intended for performance. Using these criteria she compiles a list of 103 plays.

For the sake of thoroughness, I have included here a list of plays that encompasses both Ryan's and Bowers's appendices. (There are no Stein plays not listed in one or both of these lists.) These plays are listed by their date of composition according to the chronology established by Richard Bridgman in Appendix C of *Gertrude Stein in Pieces* (1970). His list of works before 1940 is based on the Gallup and Haas list in the *Yale Catalogue,* Part 4, located in the Beinecke Library of Rare Books and Manuscripts at Yale University. Bridgman's list after 1940 is based on the Julian Sawyer extension of the Gallup-Haas chronological list in the *Yale Catalogue,* also located in the Bei-necke Library. As did Ryan and Bowers, I have included the title of the book in which each play was first published, followed by the first page number of the work in that book. Plays published individually are listed with their specific citation. The volumes are designated by the following abbreviations:

BTV	*Bee Time Vine*
FOUR	*Four in America*
G&P	*Geography and Plays*
GSFR	*Gertrude Stein First Reader*
LO&P	*Last Operas and Plays*
O&P	*Operas and Plays*
PL	*Painted Lace*
P&P	*Portraits and Prayers*
RAB	*Reflection on the Atomic Bomb*
SIM	*Stanzas in Meditation*
SW	*Selected Writings*
UK	*Useful Knowledge*
WAM	*What Are Masterpieces*
YCAL	Yale Collection of American Literature, Gertrude Stein Papers.

Those plays included in only one appendix, Ryan's or Bowers's, are followed by the initial "R" or "B" in brackets.

While some of the following texts were certainly intended as drama (for example, *Four Saints in Three Acts* and *Doctor Faustus Lights the Lights*), others probably were not. As previously argued in this study, I believe that many of Stein's shorter works, particularly those before 1920, were merely writing exercises and not intended for production. However, I leave the final determination of what constitutes a Gertrude Stein play to the reader.

1913

What Happened. A Play in Five Acts	G&P, 205
One. Carl Van Vechten [R]	G&P, 199
White Wines. Three Acts	G&P, 210
IIIIIIIIII [R]	G&P, 189
Old and Old	O&P, 219
A Curtain Raiser	G&P, 202
Simons A Bouquet [R]	O&P, 203

1915

Not Slightly. A Play	G&P, 290
Farragut or a Husband's Recompense [B]	UK, 5
This One Is Serious [B]	PL, 20
He Didn't Light the Light [B]	PL, 17
Independent Embroidery [B]	PL, 81
He Said It. Monologue	G&P, 267

1916

For the Country Entirely. A Play in Letters	G&P, 227
Henry and I [B]	PL, 273
Water Pipe [B]	RAB, 31
Ladies' Voices. Curtain Raiser	G&P, 203
Every Afternoon. A Dialogue	G&P, 254
Advertisements [B]	G&P, 341
Do Let Us Go Away. A Play	G&P, 215
Let Us Be Easily Careful [B]	PL, 35
Bonne Annee. A Play	G&P, 302
Captain Walter Arnold. A Play	G&P, 260
In Memory (Polybe Silent) [B]	PL, 29
Please Do Not Suffer. A Play	G&P, 262
I Like It to Be a Play. A Play	G&P, 286
A Very Good House [B]	PL, 26
Turkey and Bones and Eating and We Liked It. A Play	G&P, 239
I Often Think about Another [B]	PL, 32
Polybe In Port: A Curtain Raiser (Part of A Collection)	G&P, 23
I Must Try to Write the History of Belmonte [B]	G&P, 70
Look at Us [B]	PL, 259
Mexico. A Play	G&P, 304
Decorations [B]	BTV, 185
A Poem about Waldberg [B]	G&P, 166

1917

The King of Something (The Public Is Invited to Dance)	G&P, 122
Counting Her Dresses. A Play	G&P, 275
Have They Attacked Mary. He Giggled (A Political Caricature) [B]	SW, 533
An Exercise in Analysis. A Play	LO&P, 119
I Can Feel the Beauty [B]	PL, 84
Will We See Them Again [B]	PL, 275
Why Can Kipling Speak [B]	BTV, 188

1918

In Their Play [B]	BTV, 206
What Is the Name of a Ring [B]	BTV, 180
Can You See the Name [B]	BTV, 204
Making Sense [B]	BTV, 202
Work Again [B]	G&P, 392

1919

Monday and Tuesday. A Play [R]	YCAL
Accents in Alsace. A Reasonable Tragedy	G&P, 409
A Poetical Plea [B]	BTV, 195
The Work [B]	BTV, 189
Tourty or Tourtebattre. A Story of the Great War [B]	G&P, 401

1920

A Movie	O&P, 395
Photograph. A Play in Five Acts	LO&P, 152
Scenery [B]	BTV, 217
Coal and Wood [B]	PL, 3
A Circular Play. A Play in Circles	LO&P, 139
Woodrow Wilson [B]	UK, 104

1921

B.B. or The Birthplace of Bonnes [B]	P&P, 162
Capture Splinters	BTV, 218
Reread Another. A Play. To Be Played Indoors and Out. I Wish to Be a School	O&P, 123

1922

Objects Lie on a Table. A Play	O&P, 105
Saints and Singing. A Play	O&P, 71
A Saint in Seven [R]	WAM, 41
Lend a Hand or Four Religions	UK, 170

1923

A List	O&P, 89
Capital Capitals	O&P, 61
Jonas Julian Caesar and Samuel [B]	PL, 286
A Village. Are You Ready Yet Not Yet. A Play in Four Acts. Paris: Galerie Simon, 1928.	
Am I to Go or I'll Say So	O&P, 113

1927

Four Saints in Three Acts. A Opera to Be Sung	O&P, 11

1928

A Lyrical Opera Made by Two. To Be Sung.	O&P, 49
Paiseu. A Play. A Work of Pure Imagination in Which No Reminiscences Intrude	LO&P, 155
A Bouquet. Their Wills	O&P, 195

1929

Film. Deux Soeurs Qui Ne Sont Pas Soeurs	O&P, 399

1930

Parlor. A Play between Parlor of the Sisters and Parlor of the Earls	O&P, 325
At Present. A Play. Nothing but Contemporaries Allowed	O&P, 315
Madame Recamier. An Opera	O&P, 355
They Weighed Weighed-Layed. A Drama of Aphorisms	O&P, 231
To Help. In Case of Accident [B]	SIM, 253
An Historic Drama in Memory of Winnie Elliot	LO&P, 182
Will He Come Back Better. Second Historic Drama. In the Country	LO&P, 189
Third Historic Drama	LO&P, 195
Politeness [B]	PL, 142
Louis XI and Madame Giraud	O&P, 345
Play I [–III]	LO&P, 200

1931

Say It with Flowers	O&P, 331
The Five Georges	O&P, 293
Lynn and the College de France	O&P, 249
They Must. Be Wedded. To Their Wife. A Play	O&P, 161
Civilization. A Play. In Three Acts	O&P, 131

1932

A Play without Roses. Portrait of Eugene Jolas	P&P, 200
A Play of Pounds	LO&P, 239
A Manoir. An Historical Play in Which They Are Approached More Often	LO&P, 277
Short Sentences	LO&P, 317
A Play. A Lion. For Max Jacob	P&P, 28
Scenery and George Washington. A Novel or a Play [R]	FOUR, 161

1933

Byron a Play. But Which They Say Byron a Play   LO&P, 333

1935

Identity. A Poem [R]   WAM, 71

1936

Listen to Me. A Play   LO&P, 387
A Play Called Not and Now   LO&P, 422

1937

Daniel Webster. Eighteen in America. A Play   RAB, 95

1938

Doctor Faustus Lights the Lights   LO&P, 89
Lucretia Borgia. A Play   RAB, 118

1941

Lesson Sixteen. A Play   GSFR, 42

1943

In a Garden. A Tragedy in One Act   GSFR, 59
Three Sisters Who Are Not Sisters. A Melodrama   GSFR, 63
Look and Long. A Play in Three Acts   GSFR, 73

1944–45

Yes Is for a Very Young Man   LO&P, 1

1945–46

The Mother of Us All   LO&P, 52

1946

John Breon. A Novel or a Play   YCAL

Appendix B
A Chronological List
of Professional Productions

The following list includes professional productions of Stein's drama with as much detail as is currently available. In several instances, the original play has been set to music, or in other ways interpreted for the stage as, for example, Mark Morris's ballet *Four Saints in Three Acts* (2000). In no instance here, however, has the actual text been significantly altered. If the form of the production differs from the original, this has been noted in parentheses following the title. Productions that have fundamentally altered Stein's original text are included in Appendix C, "Dramatic Adaptations."

1927   *Capital, Capitals* (Concert)
Music and conducted by Virgil Thomson
Duchess de Clermont-Tonnerre, Costume Ball
Paris, France

Also presented at:
Salle d'Orgue, Vieux Conservatoire, Paris, France (1928)
Copland-Sessions Concert Series, New York, NY (1929)
Harvard Glee Club, Cambridge, MA (1929)
Barre Woman's Club (Barre, MA 1929)
Aeolian Hall, London, England (1931)

1934   *Four Saints in Three Acts*
Directed by John Houseman
Conducted by Alexander Smallens
Sets and costumes by Kate Lawson
Lighting by Abe Feder
Choreography by Frederick Ashton
Wadsworth Atheneum
Hartford, CT

Also presented at:
44th Street Theater, New York, NY
Empire Theater, New York, NY
Sullivan Opera House, Chicago, IL
Ritz Tower, New York, NY (Concert)

1936   *Identity a Poem*
Directed and designed by Donald Vestal
First American Puppetry Festival
Institute of Arts
Detroit, MI

1940   *Turkey and Bones and Eating and We Like It*
"One Carl Van Vechten" and "Captain Walter Arnold"
Gate Theatre
Dublin, Ireland

1941   *Four Saints in Three Acts* (Concert)
Museum of Modern Art
Conducted by Virgil Thomson
New York, NY

Four Saints in Three Acts (Concert)
Conducted by Alexander Smallens
Town Hall
New York, NY

1942   *Four Saints in Three Acts* (Concert)
Conducted by Alfred Wallenstein
Station WOR Broadcast
New York, NY

1943   *The Gertrude Stein First Reader and Three Plays*
Directed by Pierre Balmain
Paris, France

1946   *Yes Is for a Very Young Man*
Directed by Tom Browne Henry
Sets by Donald Finlayson
Pasadena Playhouse
Pasadena, CA

1947   *Four Saints in Three Acts* (Concert)
Original cast trained by Leonard de Paur
Conducted by Virgil Thomson
CBS: Philharmonic Hour Broadcast
New York, NY

The Mother of Us All
Brander Matthews Theater
Columbia University
Conducted by Virgil Thomson
Station WNYC Broadcast
New York, NY

Yes Is for a Very Young Man
ANTA Experimental Theater
New York, NY

1948 *Yes Is for a Very Young Man*
48 Theater
Anglo-French Art Center
London, England

1949 *In a Garden* (Opera)
Music by Meyer Kupferman
Directed by Richard Flusser
After Dinner Opera Company
New York, NY

Revivals:
Phoenix Theater, New York, NY (1957)
   (Dir. Lawrence Kornfeld)
White Barn Theater, Westport, CT (1971)

The Mother of Us All (Concert)
Cleveland Orchestra
Cleveland, OH

Yes Is for a Very Young Man
Directed by Lamont Johnson
Sets and lighting by Edwin Wittstein
Costumes by Marlin Maclintock
Cherry Lane Theater
New York, NY

1950 *What Happened*
Directed by Lindley Williams Hubbell
Randall Playhouse
Hartford, CT

Yes Is for a Very Young Man
Brattle Theater Company
Cambridge, MA

Yes Is for a Very Young Man
Actor's Colony
Dennis Dance Theater
Baltimore, MD

1951   *Doctor Faustus Lights the Lights*
Directed by Judith Malina
Music by Richard Banks
Designed by Julian Beck
Choreographed by Remy Charlip
The Living Theater
The Cherry Lane Theater
New York, NY

Ladies Voices
Directed by Julian Beck
The Living Theater
The Cherry Lane Theater
New York, NY

1952   *Four Saints in Three Acts* (Revival)
Conducted and musical direction by Virgil Thomson
Book directed by Maurice Grosser
Designed by William Morrison (from the original designs by
    Florine Settheimer)
Choreographed by William Dollar
Broadway Theater
New York, NY

Also presented at:
Théâtre des Champs-Elysees (Exposition: L'Art du Vingtieme Siecle)
Paris, France

1953   *Four Saints in Three Acts* (Concert; abridged)
Conducted by Virgil Thomson
Lewisohn Stadium
New York, NY

Four Saints in Three Acts (Concert)
Directed by Kojiro Kobune
Yokohama Symphony Orchestra
Octagon Theater
Yokohama, Japan

1954   *Doctor Faustus Lights the Lights* (Concert)
Directed by Sydney Walker
Space sculpture by Tom Hall
Playhouse Repertory

Little Theater on Hyde Street
San Francisco, CA

Four Saints in Three Acts (Concert)
Lewisohn Stadium
New York, NY

Yes Is for a Very Young Man
Provincetown Playhouse
Provincetown, MA

1955   *In a Garden; Three Sisters Who Are Not Sisters*
Directed by Strowan Robertson
Designed by Lester Hackett
Tempo Playhouse
New York, NY

1956   *Ladies Voices; In a Garden*
Produced by Addison Metcalf
Little Theater
Newton, CT

The Mother of Us All
Directed by Bill Butler
Conducted by Virgil Thomson
Phoenix Theater
New York, NY

1957   *Doctor Faustus Lights the Lights* (Dance)
Directed and designed by Paul Sanasardo
Music by Charles Wuorinen
Rooftop Theater
New York, NY

In a Garden (Opera)
Directed by Lawrence Kornfeld
Music by Meyer Kupferman
Phoenix Theater
New York, NY

1958   *Doctor Faustus Lights the Lights* (Staged reading)
Adapted by Marvin Goldstein, Bernice Loren, and Bennes
    Mardenn
Directed by Marvin Goldstein
Music by Charles Wuorinen
Conducted by Laurence Siegel
Chapter Hall, Carnegie Hall
New York, NY

1960   *Doctor Faustus Lights the Lights* (Concert)
Music by Meyer Kupferman
Two arias: "I Am a Dog," "I Am the Only She"
Carnegie Recital Hall
New York, NY

1963   *What Happened* (Musical)
Directed by Lawrence Kornfeld
Music by Al Carmines
Sets by Larry Siegel
Judson Poets' Theater
Judson Memorial Church
New York, NY

Yes Is for a Very Young Man
Directed by Philip Minor
Sets and lighting by David Moon
Players Theater
New York, NY

1964   *The Mother of Us All* (Concert)
American Opera Society
Carnegie Hall
New York, NY

Photograph
American Theater for Poets
New York, NY

1965   Homage a Gertrude Stein:
Ladies' Voices; Yes Is for a Very Young Man (partial); *The Gertrude
   Stein First Reader and Three Plays*
Directed by Christian Bagot
Designed by Pablo Picasso
Centre Cultural Americain
Paris, France

Play I(–III)
Directed by Lawrence Kornfeld
Judson Poets' Theater
Judson Memorial Church
New York, NY

Three Sister Who Are Not Sisters (Musical)
Directed by Michael Smith
Music by John Herbert McDowell

Judson Poets' Theater
Judson Memorial Church
New York, NY

Yes Is for a Very Young Man
Theater Company of Boston
Boston, MA

1966   *The Mother of Us All*
Minnesota Opera
Minneapolis, MN

1967   *In Circles* (Musical)
Directed by Lawrence Kornfeld
Music by Al Carmines
Sets by Roland Turner
Lighting by Jay Poswolsky
Based on "A Circular Play. A Play in Circles."
Judson Poets' Theater
Judson Memorial Church
New York, NY

The Mother of Us All
Directed by H. Wesley Balk
Conducted by Thomas Nee
Designed by Robert Indiana
City Center Opera
Guthrie Theater
Minneapolis, MN

Also presented at:
Wolf Trap Farm, Vienna, VA
Temple University Music Festival, Ambler, PA
Hunter College, New York, NY (1971)
     (Conducted by Philip Brunelle)

1969   *Four Saints in Three Acts* (Concert)
Merola Memorial Foundation
San Francisco, CA

1970   *Four Saints in Three Acts*
Directed by Dennis Rosa
Conducted by Charles Wilson
Merola Opera Company
Paul Masson Vineyards
San Francisco, CA

Four Saints in Three Acts
Opera Society
Washington, DC

1971   *The Mother of Us All*
Directed by William Vorenberg
Conducted by Marjorie Brewster
Sets by John Doepp
Costumes by Audrey Arnsdorf
St. Peter's Church
New York, NY

The Mother of Us All
Lake George Opera Festival
Saratoga, NY

The Mother of Us All
Minnesota Opera
Minneapolis, MN

Three Sisters Who Are Not Sisters (Opera)
Music by Ned Rorem
Directed by Richard Flusser
After Dinner Opera Company
Commissioned by the Metropolitan Opera Studio (rejected)
Signal Hill Playhouse
Lake Placid, NY

Opera Adaptations of Stein (Opera)
  In a Garden (Meyer Kupferman)
  Three Sisters Who Are Not Sisters (Ned Rorem)
  Look & Long (Florence Wickham and Marvin Schwartz)
  Photograph (Marvin Kalmanoff)
  Ladies' Voices (Vernon Martin)
Directed by Richard Flusser
Music directed by Cynthia Auerback
Sets by Beth Flusser
Costumes by Elissa Larrauri
After Dinner Opera Company
White Barn Theater
Westport, CT

1972   *Doctor Faustus Lights the Lights*
Directed by Maxine Klein
Café La Mama
New York, NY

The Mother of Us All
Artistic direction by Virgil Thomson
Directed by Elizabeth Keen and Roland Gagnon
Musical direction by Roland Gagnon
Sets by Oliver Smith
Lighting by Richard Nelson
Costumes by Patricia Zipprodt
Guggenheim Museum Theater
New York, NY

1973 *Four Saints in Three Acts*
Directed and choreographed by Alvin Ailey
Conducted by Roland Gagnon
Sets by Ming Cho Lee
Lighting by Shirley Prendergast
Costumes by Jane Greewood
Metropolitan's Opera Forum
Vivian Beaumont Theater
New York, NY

The Gertrude Stein First Reader and Three Plays
Directed by Wayne K. Elkins, Jr.
Offstage, Inc.
New York, NY

The Mother of Us All
Hartford Opera Theater
Hartford, CT

1974 *Listen to Me*
Directed by Lawrence Kornfeld
Music by Al Carmines
Sets by Ed Lazansky
Lighting by Edward M. Greenberg
Judson Poets' Theater
Judson Memorial Church
New York, NY

1975 *The Mother of Us All*
Directed by Nancy Rhodes
American Theater Festival
C. W. Post College
Greenvale, NY

The Mother of Us All
Madison Civic Opera
Madison, WI

The Mother of Us All
Pittsburgh Opera Festival
Pittsburgh, PA

1976   *Four Saints in Three Acts*
National Theater for the Deaf
Hartford, CT

The Mother of Us All
Associate Artist Opera Company
Boston, MA

The Mother of Us All
Chicago Opera Theater
Conducted by Robert Frisbie
Chicago, IL

The Mother of Us All (Concert)
Chicago Opera Studio
Conducted by Robert Frisbie
Station WTTW Broadcast
Chicago, IL

The Mother of Us All (Musical)
Adapted and directed by Nancy Rhodes
Simplified score by Virgil Thomson
Musical direction by William Boswell
Sets by Christina Weppner
Lighting by T. Winberry
Costumes by Mim Maxmen
Encompass Theatre
Greenwich Village Theater
New York, NY

The Mother of Us All (Concert)
Inverness Music Festival
San Anselmo, CA

The Mother of Us All
Directed by Peter Wood
Conducted by Raymond Leppard
Designed by Robert Indiana
Lighting by Jo Schreiber
Santa Fe Opera
Sante Fe, NM

1977   *Four Saints in Three Acts*
Conducted by Joel Thome
Orchestra of Our Time
Beacon Theater
New York, NY

Four Saints in Three Acts (Concert)
Oklahoma Symphony Orchestra
Oklahoma City, OK

A Manoir. An Historical Play in Which They Are Approached More
   Often (Musical)
Directed by Lawrence Kornfeld
Music by Al Carmines
Sets by Edward Lazansky
Costumes by Thoe Barnes
Lighting by Gary Weathersbee
Judson Poets' Theater
Judson Memorial Church
New York, NY

The Mother of Us All (Concert)
Camellia Symphony Orchestra
Sacramento, CA

The Mother of Us All
Minnesota Opera
Minneapolis, MN

Photograph. A Play in Five Acts
Adapted and directed by James Lapine
Music by Dwight Andrews
Sets and costumes by Maureen Connor
Lighting by Paul Gallo
Narration by Walt Jones
The Performance Group
Open Space Theater
New York, NY

1978   *Doctor Faustus Lights the Lights*
Directed by Craig Lowy
St. Peter's Church
New York, NY

What Happened
Music by John Plant

Dance Opera for Le Groupe de la Place Royale
National Arts Center
Ottawa, Canada

1979   *Doctor Faustus Lights the Lights* (Musical)
Directed by Lawrence Kornfeld
Music by Al Carmines
Judson Poets' Theater
Judson Memorial Church
New York, NY

Four Saints in Three Acts
Stockholm's Musikdramatiska Ensemble
Stockholm, Sweden

In Circles (Musical)
Adapted and directed by Amy Gale and Gerritt Timmers
Music by Al Carmines
Choreographed by Amy Gale
Independent Theater of Rotterdam
New York, NY

The Mother of Us All
Abbey Opera
London, England

1980   *Made by Two* (Musical of *A Lyrical Opera Made By Two*)
Composed and directed by William Turner
The Theater Express Company
Pittsburgh, PA

Also presented at:
La Mama E.T.C., New York, NY

1981   *Four Saints in Three Acts* (Concert)
Conducted by Joel Thome
Orchestra of Our Times
Carnegie Hall
New York, NY

The Mother of Us All
Bejar Opera Workshop
San Antonio, TX

The Mother of Us All
Seagle Colony Opera Guild
Schroon Lake, NY

1982   *Doctor Faustus Lights the Lights*
Directed and designed by Richard Foreman
Translated by Marie-Claire Pasquier
Freie Volksbuhne
Berlin, Germany

Also presented at:
Theatre de Gennevilliers (Festival d'Automne) Paris, France

1983   *Four Saints in Three Acts* (Concert)
Almeida Spring Music Festival
London, England

In Circles (Composed by Carmines)
Directed by Jeffrey B. Davis
Music directed by Roy Barber
Sets by Douglas A. Cumming
Costumes by Leslie-Marie Cocuzzo
Lighting by Geoffrey L. Grob
Choreography by Claudia Neely
Round House Theater
Washington, DC

The Mother of Us All
Directed by Stanley Silverman
Musical direction by Richard Cordova
Sets by Power Boothe
Costumes by Lawrence Casey
Music Theater Group
Lenox Arts Center
New York, NY

The Mother of Us All
Lyric Opera of Kansas City
Kansas City, MO

1984   *Four Saints in Three Acts*
Théâtre Romain-Rolland
Villejuif, France

Four Saints in Three Acts: An Olio (Concert)
Conducted by Virgil Thomson
Arranged by Paul Reuter
Hartford Symphony Orchestra
Hartford, CT

The Mother of Us All
Chicago Opera Theater
Chicago, IL

The Mother of Us All
Squaw Valley Creative Arts
Squaw Valley, CA

1986 *Doctor Faustus Lights the Lights*
Directed by David Kaplan
Music by the Ensemble Studio Theater
Lights by Scott Janush
Ensemble Studio Theater
Los Angeles, CA

Four Saints in Three Acts
Directed by John J.D. Sheehan
Conducted by Paul Dunkel
Designed by Rouben Ter-Arutunian
Opera Ensemble of New York
New York, NY

Four Saints in Three Acts
Camden Festival
London, England

In Circles (Musical)
Directed by John Sowle
Music by Al Carmines
Sets by John Sowle
Costumes by Anne Reghi
Kaliyuga Arts Theater
Los Angeles, CA

"Ladies Voices" (Concert)
Music by Charles Shere
Commissioned by Claude Duval and the Noh Oratorio Society
Berkeley Art Center
Berkeley, CA

1987 *Four Saints in Three Acts* (Concert)
Hartford Opera Theater
Hartford, CT

The Mother of Us All
San Francisco City Summer Opera
San Francisco, CA

The Mother of Us All
Directed by Stanley Silverman
Alice Tully Hall
Lincoln Center
New York, NY

1992 *Doctor Faustus Lights the Lights*
Directed and designed by Robert Wilson
Music by Hans Peter Kuhn
Lighting by Heinrich Brunke with Andreas Fuchs
Costumes by Hans Thiemann
Choreography by Suzushi Hanayagi
Dramaturgy by Peter Krumme
Hebbel Theater
Berlin, Germany

Also presented at:
Theater am Turm, Frankfurt, Germany
Teatro Goldoni, Venice, Italy
Teatro Argentina, Rome, Italy
Alice Tully Hall (Serious Fun! series), New York, NY
Szene Salzburg, Salzberg, Germany
Le Manege, Maubeuge, France
Théâtre de Gennevilliers (Festival d'Automne), Paris, France
De Singel, Antwerp, Belgium
Teatro Lirico, Milan, Italy (1993)
Salle Pierre Mercure (Festival de Théâtre Amériques, University of
    Quebec at Montreal) (1993)
    Royal Lyceum Theatre (Edinburgh Festival), Edinburgh,
    Scotland (1993)
    Teatro D. Maria II (Encontros Acarte '93), Lisbon, Portugal
    (1993)
Madách Szinház (Budapesti Tavaszi Fesztivál), Budapest, Hungary
    (1994)
    Divadle Archa, Prague, Czechoslovakia (1994)
    Lyric Theatre (Hong Kong Arts Festival), Hong Kong (1995)

Yes Is for a Very Young Man
Directed by Joumana Rizk
The Rushmore Festival
Woodbury, NY

1993 *Four Saints in Three Acts*
Conducted by Philip J. Bauman
Chicago Opera Theater
Chicago, IL

1994 *Nine Plays and a Recipe:*
"An Exercise in Analysis"; "Three Sisters Who Are Not Sisters";
    "Lucretia Borgia"; "Turkey and Bones and Eating and We Liked It";
    "Ladies Voices"; "Captain Walter Arnold"; "Please Do Not Suffer";
    "I Like It to Be a Play"; "A Curtain Raiser"; "Young Turkey with
    Truffles"
Directed and designed by Anthony McDonald
Lighting by Thomas Webster
Glasgow Citizens Theater
Glasgow, Poland

Objects Lie on a Table
Directed by David Herskovits
Sets by Sarah Edkins
Lighting by Lenore Doxsee
Costumes by David Zinn
Sound by David Hull
Target Margin Theater
La Mama E.T.C.
New York, NY

A Play Called Not and Now (Puppet play)
Constructed and performed by Hanne Tierney
Music by Jane Wang
Sound by Myles G. Tierney
Henson International Festival of Puppet Theater
New York, NY

1996 *Four Saints in Three Acts*
Directed and designed by Robert Wilson
Conducted by Dennis Russell Davies
Lighting by Jennifer Tipton
Costumes by Francesco Clemente
Houston Grand Opera
Houston, TX

Also presented at:
Lincoln Center Festival, New York, NY
Edinburgh Fringe Festival, Edinburgh, Scotland

Three Short Plays: *The King or Something; Not Slightly; Turkey and
    Bones and Eating and We Liked It*
Directed by Amy Huggans
Music by Rima Fond
Design by Bob Wander and Bob Junior
Costumes by Monica Schroeder
The Collapsable Giraffe

Access Theater Gallery
New York, NY

1997   *Doctor Faustus Lights the Lights*
Directed by Kenn Watt
The Fifth Floor
Intersection for the Arts
San Francisco, CA

The Mother of Us All
Directed by Sandra Bernhard
Conducted by Richard Cordova
Sets by Tom Macie
Lighting by Donald Edmund Thomas
Baltimore Opera Company
Baltimore, MD

The Mother of Us All
Directed by Emma Griffin
Williamstown Theater Festival
Williamstown, MA

Yes Is for a Very Young Man
Directed by Lamont Johnson
Music and sound by Paul Cuneo
Costumes by Vicki Sanchez
Interact Theatre
Hollywood, CA

2000   *A Circular Play. A Play in Circles.*
Directed and performed by Theater of Truth
Fringe Festival
Phoenix Black Box
Minneapolis, MN

Every Afternoon (A Dialogue)
Directed by Matthew Earnest
deep ellum ensemble
Rhinebeck Center for the Performing Arts
Rhinebeck, NY

Four Saints in Three Acts (Dance)
Directed and choreographed by Mark Morris
Conducted by Craig Smith
Sets by Maira Kalman
Lighting by Michael Chybowski
Costumes by Elizabeth Kurtman

The Coliseum
London, England

Also presented at:
Brooklyn Academy of Music, Brooklyn, NY (2001)

The Mother of Us All
Directed by Christopher Alden
Conducted by George Manahan
Sets by Allen Moyer
Lighting by Mark McCullough
Costumes by Gabriel Berry
New York City Opera
New York, NY

2001   *A Circular Play/In Circles*
Directed by Beng Oh
The Gertrude Stein Project
Melbourne, Austrailia

What Happened
Directed and designed by Scott Osborne
Music by Jake Brown
Choreographed by Jenn Weddel
Our Endeavors Theater Company
Bath House Cultural Center
Dallas, TX

2002   *Doctor Faustus Lights the Lights*
St. Martins Youth Arts Centre
Melbourne, Australia

Listen to Me
Directed and designed by Michael Counts
Music by Ken Roht
The Center for New Theatre
New York, NY

Saints and Singing
Directed by Beng Oh
The Gertrude Stein Project
Melbourne, Australia

Saints and Singing
Directed by Matthew Earnest
deep ellum ensemble

Midtown International Theater Festival
New York, NY

2004   *The Mother of Us All*
Directed by Christopher Alden
Conducted by Donald Runnicles
Sets by Allen Moyer
Lighting by Mark McCullough
Costumes by Gabriel Berry
Dramaturgy by Peter Littlefield
San Francisco Opera
San Francisco, CA

Appendix C
A Chronological List of Dramatic Adaptations

The following is a list of professional dramatic adaptations of Stein's writing, including source material from her plays, poetry, and prose. Because many of these adaptations have been staged multiple times, and in the interest of space, productions have been listed by the premiere production. (In a few instances, however, major revivals have been noted.) In the cases of one-person touring shows and musical compositions, only the author and year of completion is listed. Plays that merely incorporate the character of Stein, but do not use any of her text in production have not been included.

1933 "3 Songs" (Musical composition)
John Cage

1937 "A Wedding Bouquet" (Dance)
Composed by Lord Gerald Berners
Directed by Ninette Valois
Conducted by Constant Lambert
Based on *They Must. Be Wedded. To Their Wife.*
Sadler's Wells Ballet
London, England

Revivals:
New Theatre, London, England (1941)
Covent Garden, London, England (1949, 1951, 1964)
Metropolitan Opera House, New York, NY (1949, 1950)
Sadler's Wells Company, London, England (1950)

1940 "Living Room Music" (Musical compostition)
John Cage

1953   *Brewsie and Willie* (Drama)
Adapted by Ellen Violett and Lisabth Blakef
Theater de Lys
New York, NY

Revivals:
CBS Television (1954)
Directed by Seymour Robbie
Produced by Robert Saudek
Staged by John Six

Neighborhood Playhouse (1956)
Directed by Sanford Meisner
New York, NY

1956   *Paris, France; Lesson 19; The Making of Americans; Lesson 20* (Drama)
Produced by Addison Metcalf
Little Theater
Newtown, CT

1969   *The Gertrude Stein First Reader and Three Plays* (Musical revue)
Adapted and directed by Herbert Machiz
Music by Ann Sternberg
Sets by Kendall Shaw
Lighting by Patrika Brown
Astor Place Theater
New York, NY

Revivals:
Museum of Modern Art, New York, NY (1970)

Gertrude Stein's Gertrude Stein (Solo)
Adapted and performed by Nancy Cole

Mrs. Reynolds
Adapted by Philip Hansom
New York Public Library
New York, NY

*Three, Two, One (Not Much Limping, Monuments, May and December:
Selections from Stein, Diana de Prima, and James Waring* (Drama)
Mannhardt Theater Foundations
New York, NY

1970   *Gertrude* (Collage of Stein memorabilia)
Written by Wilford Leach

Music by Ben Johnston
Musical director, James Cuomo
Design by William Weldenbacher and Peter Murketty
Lighting by Beverly Emmons
Costumes by Nancy Reeder
Masks and props by Richard Laws
La Mama E.T.C
New York, NY

1972 *Lucy Church Amiably* (Drama)
Adapted by Scott Fields
Washington Square Church
New York, NY

The Making of Americans (Musical)
Adapted by Leon Katz
Directed by Lawrence Kornfeld
Composed by Al Carmines
Libretto by Leon Katz
Set by Ed Lazansky
Lighting by Roger Morgan
Costumes by Reve Richards
Judson Poets' Theater
Judson Memorial Church
New York, NY

Revivals:
    The Music Theater Group/Lenox Arts Center, New York, NY (1985)
        Directed by Anne Bogart
        Sets and costumes by Nancy Winters and Jim Buff
        Lighting by Carol Mullins
        St. Clement's Church
    Center Stage, Baltimore, MD (1990)
        Directed by Lawrence Kornfeld

1975 *Everything's the Same and Everything's Different* (Selections from
    Woolf, Beckett, and Stein [Drama])
Directed by Linda Mussman
Time and Space, Ltd.
New York, NY

1977 *Play; Satie; A Very Valentine; Susia Asado; Storyette: HM*
Adapted and directed by Betsy Ryan
Armory Free Theater
Urbana, IL

1978 "Wedding Bouquet" (Dance)
      Joffrey Ballet
      New York, NY

1979 *If You Had Three Husbands* (Drama)
      Soho Repertory
      New York, NY

      Gertrude Stein, Gertrude Stein, Gertrude Stein (Drama)
      Written by Marty Martin
      Directed by Milton Moss
      Performed by Pat Carroll
      New York, New York, tour

      The (Re)Making of Americans (Drama)
      Adapted and directed by Linda Mussman
      Time and Space, Ltd.
      New York, NY

      "Six Fragments of Gertrude Stein" (Musical composition)
      Aaron Jay Kernis

1983 "Gertrude Stein, Words, and Music" (Concert)
      Adapted by John Herbert Gill, Antonio Ramirez, Stephen Stark, and
        John Willard
      Based on *Blood on the Dining Room Floor*
      With address by Virgil Thomson
      St. Joseph's Church
      New York, NY

1984 *Blood on the Dining Room Floor* (Musical)
      Adapted and directed by Barbara Vann
      Music by William Hellerman
      The Medicine Show Theater
      New York, NY

1985 *Gertrude Stein and a Companion* (Drama)
      Written by Win Wells
      Directed by Ira Cirker
      Music by Jason Cirker
      Set by Bob Phillips
      Lighting by Richard Dorfman
      Costumes by Amanda J. Klein
      White Barn Theater
      Westport, CT

1986 "Wishing Them Well" (Musical composition)
Composed by A. Leroy
With text from "Valentine for Sherwood Anderson"
Dance Theater Workshop
New York, NY

1988 *She Always Said, Pablo* (Drama)
Adapted and directed by Frank Galati
   with images by Pablo Picasso
    music by Virgil Thomson and Igor Stravinsky
Goodman Theater
Chicago, IL

"When do they is not the same as why do they" (Musical composition)
Composed by Peter Hatch

1993 *The Marguerite Ida & Helene Annabel Opera* (Recorded opera)
Composed by François Ribac
Performed by Eva Schwabe
No Man's Land Records
Berlin, Germany

Mounting Picasso (Musical)
Adapted by Blue Rider Ensemble
Composed by Peter Hatch
Directed by David Mac Murray Smith
Maurier Theater Center
Toronto, Canada

Objects Lie on a Table (Drama)
Adapted and performed by Mary Curtin and David Miller
Music by Steve Thomas and Rhoda Bernard
Design by David Goodine
Mobius
Boston, MA

The World is Round (Opera)
Composed by James Sellars
Adapted and directed by Juanita Rockwell
Conducted by Michael Barrett
Sets by Sarah Edkins
Lighting by Randy Glickman
Costumes by Priscilla Putnam
Wadsworth Atheneum
Hartford, CT

1994   "Polyphonic Dialogues" (Dance)
Choreographed by Emma Diamond
Diamond Dance Company
Miller Theater at Columbia University
New York, NY

To Be Sung (Drama)
Adapted by Oliver Dejours
Music by Pascal Dusapin
Sets by Jame Turrell
Festival D'Automne
Paris, France

1996   "Es is sehr nett ein Berühmtheit zu sein" (Musical compostion)
Composed by Christina Fuchs

Gertrude Stein, Alice Toklas, and Pablo Picasso
Written by Alcides Nogueira
International Hispanic Theater Festival
Miami, FL

1997   "If I Told Him" (Musical composition)
Composed by Ezra Sims
Performed by Ted Mook and David Fedele
Merkin Concert Hall
New York, NY

1998   "The Boat" (Musical composition)
Lisa Bielawa
Music at the Anthology
Anthology Film Archives
New York, NY

House/Lights (Drama)
Adapted by the Wooster Group
Based on *Doctor Faustus Lights the Lights* and *Olga's House of Shame*
   (1964; film directed by Joseph Mawra)
Directed by Elizabeth LeCompte
Sound by James Johnson and John Collins
Sets by Jim Findlay
Video by Philip Bussman
Lighting by Jennifer Tipton
Costumes by Elizabeth Jenyon
Music by Hans Peter Kuhn
The Wooster Group
New York, NY

Also presented at:
    Theatre de Garoune, Toulose, France
    La Rose des Vents, Villeneuve d'Ascq, France
    Le Maillon, Strasbourg, France

1999   "Das Zimmer und die Zeit, sitting in my room in front of time" (Solo)
Adapted and performed by Elettra de Salvo
Based on "A Birthday Book"
Kunsthalle Schirn
Frankfurt, Germany

Gertrude and Alice: A Likeness to Loving
Adapted and performed by Lola Pashalinski and Linda Chapman
Directed by Anne Bogart
Sets by Myung Hee Cho
Lighting by Mimi Jordan Sherin
Sound by Darron L. West
Costumes by Gabriel Berry
Dramaturgs, Ulla E. Dydo and William Rice
Produced by The Foundry Theater
Signature Theater
New York, NY

Gertrude Stein and Friends (Drama)
Sudden Theater
Paris, France

"McIntosh—The Stein Way" (Solo)
Adapted and performed by Diana McIntosh
The Knitting Factory
New York, NY

2000   *Blood on the Dining Room Floor* (Opera)
Adapted and composed by Jonathan Sheffer
Directed by Jeremy Dobrish
Sets by Steven Capone
Costumes by Markas Henry
Produced by WPA Theater
Peter Norton Space
New York, NY

Gertrude Stein: Each One As She May (Drama)
Adapted and directed by Frank Galati
Goodman Theater
Chicago, IL

Hashirigaki (Drama)
Adapted and directed and with music by Heiner Goebbel
Lighting by Klaus Grunberg
Sound by Willi Bopp
Costumes by Florence von Gerkan
Théatre Vidy-Lausanne
Paris, France

Also presented at:
   Brooklyn Academy of Music, Brooklyn, NY (2003)

"Italians" (Solo)
Adapted and performed by Elettra de Salvo
Music by Marcel Daemgen
Romanfabrik
Frankfurt, Germany

Not Faust
Adapted and directed by Jennifer Tarver
Designed by Jan Komarek
Based on *Doctor Faustus Lights the Lights*
Theater Extasis
The Great Hall Theater
Toronto, Canada

2001   *The Autobiography of Alice B. Toklas* (Drama)
Adapted and directed by Maria Irene Fornes
Workshop production at Davidson College Theater
Davidson, NC

Gertrude Stein Project (Collection of short plays)
Adapted and directed by Frédédrique Michel
Design by Charles A. Duncombe, Jr.
City Garage Theater
Santa Monica, CA

"Look at Me Now and Here I Am" (Solo)
Adapted and performed by William Michael Collins

2002   *Faust 2002* (Drama)
Adapted by the Pilgrim Theater Research and Performance Collaborative
Directed by Kim Mancuso
Sets by Nic Ularu
Lighting by Kathy Couch
Costumes by Karen Dolmanisth

Based on *Doctor Faustus Lights the Lights* and on additional Faust texts
   by Goethe, Marlowe, Sands, Black, Byron, and Murnau
Boston Center for the Arts
Boston, MA

"Object Dances" (Dance)
Choreographed and performed by Rachel Thorne Germond
Music by Evelyn Glennie
Based on "Tender Buttons"
Motivity Theater
Chicago, IL

"The Landscape: A Series of Events Based on the Work of Gertrude Stein"
   (Solo)
Adapted and performed by Elettra de Salvo
Berlin, Germany

A Simple Thing (Musical)
Adapted and directed by Thomas Leabhart
With music by Erik Satie and Virgil Thomson
Based on *The Making of Americans*
Produced by The Necessary Stage
Shell Theatertte
Sinapore

Tender Buttons
Adapted and performed by Erkki Soininen
Helsinki ACT
Helsinki, Finland

The World Is Round (Musical)
Adapted by Scott Feldsher and Pea Hicks
Music by Pea Hicks
Produced by OperaZero
Sledgehammer Theater
San Diego, CA

The World Is Round (Drama)
Adapted and directed by Drew Pisarra
Music by Gisburg
Manhattan Theater Source
New York, NY

The World Is Round (Drama)
Adapted and directed by Jens-Uwe Sprengel

Performed by Franka Schwuchow and Manfred Olek Witt
Unidram Festival
Potsdam, Germany

2003 *Careful of Eights:*
Four [Five] Short Plays by Gertrude Stein
Adapted and directed by Jessica Brater
Original music by Jason Binnick
Polybe + Seats
The Beckman Theater
New York, NY

Gertrude Stein Invents a Jump Early On (Opera)
Directed by Nancy Rhodes
Composed by William Bonfield
Libretto by Karren L. Alenier
Encompass New Opera
New York, NY

2004 *The Making of Americans* (Drama—four play series)
Adapted and directed by Cheryl Faver
Design by Michael Oberle
Workshop production at University of Iowa (2002)
Gertrude Stein Repertory Theater
New York, NY

Notes

Chapter 1: Introduction

1. Incidentally, in the most vehement attack on Gertrude Stein, B. L. Reid used this very term.
2. Indeed, the evidence of any specific act was considered quite shaky at all three trials. This evidence consisted of servants' testimony, stained sheets, and Wilde's letters, some of which were presented in non-incriminating contexts by Wilde's defense. See Richard Ellmann's *Oscar Wilde*, pp. 435–478.
3. Of course, this is no different from avant-garde theater and film, which consciously turned their gaze on the audience. In Man Ray's *Emak Bakia*, for example, the camera lens is pointed at the audience, with a human eye superimposed at the center. In many of the Futurists' live performances they would both physically and verbally attack the audience, or induce the audience to riot themselves by selling multiple tickets to a single seat, thus turning the audience into the theatrical spectacle.
4. Samuel Sillen first used the phrase with regard to Stein in his 1937 review of her *Everybody's Autobiography*. See Sillen, "Obituary of Europe and Gertrude Stein" *New Masses* 25.11 (7 December 1937): 22–23.

Chapter 2: The Origins of Gertrude Stein's Drama in Cinema

1. One of the only considerations of Stein's interest in film is Susan McCabe's "'Delight in Dislocation': The Cinematic Modernism of Stein, Chaplin, and Man Ray" *Modernism/Modernity* 8.3 (2001): 429–452. A compelling argument for film's effect on Stein's poetry, the essay mentions neither Stein's screenplays, nor her drama.
2. Significantly, Stein would have this experience while watching herself in a newsreel covering the 1934 lecture series.
3. It should also be noted that the prominence of twins in the text might function as a signifier of homosexuality. Early sexologists often compared homosexuality

to narcissism. Freud wrote in his *Introductory Lectures on Psychoanalysis* that "Homosexual object-choice originally lies closer to narcissism than does the heterosexual kind" (426). The presence of twins and "sisters who are not sisters" clearly echo an affection for the same.

4. Beth Hutchinson. "Gertrude Stein's Film Scenarios" *Literature/Film Quarterly* 17.1 (1989): 35–38.

5. Although Deren's first film was produced more than twenty years after Stein's last screenplay, Deren's work bears a striking similarity to Stein's writing. Both explore the representation of reality, gender identity, and mechanical duplication. The central figure in Deren's *Meshes of the Afternoon* (1943), for example, eventually appears as four identical images of a woman sharing the same space and interacting with one another. Each woman touches a key, perhaps intended as a phallic image, which, after being touched by the last woman, suddenly transforms into a knife. For more on Maya Deren's films, see Bill Nichols, ed., *Maya Deren and the American Avant-Garde* (Berkeley, CA: University of California Press, 2001), P. Adams Sitney's *Visionary Film: The American Avant-Garde* (New York: Oxford University Press, 1974), and Lauren Rabinovitz's *Points of Resistance: Women, Power, and Politics in the New York Avant-Garde Cinema, 1943–1971* (Urbana, IL: University of Illinois Press, 1991).

6. Basket I was originally just Basket, but after his death, Stein and Toklas replaced him with a second dog, Basket II. Consequently, the original Basket is usually referred to as Basket I.

Chapter 3: Gertrude Stein and Avant-Garde Theater

1. It is important to note that Stein published this opinion in 1926, before her major plays and the harsh criticism that would accompany them.

2. A detailed consideration of the first performance of *Four Saints in Three Acts,* both in Hartford and on Broadway in 1934, may be found in Steven Watson's *Prepare for Saints: Gertrude Stein, Virgil Thomson, and the Mainstreaming of American Modernism* (Berkeley, CA: University of California Press, 1998).

3. The choice of the name Tiresias, as well as the title, is no accident. In Greek mythology and drama Tiresias is probably best known as the blind seer who announces to king Oedipus that he is the one who has killed his father, the former King Laius, and married his mother, Queen Jocasta. But in this case, Apollinaire alludes to Tiresias's history of gender-duality and the origin of his blindness. According to Greek mythology, Tiresias came upon two snakes copulating and killed the female snake. As a result of killing the snake, he became a woman and remained so for seven years until he came upon two more snakes copulating (some accounts state that these were the original two snakes); this time he killed the male snake, and as a result Tiresias turned back into a man. Subsequently, he was called before Zeus and Hera to settle their argument as to which gender feels greater pleasure during sexual intercourse, the man or the woman. Tiresias stated that not only did women feel greater pleasure, but that it was nine times greater than the pleasure men feel. Hera, who had argued the opposite, blinded

Tiresias in a fit of rage. Zeus then compensated Tiresias for his blindness by giving him the gift of prophesy.

4. Significantly, in his early *Theory of Semiotics,* Umberto Eco highlights the question of names and their role as signifiers in a larger semantic code. Eco challenges Stephan Ullman's (1962: 122) assertion "that a proper name out of context does not denote anything, while a common noun out of context always has lexematic meaning" (Eco 87), arguing instead that proper names of unknown persons can connote but not denote: "proper names of unknown persons are sign-vehicles with an open denotation and can be decoded as one would decode an abstruse scientific term that one has never heard of, but that certainly must correspond to something" (Eco 88).

Chapter 4: *Doctor Faustus Lights the Lights*

1. Stein is perhaps writing of herself in this character, having been bitten by a snake in 1933. In a letter to Lindley Hubbell, November 4, 1933, she called the experience "biblical" (Bridgman 292).

2. In her essay, "'Would a viper have stung her if she only has one name?': *Doctor Faustus Lights the Lights,*" Shirley Neuman traces the evolution of *Ida* first into *Doctor Faustus,* then "Arthur and Jenny" (1938), and finally *Ida, A Novel* (1941), which itself incorporated passages from Stein's *The World is Round* (1939), and "My Life with Dogs" (1939).

3. Gertrude Stein's notes regarding *Doctor Faustus Lights the Lights* and other plays are located in the Gertrude Stein and Alice B. Toklas Papers in the Beinecke Rare Book and Manuscript Library in the Yale Collection of American Literature at Yale University. References to Stein's unpublished notes, letters, and manuscripts are hereafter cited as YCAL.

4. Neuman further extends the influence of previous Faust operas to include Ferruccio Busoni's 1925 opera *Doktor Faust,* which had been performed in London in 1937. Neuman argues that "Stein did go to London on 23 April for the 27 April première of the Stein-Berners ballet *A Wedding Bouquet* [adapted from *They Must. Be Wedded. To Their Wife.*]. There she moved in musical circles in which she would certainly have heard discussion about the Busconi revival" (174). Neuman further argues that Stein incorporates Busoni's use of political allegory in *Doctor Faustus Lights the Lights.*

5. In early versions of the play, Stein's characters initially spoke in the first person in *They Must. Be Wedded. To Their Wife.* However, this construction was used only sporadically in the final version. For example, in Scene I, Stein writes, "Josephine. Because. I am married" (205), but in the very next scene, Stein follows with "Josephine. Oh Josephine" (206). The use of the first person is further complicated in *They Must* by the ambiguity of the characters' assigned dialogue. Stage directions, character descriptions, and spoken dialogue are indistinguishable from each other in *They Must,* whereas in *Doctor Faustus* the spoken dialogue is more clearly delineated. Furthermore, it is not until *Doctor Faustus* that characters consistently use "I" and "me."

6. Stein initially wrote to Thornton Wilder explaining her shift from novel to drama, "Ida has become an opera, and it is a beauty, really is, an opera about Faust" (YCAL). It was originally to be scored by Lord Gerald Berners, who also adapted *They Must. Be Wedded. To Their Wife.* as a ballet. After several months of discussion, however, Berners found himself unable to write any music for it.

7. Nonetheless, Wilder acknowledges Stein's influence on *Our Town* in a letter to her and Alice B. Toklas dated September 13, 1937: "The Play is an immersion, immersion into a New Hampshire town. It's called 'Our Town' and its third act is based on your ideas, as on great pillars, and whether you know it or not, until further notice, you're in a deep-knit collaboration already" (Burns and Dydo 175).

8. Interestingly, puppets figure prominently throughout avant-garde and modernist drama and performance. While Dada was in Zurich, Emmy Hennings, a night-club performer and Hugo Ball's wife, made and performed with puppets in addition to writing several short Dada plays, and Sophie Taeuber made numerous Dada puppets in a geometric style strikingly similar to the later puppets and costumes of Bauhaus. When Dada moved to Berlin, photomontagist Hannah Höch also made numerous "dada-puppen," two of which appeared in the avant-garde journal *Schall und Rauch*. For more on puppets in modernist and avant-garde drama, see Harold B. Segel's *Pinocchio's Progeny: Puppets, Marionettes, Automotons, and Robots in Modernist and Avant-Garde Drama* (Baltimore, MD: Johns Hopkins University Press, 1995). For more on Henning, Taeuber, and Höch, see *Women in Dada: Essays on Sex, Gender, and Identity,* ed. Naomi Sawelson-Gorse (Cambridge, MA: MIT Press, 1998).

9. There is room for speculation here as to the origins of Marguerite Ida-and-Helena Annabel's name. To repeat, Stein first wrote the play as a novel, *Ida,* which she then developed into *Doctor Faustus.* From the name Ida, she then added Isabel (presumably to be the pun, "is a belle"), later changing the name to Annabel. It is clear from her writings about the play, however, that the double name was of particular importance to Stein who wrote in her notes for the play, "Supposing she goes away part time the other half. –she is at home. she could have lots of adventures, —I do not see how she could be different but she is, which is best of all" (YCAL).

   The additions of Marguerite and Helena seem to come from the legend itself, for Margaret appears in a wide variety of Faustian tales as Faust's young bride and dutiful wife, while Helena, or Helen, is a sexual temptress of men, finding her origins in the Greek mythological figure Helen of Troy. In Christopher Marlowe's *Doctor Faustus* (1604), Helen of Troy is a significant character, while in Karl von Holtei's *Dr. Johannes Faust* (1829), Helen fights the devil, Voland, for possession of Faust's soul and in the final act threatens to abduct Faust and Margarethe's baby (Kaiser 72). In her own dramatization of the Faust legend, *The Seven Strings of the Lyre* (1869), George Sand also included Helen of Troy as a central character. Stein does use the name Marguerite elsewhere, however, as in her short novel *Marguerite or a Simple Novel of High Life* (1940–42), in which Stein writes, "It is her name which is of importance" (60).

In addition to its central role in Stein's novel, the name of Ida may have its roots in Greek mythology. As Allegra Stewart writes, "Mount Ida, the seat of worship of Cybele, is a place, not a person, the scene of orgiastic celebrations of the Great Mother of the Gods..." (163). She also notes that Ida may be a reference to Freud's concept of the id. Ida may have its roots in Stein's life as well. The name might also refer to the author of one of the first feminist interpretations of the Faust tale, Ida Hahn-Hahn, whose *Gräfin Faustine* (1841) tells the story of Faustine and Mephistophela. Ida is even similar to one of Stein's nicknames for Alice B. Toklas, Ada.

According to Stewart, Annabel may simply mean "fair Anna" and suggests the name Hannah, which in Hebrew refers to the "Anna Perenna of Italian tradition and also the mother of the Virgin Mary" (163). "-Bel," for its part, appears to be derived from the character of Belle in Stephen Vincent Benét's story *The Devil and Daniel Webster* (1937), published a year before *Doctor Faustus,* the same year in which Stein published her own *Daniel Webster. Eighteen in America. A Play.* In Benét's version of the Faust legend, Belle is a demonic maid (the evil antithesis to the heart- and hearth-warming Margaret) who terrorizes the family she serves (Kaiser 72). For more information on Faust and the feminist tradition, see Nancy A. Kaiser's essay, "Faust/Faustine in the 19th Century: Man's Myth, Women's Places," in *Our Faust?* (1987).

10. The word "hell" is used here with Stein's lower-case "h." Although it is usually written as Hell, Stein never designates the word as such in this play. This may distinguish "hell" as a place different from the biblical netherworld of everlasting torment associated with the devil. But it seems just as likely that Stein, like Jean-Paul Sartre shortly afterward in *No Exit* (1944), is constructing the notion of hell as the human condition—the unrelenting presence of other people—and not as a place of eternal damnation worthy of capitalization.

Chapter 5: Final Works

1. It is possible that Stein draws the inspiration for dynamite smuggling from a local drug store owner, described in *Wars I Have Seen* (132). In it, Stein describes the man as not only falsely accused of hiding explosives and harrassed by the Germans, but further ridiculed by the local authority when he attempts to complain.

2. For more on Stein's ambivalent gender identity, see Catherine R. Stimpson's "The Mind, The Body, and Gertrude Stein" *Critical Inquiry* 3.3 (spring 1977): 489–506; and Franziska Gygax's *Gender and Genre in Gertrude Stein* (Westport, CT: Greenwood Press, 1998).

3. The extent to which Stein would have known about Hitler's atrocities throughout Europe is unclear. By the time Stein begins writing in 1944, France had already been liberated and Pétain imprisoned at the fortress at Belfort. By April of 1945, Hitler had committed suicide. However, it seems quite possible that by the time she completed the play, Stein knew a great deal both of the Holocaust and the fallout from the atomic bombs in Japan. In an interview with *The New York Times* in August 1945, Stein critiqued American industrialism by comparing it

with the Gestapo, and her "Reflection on the Atomic Bomb" (the last thing she wrote), was written 1946. For a detailed consideration of Stein's communication between 1942 and 1944, see Edward M. Burns and Ulla Dydo's Appendix IX in their *The Letters of Gertrude Stein and Thornton Wilder* (New Haven, CT: Yale University Press, 1996).

4. This newfound political awareness was not limited only to gender rights in America. While working on *The Mother of Us All,* Stein also became increasingly critical of American capitalism, what she called "industrialism." See Richard Bridgman's *Gertrude Stein in Pieces,* pp. 337–341.

5. *Wars I Have Seen,* p. 11.

Chapter 6: Gertrude Stein and the American Avant-Garde

1. Although there were very few major productions of Stein's drama immediately following her death, there were numerous small productions, primarily at university theaters. (For a consideration of academic support for avant-garde performance, see Sally Banes's "Institutionalizing Avant-Garde Performance: A Hidden History of University Patronage in the United States"). In 1950, however, several nonacademic theaters began producing her plays, primarily *Yes,* but *What Happened* and *In a Garden* were also performed at Sadler's Wells Company and the After Dinner Opera Company, respectively. Interestingly, many of Stein's nonoperatic works are performed often as musicals or opera, lending credence to Donald Gallup's observation that Stein's plays "do take music well." For a complete list of professional productions of Stein's plays to 2003, see Appendix B.

2. Interview with the author, February 3, 2001.

3. Incidentally, Warhol silk-screened an image of Gertrude Stein for his "Ten Portraits of Jews of the Twentieth Century" series in 1980. For more information on the connection between Warhol and Stein, see Barbara Will's "Coda: Warhol's Stein" in her *Gertrude Stein, Modernism, and the Problem of "Genius"* (2000).

4. I am thinking of *United States I–IV* (1983) in particular, but this vocal style dominates nearly all of Anderson's work, even her recent projects, such as *Moby Dick* (1999).

5. For a particularly nuanced comparison of Stein's poetry with Cubism, see Marjorie Perloff's "Poetry as Word-System: The Art of Gertrude Stein" in her *The Poetics of Indeterminacy: Rimbaud to Cage* (Princeton, NJ: Princeton University Press, 1981).

6. For more on Stein and feminine writing, see Marianne DeKoven, *A Different Language: Gertrude Stein's Experimental Writing* (Madison, WI: University of Wisconsin Press, 1983) and Catherine Stimpson, "Somagrams of Gertrude Stein," *Poetics Today* 6.1–2 (1985): 67–80.

7. For more on the relationship between American underground cinema of the 1960s and its relationship to the European avant-garde cinema of the 1920s, see Suárez, pp. 52–86.

8. Christopher Innes exemplifies this position in his "Text/Pre-Text/Pretext: The Language of Avant-Garde Experiment" when he writes that before 1959 (the

year the Living Theater staged Jack Gelber's *The Connection*), "Judith Malina and her husband Julian Beck had run a fairly conventional 'little theater' company whose reputation for innovation was founded on European imports ... and poetic pieces by William Carlos Williams and Gertrude Stein" (62).

9. Foreman's essay was originally published in German, translated from the English by Bernd Samland and retranslated here by myself. While it may seem odd to translate an essay originally written in English, no copy exists in English.

10. In addition to previously cited works, other essays that examine Stein within this context include: Bonnie Marranca's "Presence of Mind," *Performing Arts Journal* 16.1 (Sept. 1994): 1–17, and "St. Gertrude," *Performing Arts Journal* 16 (Jan. 1994): 107–112; Marc Robinson's "Gertrude Stein, Forgotten Playwright," *The South Atlantic Quarterly* 91 (summer 1992): 621–43; and Steven Watson's *Prepare for Saints: Gertrude Stein, Virgil Thomson, and the Mainstreaming of American Modernism,* New York: Random House, 1999.

11. In her introduction to Richard Foreman's *Plays and Manifestos,* Davy describes Stein's distinction between the two in relation to time. Davy writes, "While being is eternal, existence is time-bound. This led [Stein] to differentiate between 'entity' in relation to 'identity' and 'knowing' in relation to 'remembering'" (x).

12. As a film critic and artist, Mekas was undoubtedly the father of American underground cinema. As P. Adams Sitney writes in his *Visionary Film,* "No artist within the American avant-garde film has equaled the influence of Jonas Mekas as a polemicist" (379). Mekas began as the publisher of the magazine *Film Culture* in 1955 and later wrote a film column for the *Village Voice.* He also founded the New American Cinema Group in 1960 and co-founded the Film-Makers Cooperative and the Film-Makers Showcase, later called the Film-Makers Cinematheque. Parker Tyler perhaps phrases it best when he refers to Mekas as "the guru of Underground Film" (30).

13. Foreman, Richard. Interview. http://www.ontological.com.

14. Although Wilson' childhood stutter has been commonly referred to in considerations of his work, Wilson's younger sister Suzanne Lambert (neé Wilson) disputes this. In his study of Robert Wilson's theater, Arthur Holmberg quotes her thus: "In junior high and high school, you could take electives. Bob always signed up for speech classes in which students practice extemporaneous speaking, public speaking, and debates. At school his success in the speech contests made me realize how intelligent he was. He had a reputation as an orator. I don't remember any speech defect. At home he talked an awful lot" (Holmberg 38).

15. Like Stein, LeCompte explicitly works from an awareness of multiple stimuli in the modern world. As she states in her interview with Nick Kaye, "Most kids have been doing their homework while watching TV all their lives, so there's this weird mishmash for them already ... We cannot continue to have playwrights write these imitations of real life and put them on a stage, trying to recreate what the TV did 20 years ago and learnt to do it better" (256).

Bibliography

Apollinaire, Guillaume, *The Breasts of Tiresias.* 1917. In *Modern French Theatre: An Anthology of Plays.* Eds. and trans. Michael Benedikt and George E. Wellwarth, 131–146. New York: E. P. Dutton, 1966.

Aragon, Louis. "On Décor." 1918. In *French Film Theory and Criticism: A History/Anthology 1907–1939.* Ed. Richard Abel, 165–167. Princeton, NJ: Princeton University Press, 1988.

Aronson, Arnold. *American Avant-Garde Theatre: A History.* London: Routledge, 2000.

Atkinson, Brooks. "Doctor Faustus Lights the Lights." Rev. of *Doctor Faustus Lights the Lights,* dir. Judith Malina. *The New York Times* 3 Dec. 1951, late ed.: 23:4.

Artaud, Antonin. "The Shell and the Clergyman." 1928. *Antonin Artaud: Collected Works, Vol. 3.* 1961. Trans. Alastair Hamilton, 19–25. London: Calder and Boyars, 1972.

———. *The Theater and Its Double.* Trans., Mary Caroline Richards. New York: Grove Press, 1958.

Arp, Hans. "Notes from a Dada Diary." In *The Dada Painters and Poets.* Ed. Robert Motherwell, 221–225. Cambridge, MA: Harvard University Press, 1979.

Baker, Christopher. "*Danton's Death* at Alley Theatre." In *The Production Notebooks.* Ed. and intro. Mark Bly, 63–125. New York: Theatre Communications Group, 1996.

Banes, Sally. "Institutionalizing Avant-Garde Performance: A Hidden History of University Patronage in the United States." In *Contours of the Avant-Garde:*

Performance and Textuality. Ed. James M. Harding, 217–238. Ann Arbor, MI: University of Michigan Press, 2000.

Bartow, Arthur. *The Director's Voice: Twenty-One Interviews.* New York: Theatre Communications Group, 1988.

Bazin, André. "The Ontology of the Photographic Image." 1945. In *What is Cinema?.* Vol. 1. Ed. and trans. Hugh Gray, 1–8. Berkeley, CA: University of California Press, 1967.

———. "The Evolution of the Language of Cinema." 1950–1955. In *What is Cinema?.* Vol. 1. Ed. and trans. Hugh Gray, 23–40. Berkeley, CA: University of California Press, 1967.

Beaver, Harold. "Homosexual Signs (*In Memory of Roland Barthes*)" *Critical Inquiry* 8.1 (autumn): 99–119.

Beck, Julian. *A Life of the Theatre: The Relation of the Artist to the Struggle of the People.* San Francisco CA: City Lights, 1972.

———. *Theandric: Julian Beck's Last Notebooks.* Ed. Erica Bilder. Notes by Judith Malina. Philadelphia, PA: Harwood, 1992.

Beckett, Samuel. *Endgame.* New York: Grove Press, 1958.

Benjamin, Walter. "The Work of Art in the Age of Mechanical Reproduction." 1936. In *Illuminations.* 1969. Ed. Hannah Arendt, 217–252. New York: Schocken Books, 1986.

Bernstein, Charles. "A Conversation with Richard Foreman" *TDR* 36 (fall 1992): 103–130.

Bigsby, C.W.E. *Dada and Surrealism.* London: Methuen, 1972.

Bloom, Harold, ed. and intro. *Gertrude Stein.* New York: Chelsea House, 1986.

Bogart, Anne. Interview with the author. 3 Feb. 2001.

Bowers, Jane Palatini. *"They Watch Me as They Watch This": Gertrude Stein's Metadrama.* Philadelphia, PA: University of Pennsylvania Press, 1991.

———. "The Writer in the Theater: Gertrude Stein's *Four Saints in Three Acts.*" In *Critical Essays on Gertrude Stein.* Ed. Michael J. Hoffman, 210–225. Boston: Hall, 1986.

Brakhage, Stan. "Gertrude Stein: Meditative Literature and Film." Boulder, CO: The Graduate School, University of Colorado at Boulder, 1990.

Bridgman, Richard. *Gertrude Stein in Pieces*. New York: Oxford University Press, 1970.

Büchner, Georg. *Woyzeck*. 1836. In *Complete Works and Letters*. Eds. Walter Hinderer and Henry J. Schmidt, 199–244. New York: Continuum, 1991.

Burns, Edward and Ulla E. Dydo, eds. *The Letters of Gertrude Stein and Thornton Wilder.* New Haven, CT: Yale University Press, 1996.

Camus, Albert. *Carnets 1942–1951*. Trans. J. O'Brien. New York: Knopf, 1963.

Cardullo, Bert, and Robert Knopf, eds. *Theatre of the Avant-Garde: 1890–1950, An Anthology*. New Haven, CT: Yale University Press, 2001.

Chekhov, Anton. *Three Sisters*. 1901. In *Chekhov: Plays*. Trans. and intro. Michael Frayn, 189–282. London: Methuan, 1995.

Chessman, Harriet Scott. *"The Public Is Invited to Dance": Representations of the Body and Dialogue in Gertrude Stein*. Palo Alto, CA: Stanford University Press, 1989.

Chiti, Remo, "Words." 1915. In *Futurist Performance*. Ed. Michael Kirby. Trans. Victoria Kirby, 258–259. New York: *Performing Arts Journal Publications,* 1986.

Churchill, Caryl. *Not Not Not Not Not Enough Oxygen*. 1971. In *Shorts: Short Plays*. London: Nick Hern, 1990. 37–56.

Cleland, John. *Memoirs of a Woman of Pleasure*. 1750. Ed. Peter Sabor. New York: Oxford University Press, 1985.

Cook, David A. *A History of Narrative Film*. 3rd ed. New York: Norton, 1996.

Curtis, David. *Experimental Cinema*. New York: Delta, 1971.

Davy, Kate. "Richard Foreman's Ontological-Hysteric Theatre: The Influence of Gertrude Stein" *Twentieth-Century Literature* 24.1 (spring 1978): 108–126.

———. Introduction. *Plays and Manifestos*. Richard Foreman. Ed. Kate Davy, iv–xvi. New York: New York University Press, 1976.

DeKoven, Marianne. *A Different Language: Gertrude Stein's Experimental Writing*. Madison, WI: University of Wisconsin Press, 1983.

Deren, Maya. "Cinematography: The Creative Use of Reality." 1960. In *The Avant-Garde Film Reader: A Reader of Theory and Criticism*. Ed. P. Adams Sitney, 60–73. New York: New York University Press, 1978.

Derrida, Jacques. *Writing and Difference.* Trans. Alan Bass. Chicago, IL: University of Chicago Press, 1978.

Dollimore, Jonathan. "Post/modern: On the Gay Sensibility, or the Pervert's Revenge on Authenticity." In *Camp: Queer Aesthetics and the Performing Subject: A Reader.* Ed. Fabio Cleto, 221–236. Ann Arbor, MI: University of Michigan Press, 1999.

Dubnick, Randa. *The Structure of Obscurity: Gertrude Stein, Language, and Cubism.* Urbana, IL: University of Illinois Press, 1984.

Dydo, Ulla, ed. and intro. *A Stein Reader.* Evanston, IL: Northwestern University Press, 1993.

Eco, Umberto. *A Theory of Semiotics.* Bloomington, IN: Indiana University Press, 1979.

Edleman, Lee. *Homographesis: Essays in Gay Literary and Cultural Theory.* New York: Routledge, 1994.

Eisenstein, Sergei. "The Cinematographic Principle and the Ideogram." In *Film Form: Essays in Film Theory.* 1949. Ed. and trans. Jay Leyda, 28–44. New York: Harcourt Brace, 1977.

Ellman, Richard. *Oscar Wilde.* New York: Vintage, 1987.

Elsaesser, Thomas, ed. *Early Cinema: Space, Frame, Narrative.* London: BFI, 1990.

Erikson, Erik. *The Life Cycle Completed.* Rev. ed. New York: Norton, 1997.

Evans, Greg. Rev. of *Doctor Faustus Lights the Lights. Variety* 27 July 1992: 69.

Fairbrother, Trevor. *Robert Wilson's Vision.* New York: Abrams, 1991.

Feingold, Michael. "Steins of Life." Rev. of *Doctor Faustus Lights the Lights,* dir. Robert Wilson. *Village Voice* 21 July 1992: 99.

Fischer-Lichte, Erika, "The Avant-Garde and the Semiotics of the Antitextual Gesture." In *Contours of the Avant-Garde: Performance and Textuality.* Ed. James M. Harding, 79–95. Ann Arbor, MI: University of Michigan Press, 2000.

Foreman, Richard. "Awful Great: On Jack Smith: Jack Smith" *Artforum* 36.2 (Oct. 1997): 74.

———. "Die Mütter von Uns allen: Richard Foreman über Gertrude Stein" *Theater Heute* 23.10 (Oct. 1982): 36–37.

————. *Plays and Manifestos*. New York: New York University Press, 1976.

————. *Symphony of Rats*. In *Unbalancing Acts: Foundations for a Theatre*. Ed. Ken Jordan, 205–258. New York: Theatre Communications Group, 1992.

————. *Unbalancing Acts: Foundations for a Theatre*. Ed. Ken Jordan. New York: Theatre Communications Group, 1992.

————. *What Did He See?*. In *Unbalancing Acts: Foundations for a Theatre*. Ed. Ken Jordan, 261–305. New York: Theatre Communications Group, 1992.

Fornes, Maria Irene. *The Danube*. 1982. *Plays*. Preface by Susan Sontag. New York: *Performing Arts Journal Publications,* 1986. 41–64.

Foucault, Michel. *The History of Sexuality: An Introduction*. 1978. Trans. Robert Hurley. New York: Vintage, 1990.

Freud, Sigmund. *Introductory Lectures on Psychoanalysis*. 1917. Trans. and ed. James Strachey. New York: Norton, 1966.

Freytag, Gustav. *Technique of the Drama: An Exposition of Dramatic Composition and Art*. Chicago, IL: S. C. Griggs, 1895.

Fuchs, Elinor. *The Death of Character: Perspectives on Theater after Modernism*. Bloomington, IN: Indiana University Press, 1996.

———— and Una Chaudhuri, eds. *Land/Scape/Theater.* Ann Arbor, MI: University of Michigan Press, 2002.

Gale, Matthew, *Dada and Surrealism.* London: Phaidon Press, 1997.

Garrett, Shawn-Marie. "The Possession of Suzan-Lori Parks" *American Theatre* 17.8 (Oct. 2000): 22–26+.

Germain, Edward B., ed and intro. *Surrealist Poetry*. Middlesex, England: Penguin, 1978.

Gordon, Mel, ed. and intro. *Dada Performance*. New York: Performing Arts Journal Publications, 1987.

Graver, David. *The Aesthetics of Disturbance: Anti-Art in the Avant-Garde*. Ann Arbor, MI: University of Michigan Press, 1995.

Gygax, Franziska. *Gender and Genre in Gertrude Stein*. Westport, CT: Greenwood Press, 1998.

Hahn-Hahn, Ida, *Gräfin Fanstine*. Berlin: A. Duncker, 1941.

Harding, James M. *Contours of the Avant-Garde: Performance and Textuality.* Ann Arbor, MI: University of Michigan Press, 2000.

Hare, David. *Plenty.* London: Faber, 1978.

Hedges, Inez. "Constellated Visions: Robert Desnos's and Man Ray's *L'Etoile de Mer.*" In *Dada and Surrealist Film.* Ed. Rudolf E. Kuenzli, 99–109. Cambridge, MA: MIT Press, 1987.

Hoffman, Michael J. *The Development of Abstractionism in the Writing of Gertrude Stein.* Philadelphia, PA: University of Pennsylvania Press, 1965.

———. *Gertrude Stein.* Boston, MA: Twayne, 1976.

Holmberg, Arthur. *The Theatre of Robert Wilson.* Cambridge, England: Cambridge University Press, 1996.

The Holy Bible: The Oxford Annotated Bible. Eds. Herbert G. May and Bruce M. Metzger. Rev. ed. New York: Oxford University Press, 1962.

Heuval, Michael Vanden. *Performing Drama/Dramatizing Performance: Alternative Theater and the Dramatic Text.* Ann Arbor, MI: University of Michigan Press, 1993.

Hutchinson, Beth. "Gertrude Stein's Film Scenarios" *Literature/Film Quarterly* 17.1 (1989): 35–38.

Innes, Christopher. "Text/Pretext/Pre-Text: The Language of Avant-Garde Experiment." In *Contours of the Avant-Garde: Performance and Textuality.* Ed. James M. Harding, 58–78. Ann Arbor, MI: University of Michigan Press, 2000.

Jarry, Alfred. "Questions of the Theatre." In *Ubu Roi: Drama in Five Acts.* Trans. Barbara Wright, 173–182. Norfolk, CT: New Directions, 1961.

———. *Ubu Roi.* 1968. In *The Ubu Plays.* Ed. Simon Watson Taylor, 17–74. Trans. Cyril Connolly and Simon Watson Taylor. New York: Grove Weidenfeld, 1969.

Kaiser, Nancy A. "Faust/Faustine in the 19th Century: Man's Myth, Women's Places." In *Our Faust?: Roots and Ramifications of a Modern German Myth.* Eds. Reinhold Grimm and Jost Hermand, 65–81. Madison, WI: University of Wisconsin Press, 1987.

Kawin, Bruce. *Telling It Again and Again: Repetition in Literature and Film.* Ithaca, NY: Cornell University Press, 1972.

Kennedy, Adrienne. *A Movie Star Has to Star in Black and White.* In *Adrienne Kennedy in One Act.* Minneapolis, MN: University of Minnesota Press, 1988. 79–104.

————. *Funnyhouse of a Negro.* In *Adrienne Kennedy in One Act.* Minneapolis, MN: University of Minnesota Press, 1988. 1–24.

Knight, Arthur. *The Liveliest Art: A Panoramic History of the Movies.* New York: Macmillan, 1957.

Koppen, Randi. "Formalism and the Return to the Body: Stein's and Fornes's Aesthetic of Significant Form" *New Literary History* 28 (fall 1997): 791–809.

Kracauer, Siegfried. "Photography." 1927. In *The Mass Ornament: Weimar Essays.* Trans, ed., and into. Thomas Y. Levin, 47–64. Cambridge, MA: Harvard University Press, 1995.

————. "The Mass Ornament." 1927. In *The Mass Ornament: Weimar Essays.* Trans, ed., and into. Thomas Y. Levin, 75–88. Cambridge, MA: Harvard University Press, 1995.

————. *Theory of Film: The Redemption of Physical Reality.* Oxford, England: Oxford University Press, 1960.

Kuenzli, Rudolf E. "Introduction." *Dada/Surrealism* 15 (1986): 5.

LeCompte, Elizabeth. *Art into Theatre: Performance Interviews and Documents.* Interview, Nick Kaye. London: Harwood, 1996.

The Living Theater. Notes for *Doctor Faustus Lights the Lights* by Gertrude Stein, 1951. Special Collections, Harlan Hatcher Graduate Library, University of Michigan, Ann Arbor, MI.

MacPherson, Kenneth. Letter to Gertrude Stein. 24 June 1927. In *Close-Up, 1927–1933: Cinema and Modernism.* Eds. James Donald, Anne Friedberg, and Laura Marcus, 14. Princeton, NJ, Princeton University Press, 1988.

Maholy-Nagy, Laszlo. *Painting, Photography, Film.* 1967. Trans. Janet Seligman. Cambridge, MA: MIT Press, 1987.

Malina, Judith, and Julian Beck. *Paradise Now: Collective Creation of the Living Theatre.* New York: Vintage, 1971.

Malraux, André. *The Voices of Silence.* Trans. Stuart Gilbert. Princeton, NJ: Princeton University Press, 1978.

Mann, Paul. *The Theory-Death of the Avant-Garde.* Bloomington, IN: Indiana University Press, 1991.

Mantle, Burns. *The Best Plays of 1945–1946.* New York: Dodd and Mead, 1946.

Marlowe, Christopher. *Doctor Faustus.* 1604. Ed. Roma Gill. Oxford, England: Clarendon, 1990.

Marranca, Bonnie, "Presence of Mind" *Performing Arts Journal* 16.1 (Sept. 1994): 1–17.

———. ed. and intro. *The Theatre of Images.* New York: Drama Book Specialists, 1977.

———. "St. Gertrude" *Performing Arts Journal* 16 (Jan. 1994): 107–112.

Martin, Robert K. "The Mother of Us All and American History." In *Gertrude Stein and the Making of Literature.* Eds. Ira Bruce Nadel and Shirley Neuman, 210–222. Boston, MA: Northeastern University Press, 1988.

Mast, Gerald. *A Short History of the Movies.* 2nd ed. Indianapolis, IN: Bobbs-Merrill, 1976.

Matthews, J. H. *Theatre in Dada and Surrealism.* Syracuse, NY: Syracuse University Press, 1974.

McCabe, Susan. "'Delight in Dislocation': The Cinematic Modernism of Stein, Chaplin, and Man Ray" *Modernism/Modernity* 8.3 (2001): 429–452.

Melzer, Annabelle. *Dada and Surrealist Performance.* Baltimore, MD: Johns Hopkins University Press, 1976.

Motherwell, Robert. *The Dada Painters and Poets.* 2nd ed. Cambridge, MA: Harvard University Press, 1981.

Myers, Steven. *Irresistible Dictation: Gertrude Stein and the Correlation of Writing and Science.* Pals Alto, CA: Stanford University Press, 2001.

Neuman, Shirley. "'Would a viper have stung her if she had only had one name?': *Doctor Faustus Lights the Lights.*" In *Gertrude Stein and the Making of Literature.* Eds. Ira Bruce Nadel and Shirley Neuman, 168–193. Boston, MA: Northeastern University Press, 1988.

Nichols, Bill, ed. *Maya Deren and the American Avant-Garde.* Berkeley, CA: University of California Press, 2001.

Oxford Dictionary of Slang. New York: Oxford University Press, 1998.

Oxford English Dictionary. 2nd. ed. New York: Oxford University Press, 1989.

Parks, Suzan-Lori. *The America Play.* 1990–1993. In *The America Play and Other Works.* New York: Theatre Communications Group, 1995. 157–199.

————. "From Elements of Style." In *The America Play and Other Works*. New York: Theatre Communications Group, 1995. 6–18.

————. *Venus*. 1990. New York: Theatre Communications Group, 1997.

Perloff, Marjorie. *The Futurist Moment: Avant-Garde, Avant-Guerre, and the Language of Rupture*. Chicago, IL: University of Chicago Press, 1986.

————. *The Poetics of Indeterminacy: Rimbaud to Cage*. Princeton, NJ: Princeton University Press, 1981.

Picabia, Francis. *391*. 1917–1924. Ed. Michel Sanouillet. Paris, France: Le Terrain Vague, 1960.

Pladott, Dinnah. "Gertrude Stein: Exile, Feminism, Avant-Garde in the American Theater." In *Modern American Drama: The Female Canon*. Ed. June Schlueter, 111–129. Cranbury, NJ: Association of University Presses, 1990.

Pronko, Leonard Cabell. *Avant-Garde: The Experimental Theater in France*. Berkeley, CA: University of California Press, 1966.

Puchner, Martin. *Stage Fright: Modernism, Anti-Theatricality, and Drama*. Baltimore, MD: Johns Hopkins University Press, 2002.

Quadri, Franco, Franco Bertoni, and Robert Stearns. *Robert Wilson*. Trans. Richard Fremantle and Jenny McPhee. New York: Rizzoli, 1997.

Rabinovitz, Lauren. *Points of Resistance: Women, Power, and Politics in the New York Avant-Garde Cinema, 1943–1971*. Urbana, IL: University of Illinois Press, 1999.

Reid, B. L. *Art by Subtraction: A Dissenting Opinion of Gertrude Stein*. Norman, OK: University of Oklahoma Press, 1958.

Robinson, Marc. "Gertrude Stein, Forgotten Playwright" *The South Atlantic Quarterly* 91 (summer 1992): 621–43.

————. *The Other American Drama*. New York: Cambridge University Press, 1994.

Rostagno, Aldo, Julian Beck, and Judith Malina. Introduction. In *We, The Living Theatre: A Pictorial Documentation by Gianfranco Mantegna of the Life and Pilgrimage of The Living Theatre in Europe and in the U.S.* Ed. Gianfranco Mantegna. New York: Ballantine, 1970.

Rosten, Bevya. "The Gesture of Illogic: Interview with Kate Valk" *American Theatre* 15 (Feb. 1998): 16–19.

Ryan, Betsy Alayne. *Gertrude Stein's Theatre of the Absolute.* Ann Arbor, MI: UMI Research Press, 1984.

Sand, George. *A Woman's Version of the Faust Legend: The Seven Strings of the Lyre.* 1869. Ed., trans., and intro. George A. Kennedy. Chapel Hill, NC: University of North Carolina Press, 1989.

Saussure, Ferdinand de. *Course in General Linguistics.* 1915. Eds. Charles Bally and Albert Sechehaye in collaboration with Albert Riedlinger. Trans., intro., and notes Wade Baskin. New York: McGraw-Hill, 1966.

Savran, David. "Queer Theater and the Disarticulation of Identity." In *The Queerest Art: Essays on Lesbian and Gay Theater.* Eds. Alisa Solomon and Framji Minwalla, 152–167. New York: New York University Press.

———. "Whistling in the Dark." Rev. of *Doctor Faustus Lights the Lights,* dir. Robert Wilson. *Performing Arts Journal* 15 (Jan. 1993): 25–27.

Sawelson-Gorse, Naomi, ed. *Women in Dada: Essays on Sex, Gender, and Identity.* Cambridge, MA: MIT Press, 1998.

Schaefer, James F., Jr. "An Examination of Language as Gesture in a Play by Gertrude Stein" *Literature in Performance* 3 (1982): 1–14.

Sedgwick, Eve Kosofsky. *Tendencies.* Durham, NC: Duke University Press, 1993.

Segel, Harold. *Pinocchio's Progeny: Puppets, Marionettes, Automotons, and Robots in Modernist and Avant-Garde Drama.* Baltimore, MD: Johns Hopkins University Press, 1995.

Sellars, Peter. Interview. In *The Director's Voice: Twenty-One Interviews.* Ed. Arthur Bartow, 268–285. New York: Theatre Communications Group, 1988.

Senelick, Laurence. "The Queer Root of Theater." In *The Queerest Art: Essays on Lesbian and Gay Theater.* Eds. Alisa Solomon and Framji Minwalla, 21–39. New York: New York University Press, 2002.

Shank, Theodore. *Beyond the Boundaries: American Alternative Theatre.* Rev. ed. Ann Arbor, MI: University of Michigan Press, 2002.

Shattuck, Roger. *The Banquet Years: The Arts in France, 1885–1918.* Garden City, NJ: Doubleday, 1961.

Shyer, Laurence. *Robert Wilson and His Collaborators.* New York: Theatre Communications Group, 1989.

Sillen, Samuel. "Obituary of Europe and Gertrude Stein" *New Masses* 25.11 (Dec. 1937): 22–23."

Simmel, Georg. "The Metropolis and Mental Life." In *The Sociology of Georg Simmel.* 1950. Trans. and ed. Kurt H. Wolff, 409–424. New York: The Free Press, 1969.

Simon, John. "The Living Theatre" *New York* 11 Nov. 1968: 54.

Sitney, P. Adams. *Visonary Film: The American Avant-Garde.* New York: Oxford University Press, 1974.

Sprigge, Eliabeth. *Gertrude Stein: Her Life and Work.* New York: Harper, 1957.

Stam, Robert, Robert Burgoyne, and Sandy Flitterman-Lewis. *New Vocabularies in Film Semiotics: Structuralism, Post-Structuralism, and Beyond.* London: Routledge, 1992.

Stein, Gertrude. *The Autobiography of Alice B. Toklas.* 1933. In *Selected Writings of Gertrude Stein.* 1946. Ed. Carl Van Vechten, 1–237. New York: Vintage, 1990.

———. *Bee Time Vine and Other Pieces.* New Haven, CT: Yale University Press, 1953.

———. "Composition as Explanation." 1925. In *Gertrude Stein: Writing and Lectures, 1911–1945.* Ed. Patricia Meyerowitz, 21–30. London: Peter Owen, 1967.

———. Correspondence and Manuscript Notebooks, Gertrude Stein and Alice B. Toklas Papers, Yale Collection of American Literature, Beinecke Rare Book and Manuscript Library, Yale University.

———. *Doctor Faustus Lights the Lights.* 1938. In *Last Operas and Plays.* 1949. Ed. and intro. Carl van Vechten, 89–118. New York: Vintage, 1975.

———. *Everybody's Autobiography.* 1938. Cambridge, MA: Exact Change, 1993.

———. *Film. Duex Soeurs Qui Ne Sont Pas Soeurs.* 1929. In *Operas and Plays.* 1932. Barrytown, NY: Station Hill Arts, 1998. 399–400.

———. *Four in America.* New Haven, CT: Yale University Press, 1947.

———. *Four Saints in Three Acts.* 1927. In *Opera and Plays.* 1932. Foreword James R. Mellow. Barrytown, NY: Station Hill Press, 1998. 11–47.

———. *Geography and Plays.* 1922. Intro. Cyrena N. Pondrom. Madison, WI: University of Wisconsin Press, 1993.

————. *The Gertrude Stein: A First Reader and Three Plays.* Boston, MA: Houghton Mifflin, 1948.

————. "How Writing Is Written." 1935. *How Writing Is Written: Previously Unpublished Writing of Gertrude Stein.* Ed. Robert Barlett Haas, 151–160. Los Angeles, CA: Black Sparrow Press, 1974.

————. "Identity." 1935. In *A Stein Reader.* Ed. Ulla Dydo, 588–594. Evanston, IL: Northwestern University Press, 1993.

————. *Last Operas and Plays.* 1949. Ed. and intro. Carl van Vechten. New York: Vintage, 1975.

————. *Lend a Hand or Four Religions.* 1922. In *Useful Knowledge.* New York: Payson and Clark, 1928. 170–209.

————. *Listen to Me. A Play.* 1936. *Last Operas and Plays.* 1949. Ed. and intro. Carl van Vechten, 387–421. New York: Vintage, 1975.

————. "A Message from Gertrude Stein." In *Selected Writings of Gertrude Stein.* 1946. Ed. Carl Van Vechten, vii. New York: Vintage, 1990.

————. *The Mother of Us All.* 1945–46. In *Last Operas and Plays.* 1949. Ed. and intro. Carl van Vechten, 52–88. New York: Vintage, 1975.

————. *A Movie.* 1920. In *Operas and Plays.* 1932. Barrytown, NY: Station Hill Arts, 1998. 395–398.

————. "Mrs. Emerson." 1914. *Close-Up* 1.2 (Aug. 1927): 28–33.

————. "Near East or Chicago." In *Useful Knowledge.* New York: Payson and Clarke, 1928. 51.

————. "The New Hope in Our 'Sad Young Men'" *New York Times Magazine* 3 June 1945: 5+.

————. *Not Slightly [A Play].* 1914. In *Geography and Plays.* 1922. Intro. Cyrena N. Pondrom, 290–301. Madison, WI: University of Wisconsin Press, 1993.

————. *Opera and Plays.* 1932. Foreword James R. Mellow. Barrytown, NY: Station Hill Press, 1998.

————. *Painted Lace.* New Haven, CT: Yale University Press, 1955.

————. *A Photograph.* 1920. In *A Stein Reader.* Ed. Ulla E. Dydo, 343–346. Evanston, IL: Northwestern University Press, 1993.

————. *Picasso*. London: C. Scribner's Sons, 1939.

————. "Plays." In *Lectures in America*. New York: Random House, 1935. 91–131.

————. "A Poem about the End of the War." 1944. In *Gertrude Stein and the Making of Literature*. Eds. by Shirley Neuman and Ira B. Nadel, 232–236. Boston, MA: Northeastern University Press, 1988.

————. "A Portrait of Constance Fletcher." 1911. In *Geography and Plays*. 1922. Madison, WI: University of Wisconsin Press, 1992. 157–165.

————. *Portraits and Prayers*. New York: Random House, 1934.

————. "Portraits and Repetition." In *Lectures in America*. New York: Random House, 1935. 165–208.

————. "Reflection on the Atomic Bomb." 1946. In *Reflection on the Atomic Bomb: Volume I of the Previously Uncollected Writings of Gertrude Stein*. Ed. Robert Bartlett Haas, 179. Los Angeles, CA: Black Sparrow Press, 1973.

————. *Selected Writings of Gertrude Stein*. 1946. Ed. Carl Van Vechten. New York: Vintage, 1990.

————. "Sentences." In *How to Write*. 1931. Intro. Patricia Meyerowitz, 113–214. New York: Dover, 1975.

————. *Stanzas in Meditation and Other Poems*. New Haven, CT: Yale University Press, 1956.

————. *Useful Knowledge*. New York: Payson and Clark, 1928.

————. *They Must. Be Wedded. To Their Wife*. 1931. In *Opera and Plays*. 1932. Foreword James R. Mellow, 161–194. Barrytown, NY: Station Hill Press, 1998.

————. *Three Sister Who Are Not Sisters: A Melodrama*. In *The Gertrude Stein First Reader and Three Plays*. Boston, MA: Houghton Mifflin, 1948. 63–71.

————. *Wars I Have Seen*. New York: Random House, 1945.

————. "What Are Master-Pieces and why are there so few of them." 1935. In *Gertrude Stein: Writing and Lectures, 1911–1945*. Ed. Patricia Meyerowitz, 146–154. London: Peter Owen, 1967.

————. "What Happened. A Play in Five Acts." 1913. In *Geography and Plays*. Madison, WI: University of Wisconsin Press, 1993.

————. *Yes Is for a Very Young Man.* 1944–45. In *Last Operas and Plays.* 1949. Ed. and intro. Carl van Vechten, 3–51. New York: Vintage, 1975.

Stewart, Allegra. *Gertrude Stein and the Present.* Cambridge, MA: Harvard University Press, 1967.

Stimpson, Catherine. "The Mind, the Body, and Gertrude Stein" *Critical Inquiry* 3.3 (spring 1977): 489–506.

————. "The Somograms of Gertrude Stein" *Poetics Today* 6.1–2 (1985): 67–80.

Suárez, Juan. *Bike Boys, Drag Queens, and Superstars: Avant-Garde, Mass Culture, and Gay Identities in the 1960s Underground Cinema.* Bloomington, IN: Indiana University Press, 1996.

Sullivan, Ceri. "Faustus and the Apple" *Review of English Studies: A Quarterly Journal of English Literature and the English Language* 47 (1996): 47–50.

Sutherland, Donald. *Gertrude Stein: A Biography of Her Work.* Westport, CT: Greenwood Press, 1951.

Tyler, Parker. *Underground Film: A Critical History.* New York: De Capo, 1995.

Tzara, Tristan. "An Introduction to Dada." In *The Dada Painters and Poets: An Anthology.* 2nd ed. Ed. Robert Motherwell, 402–406. Cambridge, MA: Harvard University Press, 1981.

————. *The Gas Heart.* In *Modern French Theatre: An Anthology of Plays.* Eds. and trans. Michael Benedikt and George E. Wellwarth, 131–146. New York: E. P. Dutton, 1966.

————. "Dada Manifesto. 1918." In *The Dada Painters and Poets: An Anthology.* 2nd ed. Ed. Robert Motherwell, 76–82. Cambridge, MA: Harvard University Press, 1981.

Ullman, Stephen. *Semantics: An Introduction to the Science of Meaning.* Oxford, England: Blackwell, 1962.

Van Vechten, Carl. Introduction. *Last Operas and Plays.* 1949. Ed. and intro. Carl van Vechten, vii–xix. New York: Vintage Books, 1975.

————. Program Notes for *Four Saints in Three Acts.* By Gertrude Stein and Virgil Thomson. Forty-fourth Street Theater. March 1934. Gertrude Stein Papers, Yale Collection of American Literature, Beinecke Rare Book and Manuscript Library, Yale University.

Vaughan, Dai. "Let There Be Lumière" *Sight and Sound* 50.2 (spring 1981): 126–127.

Watson, Steven. *Prepare for Saints: Gertrude Stein, Virgil Thomson, and the Mainstreaming of American Modernism.* Berkeley, CA: University of California Press, 1998.

Watts, Linda S. *Rapture Untold: Gender, Mysticism, and the "Moment of Recognition" in Works by Gertrude Stein.* New York: Peter Lang, 1996.

Weightman, John, *Concept of the Avant-Garde: Explorations in Modernism.* London: Alcove, 1973.

Weinstein, Norman. "'Four Saints in Three Acts': Play as Landscape." In *Gertrude Stein.* Ed. and intro. Harold Bloom, 113–120. New York: Chelsea, 1986.

———. *Gertrude Stein and the Literature of Modern Consciousness.* New York: Frederick Unger, 1970.

Wilder, Thornton. *Our Town: A Play in Three Acts.* New York: Coward McCann, 1938.

Will, Barbara. *Gertrude Stein, Modernism, and the Problem of "Genius."* Edinburgh, England: Edinburgh University Press, 2000.

Wilson, Robert. "Director's Notes." *Four Saints in Three Acts.* Houston Grand Opera Stagebill (winter 1996). Byrd Hoffman Foundation Collection.

———. Interview. *The New Yorker.* 27 Mar. 1971. 30.

———. ". . . I thought I was hallucinating" *The Drama Review.* 21.4 (Dec. 1977): 76.

Wineapple, Brenda. *Sister Brother: Gertrude and Leo Stein.* New York: G. P. Putnam's Sons, 1996.

Wirth, Andrzej. "Gertrude Stein und ihre Kritik der dramatischen Vernunft." *Lili: Zeitschrift für Literaturwissenschaft und Linguistik.* Jahrgang 12 (1982): 64–74.

Wren, Celia. "Loving Repetition: Why Has Gertrude Stein Become a Recurrent Character on America's Stages?" *American Theatre* (May/June 2001): 30–33+.

Index

Abdoh, Reza: 130, 139–40
Abdy, Robert "Bertie": 65
Absurdism: 110
Académie Nationale de Musique et de Danse: 74–76
Akalaitis, JoAnne: 130
American Civil War, The: 103
American theater: 2–3, 47
Anderson, Laurie: 116
   Moby Dick, 182n; *The United States I–IV*, 182n
Anderson, Sherwood: 47
Anger, Kenneth: 131
anti-theatricalism: 35
Apollinaire, Guillaume: 49, 50
   Breasts of Tiresias, 19, 60–61; and Surrealism, 60–61
Aragon, Louis: 37
aria: 110
Aronson, Arnold: 3, 114, 119, 129
Arp, Hans: 80
Artaud, Antonin: 8–9, 117
atomic bomb, the: 181n
atomic energy: 128
The Autobiography of Alice B. Toklas (Stein): 50, 69, 79, 99
automatic writing: 53, 138
avant-garde, the: 1–8, 103
   audience of, 51–52; and cinema, 4–7, 118; decline of, 69, 110–11; definition of, 9, 48–49; history of, 118; and military, 52; and modernity, 4; origins of, 4; in painting, 1; puppets in, 180n; and queerness, 118; simultaneity in, 59, 81
avant-garde cinema: 4, 8–18, 27–33, 38, 40, 55
   and homosexuality, 4, 8–18; origins of, 4; and visual arts, 32, 37

avant-garde drama: 115–16, 119
   in America, 116, 117, 138; as antagonistic, 52; as anti-textual, 10, 125; and cinema, 4–7, 37, 116; definition of, 8–10; the gaze in, 177n; individual in, 82–83; and machine aesthetic, 6; morality of, 4–5, 36; negation in, 46; non-linear structure of, 13, 59; origins of, 4; painting, 1; and realism, 104; repetition in, 46; and science, 52–53; similarities to homosexuality, 12; techniques of, 110; and visual arts, 14; and World War I, 51–53
avant-garde theater. *See* avant-garde drama.

Ball, Hugo: 49
   on Futurism, 50
Banes, Sally: 182n
Baraka, Amiri: 125
Bauhaus: 36
Bazin, André: 15
Beatles, The:
   "Strawberry Fields Forever," 123
Beaver, Harold: 12
Beck, Julian: 125–26, 128–29, 183n
Beckett, Samuel: 25, 66
   Endgame, 92; *Film*, 44
Benét, Stephen Vincent:
   The Devil and Daniel Webster, 181n
Benjamin, Walter: 33, 35
Bentley, Eric: 125
Berlioz, Hector:
   The Damnation of Faust, 76
Berners, Lord Gerald: 114
Bernstein, Charles: 131
Black Mountain College: 117
Bogart, Anne: 116, 130